Promotional Screen Industries

From the trailers and promos that surround film and television to the ads and brand videos that are sought out and shared, promotional media have become a central part of contemporary screen life. *Promotional Screen Industries* is the first book to explore the sector responsible for this thriving area of media production.

In a wide-ranging analysis, Paul Grainge and Catherine Johnson explore the intermediaries – advertising agencies, television promotion specialists, movie trailer houses, digital design companies – that compete and collaborate in the fluid, fast-moving world of promotional screen work.

Through interview-based fieldwork with companies and practitioners based in the UK, US and China, *Promotional Screen Industries* encourages us to see promotion as a professional and creative discipline with its own opportunities and challenges. Outlining how shifts in the digital media environment have unsettled the boundaries of 'promotion' and 'content', the authors provide new insight into the sector, work, strategies and imaginaries of contemporary screen promotion.

With case studies on mobile communication, television, film and live events, this timely book offers a compelling examination of the industrial configurations and media forms, such as ads, apps, promos, trailers, digital shorts, branded entertainment and experiential media, that define promotional screen culture at the beginning of the twenty-first century.

Paul Grainge is Associate Professor of Film and Television Studies at the University of Nottingham. He is the author of *Brand Hollywood* (2008) and *Monochrome Memories* (2002), editor of *Ephemeral Media* (2011) and *Memory and Popular Film* (2003), and co-author of *Film Histories* (2007).

Catherine Johnson is Associate Professor of Film and Television Studies at the University of Nottingham. She is the author of *Branding Television* (2012) and *Telefantasy* (2005) and the co-editor of *Transnational Television History* (2012) and *ITV Cultures* (2005).

'This is a landmark study and a compelling account of productive fieldwork across media in the promotional screen industries. Sets a methodological standard for future production studies research. Its careful, interview-based, multi-year ethnography mines theoretical insights from complex creative labor and institutional practices rather than from textual theories. The book effectively underscores the clear value of scholar-practitioner interactions and systematically integrated cultural-industrial analysis. Well-written and astutely reasoned, a must-read for anyone studying the contemporary media industries.'

John T. Caldwell, *Professor of Film, Television, and Digital Media, UCLA*

'This is a truly superb book that throws down a gauntlet to media studies to expand in interesting, vital ways, and that then picks that gauntlet back up and uses it with skill and panache, showing us how to study promotional screen industries. It's pathbreaking, exciting, and excellent, full of raw information and smart, thoughtful ideas.'

Jonathan Gray, *Professor of Media and Cultural Studies, University of Wisconsin, Madison*

'Read as a guide to today's hybridized marketing, branding and advertising screen industries this is undoubtedly an impressive book. But approached as an intervention in the field from two leading members of the 'paratextual cohort', it is even more dazzling. Drawing on international fieldwork and an instructive range of case studies, Grainge and Johnson convincingly make the case for just how creative, aesthetically vibrant, and culturally significant the work of the promotional screen industries can be.'

Matt Hills, *Professor of Film and TV Studies, Aberystwyth University*

Promotional Screen Industries

Paul Grainge and Catherine Johnson

Routledge
Taylor & Francis Group

LONDON AND NEW YORK

First published 2015
by Routledge
2 Park Square, Milton Park, Abingdon, Oxon, OX14 4RN

and by Routledge
711 Third Avenue, New York, NY 10017

Routledge is an imprint of the Taylor & Francis Group, an informa business

British Library Cataloguing in Publication Data
A catalogue record for this book is available from the British Library

Library of Congress Cataloging in Publication Data
Grainge, Paul, 1972-
Promotional screen industries / by Paul Grainge and Catherine Johnson.
pages cm
Includes bibliographical references and index.
1. Motion pictures--Marketing. 2. Television programs--Marketing.
I. Johnson, Catherine, 1973- II. Title.
PN1995.9.M29G733 2015
384'.84--dc2
2014037789

ISBN: 978-0-415-83162-8 (hbk)
ISBN: 978-0-415-83166-6 (pbk)
ISBN: 978-1-315-71868-2 (ebk)

Typeset in Sabon
by Taylor & Francis Books
Printed in Great Britain by Ashford Colour Press Ltd.

For my Dad, David Grainge (PG)
For my parents, Maria Amalia and Ron Haller-Williams,
and Peter and Liz Johnson (CJ)

Contents

List of Figures

Acknowledgements

This book has grown out of an extended period of industry fieldwork with companies and individuals who work in the sector that we call the 'promotional screen industries'. This fieldwork was made possible by a Follow-On Fund award by the Arts and Humanities Research Council (grant number AH/J006475/1), and we would like to thank the AHRC for their generous support. We are also grateful to the University of Nottingham's Centre for Advanced Studies for an External Engagement Challenge Fund award that helped fund some of our early visits to London to explain our project to personnel at various key companies.

We could not have written this book without a wide range of industry professionals being willing to talk at length about their work. We are especially indebted to staff in the Creative department of Red Bee Media who were incredibly generous with their time during our many visits to their London office in 2012, and who have made industry–academic collaboration meaningful on a number of fronts since. Most notably, our thanks go to Andy Bryant who not only made things possible at Red Bee Media, but who has been a tremendous advocate of the relation between Red Bee and the Institute for Screen Industries Research (ISIR) at the University of Nottingham. We are equally grateful to the many staff at Red Bee who gave (multiple) interviews, provided access to workshops and discussions, and let us generally linger around their desks. Our thanks go to Charlie Mawer (where everything began), Clare Phillips, Mandy Combes, Tim Whirledge, Michael Reeves, Kath Hipwell, Emma James, Frazer Jelleyman, Michelle Marks, Kris Hardiman, Laura Gould, Ruth Shabi, Victoria Findlay, Aileen Madden, Eve Hacking, Elinor Jones, Paul Fennell, Bruce Collingwood and Jenny Good for their openness, insight and good humour.

Beyond Red Bee our industry acknowledgements extend in various directions. Paul visited Crystal CG's Beijing headquarters in January 2011 and his thanks go to Rachel Wang and Jet for the time they gave to the delegation from Nottingham. We would both like to thank Gilles Albaredes and Will Case for explaining the work of Crystal CG International at the company's London office before, during and after their intensely busy period of work for the 2012 Olympic and Paralympic Games. At Create Advertising, Suneil Beri, David Stern and Frank Frumento gave illuminating interviews on the world of trailers, and Katie Sexton has been extremely generous both in interviews and by returning to Nottingham to share her film-marketing experience with staff and students. It was a pleasure to reconnect with Victoria Jaye at the BBC who was typically insightful about multiplatform television, and our thanks go to Tim Hughes at Discovery Networks, Dean Baker at JWT, Matt Andrews at Mindshare, and Neil Mortensen at Thinkbox for giving us much more interview time than we ever expected.

Our thinking and approach to the promotional screen industries has been enriched by discussions with numerous friends and colleagues along the way. Jonathan Gray, James Bennett and Max Dawson were kind enough to offer feedback on our book proposal at an early stage and have always provided food (gnocchi in one case) for thought. We have also enjoyed discussions with Jennifer Gillan, James Lyons, Derek Kompare, Charles Acland, Denise Mann, Keith Johnston and Annette Davison at conferences at SCMS and elsewhere. Closer to home, we have been supported by an excellent band of colleagues in the Department of Culture, Film and Media. We would like to thank, in particular, Paul McDonald, Liz Evans, Mark Gallagher, Roberta Pearson, Gianluca Sergi, Julian Stringer, Alex Simcock and Ian Brookes for making the University of Nottingham such an exciting place to teach and research the screen industries. Thanks also to Michele Hilmes and Bruce Croushore for the perfect martinis during their Fulbright stay. In providing the opportunity to road-test ideas, we are grateful for invitations to give plenaries at the 'Titles, Teasers and Trailers' conference at the University of Edinburgh and the 'Media Mutations' symposium at the University of Bologna, and to give guest lectures at the Universities of Birmingham, East Anglia, Exeter and Hertfordshire.

We are both indebted to our editor Natalie Foster who has been constantly supportive throughout the project. As ever, the team at Routledge have been brilliant. Thanks to Sheni Kruger and Stacey Carter for their sterling work producing the book. A very different version of Chapter 3 appeared as 'A Song and Dance: Branded Entertainment and Mobile Promotion' in the *International Journal of Cultural Studies* 15(2) 2011: 165–180 and Paul would like to thank Sage for permission to reprint.

In bringing this book to fruition, we have both relied on the patience and support of those who put up with multiple London visits, over-enthusiastic talk of idents, and much more besides. David Hesmondhalgh has provided the perfect template for academic book dedications by ending one of his with the words 'blah, blah, blah'. In the same vein Paul would like to thank, as always, his wife Claire and his children Daniel and Joseph for listening to him jabber on when he should have been doing something more useful or fun – 'promos, trailers, blah, blah, blah'. He would like to dedicate this book to his Dad, whose generosity and support in all things (and belief in grammatical precision) has always been a compass. Cathy would like to dedicate this book to her parents, who are so generous in their unwavering support and who have taught her that there is more to life than work. She is eternally grateful to Rob for getting the perfect balance between being interested in her research and encouraging her to put it to one side and go for a walk instead.

Introduction

Once a year, the professional community of British television marketers gathers for its major trade conference and awards, Promax UK. The awards are a gala event in the television marketing calendar. With forty separate prize categories, nominees from broadcast marketing departments and communication agencies compete to win a Promax Gold, a statuette bearing an uncanny resemblance to an Oscar and made by the same manufacturer. In November 2012 we attended Promax UK (Grainge and Johnson 2015). As one of eight major events licensed by PromaxBDA – a US-based organization representing 'the global community of those passionately engaged in the marketing of television and video content on all platforms' (PromaxBDA 2014)[1] – the conference ran over two days and culminated in a black-tie ceremony held at the Hilton Hotel in London's Park Lane. A mixture of panel sessions, creative activities, networking opportunities and rituals of reward, Promax UK brought together the individuals and companies responsible for the vast majority of programme trailers and channel promos seen on British television screens.

The conference and awards were no small affair. According to Tim Hughes, co-chair of Promax UK's executive committee (and On-Air Marketing Director for Discovery Networks UK),

> people would probably think [television marketing] is quite a small industry, but it's not, it's huge in the UK. Every TV company has an in-house team, every TV company to some extent works with agencies, and we're looking at a market that's got nearly 600 channels. All of those channels have been branded, all of those channels have promotions.
>
> (Hughes 2012)

Beyond the UK, PromaxBDA professes to represent 'more than 10,000 companies and individuals at every major media organization, marketing agency, research company, strategic and creative vendor and technology provider', the association's membership spanning sixty-five countries (PromaxBDA 2014). As the main trade organization for the television marketing sector, Promax is a 'resource for education, community, creative inspiration and career development' (ibid.) for those in the business of producing the audiovisual materials that promote networks, stations and television shows. In a period when audiences are fragmented across a wide range of sites for media content, this work has become increasingly strategic and complex. According to one leading company, the goal of television marketing is no longer simply to persuade people to watch programmes on broadcast channels but to navigate audiences in rich visual environments, and to 'connect viewers to content' in a burgeoning multiplatform world (Red Bee Media 2012).

The clear winner at the Promax awards in 2012 was a long-form trailer called 'Meet the Superhumans'. This was made by 4Creative (the marketing department of UK broadcaster Channel 4) to promote the broadcaster's coverage of the London Paralympic Games. Ninety seconds in length, the trailer swept the board in terms of major awards, winning Promax Gold in the categories of Best Direction, Best Editing, Best Long Form, Best Launch, and Best Sports Promo (Originated), and also picking up the People's Award, a prize based on a vote for 'best promo of the year' among delegates at the Promax conference. In addition, the wider Paralympic campaign devised by 4Creative won Best On-Air Campaign and was awarded Promax Silver awards in the categories for Best Cross-Media Campaign and Best On-Air Media Planning. By the end of the award ceremony, 'Meet the Superhumans' and the Paralympic campaign were instrumental in helping Channel 4 to win the prestigious Promax Gold for 'Channel of the Year'.

'Meet the Superhumans' became a familiar, even iconic, media text in the British television landscape in 2012. The trailer became integral to Channel 4's coverage of the Paralympic Games as host broadcaster. Promoted in the press before transmission and broadcast on 17 July 2012 at 9 pm across seventy-eight television channels – what the TV marketing industry calls a 'roadblock' – 'Meet the Superhumans' was purportedly seen by 50 percent of the UK population in

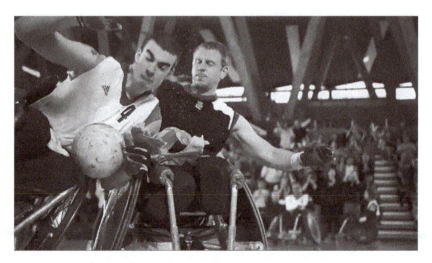

Figure 0.1 'Meet the Superhumans' promo (2012).

one go (Walker 2012). In representational terms, the trailer showcased the physical strength and resilience of a range of British Paralympic athletes against the thumping soundtrack of Public Enemy's 'Harder Than You Think'. The film not only confronted fears and prejudices about the physically disabled body, but also asked the audience to reflect on the cause of individual disabilities in ways that humanized the 'superhumans' without undermining the broader representation of them as exceptional athletes.[2] While ostensibly a film designed to promote Channel 4's coverage of the Paralympics, the trailer challenged assumptions about disabled sport and set the tone for Channel 4's coverage of the Games, reinforcing the broadcaster's aim 'to make people not worried about talking about disability' (Walker 2012). With an affective power that welcomed repeat viewing 'Meet the Superhumans' became a fixture on broadcast television before and during the Paralympics, but was also widely shared across social networks. The trailer received 1.5 million views on YouTube before the Games began, and was spread through Channel 4's own use of websites, apps, social media and online video as part of its multiplatform approach to the Paralympics. As a text, the production and distribution of 'Meet the Superhumans' blurred distinctions between 'promotion' and 'content' – it was an interstitial trailer but at the same time a discrete form of screen output that assumed a status and circulatory life of its own.

Promax is one of many trade gatherings within the advertising, marketing and media industries; it can be set alongside advertising festivals such as the Cannes Lions, galas for movie marketing such as the Key Art Awards, and prize ceremonies for design and art direction such as D&AD. Each year these events bring together, nationally and internationally, the community of practitioners that sit behind the promotional materials that populate the media landscape. Such awards are designed to highlight the skills that go into the production of trailers, promos, idents and new disciplinary forms like companion apps and experiential media content.[3] This serves its own industrial function. Rewarding promos like 'Meet the Superhumans' allows a relatively unseen professional community to forge its identity and legitimise its value within the transactional markets that surround media industries. However, the awards also point more generally to *promotional work as a field of screen practice*. This extends beyond the realm of television marketing to include a wide range of companies and occupations that operate in the fertile space between the worlds of marketing and media. This can be seen to encompass the work and output of film and television marketing departments, broadcast promotion specialists, movie trailer houses, 'content' divisions within advertising and media agencies, and digital media firms selling expertise in visual effects and user-experience design. Working variously with media and consumer brands, these companies function as intermediaries in the hybrid sector that we call the *promotional screen industries*.

Within scholarly accounts of the influence of promotion in the cultural industries, promotional intermediaries such as film and television marketers are often regarded as a constraining force upon the media producers who actually make movies, television programmes and other popular cultural forms. Discussing the 'organizational tensions between cultural producers and creative artists' that characterize the cultural industries, Aeron Davis writes:

> Promotional intermediaries think about the commercial while artists think about the creative. Intermediaries think about what is predictable and reliable, based on their research of past work, while artists focus on the new and original and look to future fashions. Intermediaries think about mass markets while artists think about their peers, critics and industry awards.
>
> (2013: 100–101)

Within Davis' account, promotional work is measured in terms of the degree to which intermediaries restrict (or not) the creative autonomy of those who make entertainment media. What risks getting lost in this dialectic between 'intermediaries' and 'artists' is the importance placed on creativity, originality, awards, and peer recognition by members of bodies like Promax. This book is ostensibly concerned with companies and occupations that make up the promotional screen industries. Behind this discussion, however, is an argument about promotional screen work as a *professional and creative discipline*. We suggest that the products, practices and socio-professional world of promotional intermediaries should be taken seriously if we are to understand contemporary developments in screen culture and the media industries. This means stepping beyond critical dualisms that set creativity against marketing as the default of promotional analysis.

By positing the term 'promotional screen industries', we draw together three strands of contemporary academic debate – the discussion of paratexts, promotional culture and production studies. A recurring theme in each strand, demonstrated in the 'Meet the Superhumans' example, is the blurring boundary of promotion and content in the contemporary media landscape. Within film and television studies, screen forms such as logos, promos, trailers and idents have been increasingly taken up as subjects worthy of study in their own right (Kernan 2004, Grainge 2008, 2011, Johnston 2009, Gray 2010, Johnson 2012, Gillan 2015). This scholarship responds to the burgeoning role of marketing and branding across the film and television industries since the 1970s but also to growing recognition that promotional texts have distinctive aesthetic and affective pleasures. Such arguments have been notably developed in the discussion of media paratexts. According to Jonathan Gray, paratexts are audiovisual forms and artefacts that surround the viewing experience of films and television shows, and can include anything from trailers, spoilers and opening credits to video games, podcasts, DVD bonus materials and toys. Instead of dismissing these media materials as the bad objects of marketing and merchandising, Gray suggests that paratexts create and amplify meanings that shape the 'DNA' of film and television texts. Rather than peripheral, ancillary or tertiary texts that are purely commercial in purpose, he argues that paratexts bear on the way that audiences anticipate, interpret and engage with movies and television shows.

This has become marked in a period when film and television franchises have looked to extend their textual presence across platforms, resulting in a greater range of screen forms that interlock promotional and narrative functions. As Gray writes: 'paratexts confound and disturb many of our hierarchies and binaries of what matters and what does not in the media world, especially the long-held notion that marketing and creativity are or could be distinct from one another' (2010: 209).

Paratextual analysis considers the aesthetic and interpretive function of established film and television content such as trailers and title sequences, but also that of emergent audiovisual forms. Focusing on the instrumental role of the digital short in television's merger with digital media, for example, Max Dawson (2011) examines the rise of mobile and web videos in the 2000s (otherwise known as 'mobisodes' and 'webisodes', referring to short-form content produced for mobile phones and web playback respectively). These can be seen as indicative promotional storytelling hybrids. Surrounding serial dramas as part of the multiplatform programme strategies of television networks, Dawson suggests that television digital shorts have their own native aesthetic characterized by 'streamlined exposition, discontinuous montage and ellipsis, and decontextualized narrative or visual spectacle' (ibid.: 206). Theorizing what he calls the 'aesthetic of efficiency' of such texts, Dawson proposes new evaluative criteria for the digital short forms that often now surround complex serial dramas. This involves moving 'beyond the simple dualism of the distinction between promo and content' and towards criteria that 'is as open to the artistry of the seventy-second promo as it is to that of the seventy-hour serial' (ibid.: 225). Neither Gray nor Dawson suggests that we should uncritically celebrate media paratexts; both cite examples that are poorly conceived or that 'visibly strain under the pressure of containing [the] antagonistic demands' of being promos and content at the same time (ibid.: 221). However, they do suggest that derision of promotional forms like trailers or mobisodes can limit understanding of paratextual creativity, both in the function these objects serve in constituting the films and television programmes they surround, and in the way they have become a more commonplace component of audiences' media diets.

A trailer like 'Meet the Superhumans' is an exemplary paratext, a promotional artefact that helped shape and control 'entrance' to Channel 4's coverage of the Paralympics and that was an accomplished short-form on its own terms. More broadly, Channel 4's use of websites, Twitter feeds and online video leading up to and during its Paralympic coverage would demonstrate the development of digital paratextual strategies in the era of 'connected viewing' (Holt and Sanson 2014). Dispersing content across multiple devices and platforms, Channel 4's digital campaign included online video diaries of Paralympic athletes, user-generated audition tapes to discover disabled television presenters and reporters, and online tools such as an 'impactometer' for measuring the speed of collisions during wheelchair basketball games. Integrating broadcast and digital materials, the Channel 4 Paralympic campaign would not only claim a raft of Promax awards but also a BAFTA, the main award of the British film and television industry. Winning the 2013 award category for 'digital creativity', the campaign's BAFTA success would demonstrate the status accorded to promotional work by the film and television industry. More specifically, it would indicate this industry's recognition of such work *as* creative content.

The study of paratexts helps deepen thinking about the relation of promotional screen media to the textual construction of film and television. However, paratextual analysis has less to say about the screen output of the 'promotional industries' more generally (Powell 2013c), focusing as it does on film- or television-related artefacts. The term promotional industries designates the professional fields of advertising, marketing, branding and public relations – areas that cross-connect with the screen industries but that are not synonymous with them. Within recent books on 'promotional culture' by Aeron Davis (2013), Helen Powell (2013a), and Matthew P. McAllister and Emily West (2013), the promotional industries describe an area of professional practice whose activities and influence have become far more widespread and systematic. This provides a second area of academic debate that informs this book. In different ways, these studies offer interdisciplinary analyses of the extension of promotional logics within cultural, political and media life; they consider the ways and means by which media content, institutional settings and everyday experience have become infused with promotion. These sites of permeation range from the heightened value given to promotional skill-sets in occupations, to the growing will-to-brand among corporations and institutional bodies, to the dynamics of individual self-promotion encouraged by new media such as social networks. Wide-ranging in scope, the analysis of promotional culture examines a series of questions about the penetration of promotional forms and values within cultural and social practice. In these accounts, the collapsing boundaries of promotion and content relate to a wider set of changes in contemporary market (and media) conditions.

Unlike early social theories of promotional culture that proposed a new social formation based on the saturation of signs (Wernick 1991), recent work within political communication, media sociology and advertising studies has looked to the more precise working practices of the promotional industries to understand the shifts and stakes of cultural and economic change. Taking a broad view of transitions in media technologies, regulations and values at the beginning of the twenty-first century, Emily West and Matthew McAllister observe that advertising and promotional culture are in the throes of rapid transformation and rethinking. They write:

> It seems that, everywhere we look, boundaries that once seemed fixed and knowable are blurring and destabilizing. Practitioners and scholars are rethinking the boundaries between media content and promotion, promotion and advertising, advertiser and audience, community and target market.
>
> (2013: 1)

This sense of destabilization is linked in their account to the consequences of digital transformations in the media world. Helen Powell draws a similar connection, explicitly associating the changing relationship between media and the promotional industries with a 'culture of convergence'. Powell suggests that changes across the communication landscape, driven by new technologies, has led to a revision of fundamental intrinsic practices within the promotional field. This has brought with it a number of key questions: 'how audiences might be assembled; which platforms are now available for promotional purposes; what kinds of competition do traditional media face; what does the consumer want from promotion and how can they be reached accordingly?' (2013b: 3). In these arguments, the dispersal of audiences across screens and platforms, and the more fugitive nature of audience attention, has put under pressure traditional advertising practice symbolized by the thirty-second commercial spot. While for Powell the changing media ecology asks 'how traditional media present themselves as suitable vehicles of promotion in the digital age' (ibid.: 2), for West and McAllister it raises the parallel question of how consumers, citizens and scholars develop new approaches to media literacy that 'detect promotional intent' (2013: 7). Here, the blurring of media content and promotion extends beyond the relationship between paratexts and film and television properties; as we shall see in our discussion of branded entertainment in Chapters 1 and 3, it invites thinking about the way that advertising has sought to engage audiences and involve consumers in the co-creation of value.

Aeron Davis argues that 'promotional culture's influence is based on the notion that individuals and organizations have become more promotionally oriented. That is to say, they give promotion a greater priority, more resources and more time' (2013: 4). This observation is instructive. Indeed, the media companies and organizations that we consider in Part II of this book, from television broadcasters like the BBC to bodies such as the London Olympic Organization Committee, all bear witness to a growing 'promotional orientation'. Rather than see this as a purely negative consequence of marketization, we want to build on work that understands promotion as having complex meanings and functions, and as developing from particular material and discursive practices. Although promotional texts emerge from commercial systems, Davis suggests that we should not 'assume that promotion is an autonomous all-powerful force that "determines" or "performs" all it touches' (ibid.: 5). Rather, he suggests that 'promotion combines and interacts with social, economic, technical and other forces' (ibid.). Davis is sensitive to the way that promotion has developed as a professional field and suggests that 'many promotional practices and practitioners have a fairly neutral or even positive role' in the way that issues, objects, organizations, and causes are brought to the fore (ibid.: 192). Equally, he notes that consumers are not easily duped by promotional campaigns and that campaigns 'fail far more often than they succeed' (ibid.). These qualifications are important in tempering views that equate promotion with the inexorable commodification of culture. And yet, what can often be missed in the discussion of both paratexts and promotional culture, despite the nuance they provide, is the particular nature of promotional work as a field of screen production. This brings into focus a third area of critical debate that informs this book, that of production studies.

Production studies has become a vibrant site of discussion within contemporary film and television scholarship (Caldwell 2008, Mayer, Banks and Caldwell 2009, Mayer 2011). This work has opened up an expanded conceptual field for thinking about screen production, specifically hidden or less-regarded communities of producers. At the same time, production studies has offered a range of analytic methods for examining the practices, collective rituals and industrial theorizations attached to professional work worlds. John Thornton Caldwell's (2008) analysis of production culture in the Los Angeles-based film and television industry, for example, seeks to understand the conditions and cultural interactions of contemporary production workers, including the mechanisms through which socio-professional groups represent themselves to each other. Similar to West and McAllister's description of advertising and promotion, Caldwell suggests that production in the screen industries has become increasingly destabilized, made volatile by 'unruly' work worlds, technologies and audiences. Within film and television industry practice, one site of volatility and self-theorizing has been the 'collapsing distinctions between creative content and marketing' (2009a: 175). Caldwell writes: 'Twenty years ago, to say that marketing had merged with creative content might have suggested two minor industrial practices: product placement and informercials. Today all films and series market other versions of the same films and series in various franchises and brands' (ibid.: 176). This merging has made the division between the 'creators' of films and television programmes and those who make paratexts far less clear. In a blurring of production labour, writers, directors, marketers, users and fans have variously participated in the creation of promotion/content (videos, games, commentaries, trailers, extras, blogs, mash-ups) that surrounds entertainment brands.

The sense of blurring in production identity and practice applies to the study of media work more generally. According to Mark Deuze, 'what typifies media professions in the digital age is an increasing complexity and ongoing liquefaction of the boundaries between different fields, disciplines, practices and categories that used to define what media work was' (2007: 112). This widens the picture of media production and helps us to think about the ways in which industrial sectors such as film and television, advertising and marketing, and digital design have become more porous in their practices, interactions and claims of market territory. Indeed, one of the arguments of this book is that the promotional screen industries are not a clearly defined sector, but a fluid, fast-moving site of industrial collaboration and competition, with promotional intermediaries from different fields moving into each other's territory. Analyzing the 'media logic' that distinguishes professions such as advertising and film and television, Deuze suggests that, in a convergent media era, the forms and processes that organize the work done within a particular area and medium have begun to bleed into each other (2007: 110–112). This can be understood, not least, in the way that new media technologies have accelerated the flow of people, processes and ideas within organizations and between different sectors of the media (ibid.: 235). This fluidity complicates any sense of there being contained, or cleanly bounded, production cultures in the media industries; as the likes of Deuze and Caldwell (2013) both suggest, media work is liquid, industry structures a mess.

Promotional Screen Industries straddles discussions about the textual, cultural and industrial significance of promotional screen content and the hybrid professional sector that produces it. Our approach is interdisciplinary and draws on debates within screen studies, advertising studies, cultural studies and the burgeoning sub-field of media industries studies (Holt and Perren 2009, Havens and Lotz 2011). In methodological terms, this approach is underpinned by interview-based fieldwork with a range of promotional intermediaries primarily located in the media capital of London. Our point of entry was a period of sustained engagement and field research with Red Bee Media, a leading digital and communications company with specialist expertise in television promotion. For an eleven-month period between January and November 2012, we were given access to Red Bee. This enabled us to interview personnel within the company's Creative division (including staff in creative, strategic planning, client services, production and operations teams) and to follow a number of projects from client brief to realization, some of which form the basis of the case studies within this book. During the same period, however, we also interviewed senior executives at a range of other promotional intermediaries, including the advertising agency JWT, the media agency Mindshare, the LA and London-based trailer house Create Advertising, China's largest digital design company Crystal CG, marketing directors at Discovery Networks and Lionsgate, and media executives at the BBC and the marketing body for commercial television in the UK, Thinkbox.

To borrow a phrase from Vicki Mayer's (2008) account of ethnographic interviewing in production studies, we have 'studied up' rather than 'studied down'. That is to say, we have studied up production hierarchies and engaged with senior executives, rather than focus down on ground-level workers. Critically, *Promotional Screen Industries* is concerned with the management and organization of media work rather than below-the-line labour. While we draw attention to macro industry structures and micro interactions, our study concentrates on the 'meso' level of media work. According to Mark Deuze and Brian Steward, of particular concern at this level are 'the organizational management techniques incorporated by (professionals working in or for) media companies' (2011: 6). Within their account, it is at the meso level that negotiations over the 'new identity' of content have been pushed to the fore within industrial theorizing and practice. Although Mayer warns of the dangers of studying up, in particular the tendency for senior (Hollywood) executives to obfuscate and give packaged responses, our experience was defined by openness and enthusiasm on the part of our interviewees. This does not mean to say that we treat interview materials as transparent windows into the promotional professions. They clearly offer partial perspectives and can be slippery forms of evidence. However, whether by luck in our selection of interviewees or the fact that we were engaging with a media profession less called upon to give interviews to academics interested in their work, we found that our interview transcripts offered much more than 'scripted performances' (Caldwell 2009a: 172). Indeed they were vital in offering a viewpoint, and form of discourse, beyond that available in corporate materials and the trade press. Acknowledging that interviews often require subsequent textual analysis, we were afforded rich insight into the practices, vocabularies and self-theorizations of promotional work, in particular the challenges and opportunities that executives at leading companies perceived as key in the early 2010s.

Rather than stand on their own, interviews form one part of our evidentiary base. Developing a production-centred methodology, our analysis is influenced by Caldwell's 'integrated cultural-industrial' approach (2009b). This combines practitioner interviews and fieldwork observation (of production spaces and professional gatherings) with institutional research and textual analysis of promotional screen forms and industrial 'deep texts' such as company workshops, white papers and other semi-public materials. Unlike Caldwell, however, our analysis of the promotional screen industries moves away from a focus on Los Angeles, and towards a different centre of media production in London. This is intended to contribute to the emerging body of work in screen studies expanding the scope of production studies beyond North America (Szczepanik and Vonderau 2013, Banks, Conor and Mayer 2015). At the same time, our chosen focus picks up a rich strain of production-centred analysis in advertising studies; it contributes to work on promotional practice by the likes of Chris Hackley (2010) and Jing Wang (2008) who examine agency culture in established promotional centres like London and emerging media capitals such as Beijing.

While the industrial changes being mapped in this book are not confined to a single regional territory or city, London provides a site to tease out the complex configurations that make up the promotional screen industries. In Part II, London provides a particular basis for our case chapters, all of which focus on companies that have either headquarters or international hubs in the city. London is a useful site for mapping the promotional screen industries because it is unusually clustered in terms of the creative sectors that operate within the city.[4] In advertising, according to one creative industry consultancy document,

> London is acknowledged as one of the three global capitals for the industry (along with New York and Tokyo). London has often been used as a base for targeting pan-European and global markets, with two thirds of all international agencies having their European headquarters in the city.
>
> (BOP Consulting et al. 2006: 11)

While advertising was London's third largest sector in terms of employment in 2010 (after publishing, and software and electronic publishing) (Freeman 2011: 3), the city is also a hub for specialist services for the screen industries such as special effects and post-production. These services tend to be based in Soho, alongside film funders, distributors, international television companies and technical and artistic specialists (Pratt and Gornostaeva 2009: 129–30). As Pratt and Gornostaeva argue, London is 'a global city and an international node of image production (film, theatre, fine art, new media and advertising)' (ibid.: 133). However, it is not just in these areas that London has emerged as a global hub. The growth of the international design industry in the 1980s and 1990s also saw London emerge as a global centre with an especially high concentration of design practices. Around the areas of Shoreditch, Hoxton and Old Street (often termed the 'Silicon roundabout') a cluster of design, technology and digital companies emerged in the 2000s, supported by the establishment of the Tech City Investment Organization by the British government in 2010 to drive development of the digital technology sector in the east of the city. According to Gilles Albaredes, former managing director of the London hub of Chinese digital company Crystal CG,[5] 'London is unique in design terms as everything is in one city' (2011). As this comment suggests, London brings together a range of creative industry sectors within a single place and on a significant scale.[6] This includes advertising, design, film and television, digital and new media, all of which are central to the business of promotion. London, therefore, offers a useful focal point to map out the complex interrelationships between the types of companies, agencies and boutiques that operate and compete in the promotional screen industries.

London is also relevant in terms of our period of study. This spans the 2000s and early 2010s but looks, in particular, at the period between 2005 and 2014. These timeframes correspond with key (if uneven) developments in digital media culture, notably the rise of online video (prefigured by the launch of YouTube in 2005), the development of socially networked communication, the switchover to digital television and other modes of connected viewing, and the rise of the smartphone and tablet. London, and the UK more generally, became an especially active site for digital media developments in the first decades of the twenty-first century. In 2011 the UK had the highest penetration of digital television in any global market and the second highest use of online television on-demand services behind the United States (Strange 2011: 133). It also had the heaviest users of social media in the world, London being the Twitter capital according to the managing director of consumer and online for Microsoft UK (Highfield 2011). Moreover, as we shall see in Chapter 3, the UK became a host for government-led policy discussion about 'being digital' (Carter 2009). While this book is not about the British market specifically, the UK provides a backdrop for analysing the response of the promotional screen sector to transitions in the digital environment. These transitions, which can be linked to shifts in the ecology of media content, provide the frame for the book as a whole.

As a form of cultural analysis, our study is informed by William Boddy's rich historicization of media conjunctures. Focusing on the precise contexts in which promotional forms and practices emerge, we consider, in particular, 'the new strategic imperatives of ubiquity, mobility and interactivity' that Boddy suggests took hold in the media and marketing industries in the mid to late 2000s (2011: 76). In examining screen promotion in a specific period of time, we do not claim that promotional forms have only ever been seen or configured as 'content' in the 2000s, or that the sectors of advertising, film and television, and design have never developed relationships before. There are strong residual elements in the kinds of promotional blurring we discuss throughout this book (see Spigel 2008, Gillan 2015). However, we do claim that there have been substantive changes in the media landscape in the last two decades, and that the industries of advertising, film and television, and digital design have come to exist, interact and respond to these changes in certain ways. It is our contention that these responses warrant examination if we are to understand the particularity and significance of the blurring taking place within contemporary screen practice.

In structuring our argument, we move from the contextual to the case-specific. *Promotional Screen Industries* is organized in two parts. Part I examines the status of promotional screen content and the sector and work of the inter-mediaries that produce it. Chapter 1 explores the set of transformations in media culture that lie behind the reconceptualization of promotion as content; it examines how three key areas of promotional practice – screen advertising, film and television marketing, and corporate and organizational promotion – have responded to digital media shifts that have unsettled distinctions between pro-motion and content. During the 2000s, media and consumer brands increasingly sought to transform promotional texts into entertaining or useful media that audiences would be motivated to seek out and interact with. We explore this content ecology both in broad terms and in relation to the specific case of 'branded entertainment', a site that is especially revealing of the blurred lines of adver-tising and entertainment media within contemporary screen practice (specifically in nascent areas like online video). Chapter 2 takes a more production studies approach. First, it examines the fluid configurations that have seen promotional intermediaries from the sectors of advertising, film and television marketing, and digital design compete and collaborate for promotional screen work. Second, it explores the operational management of such work, using Red Bee Media to draw out divisions, roles, spaces and routines within a company that purposefully blurs the 'media logic' of advertising and broadcasting. Finally, the chapter considers promotion as a form of creative labour, examining the values (and hierarchies) of creativity revealed in trade awards, labour disputes and expectations around skill-sets. In critical terms, Part I examines how shifts in the media environment since the 2000s have shaped the production, circulation and status of promotional screen texts, and considers the extent to which tex-tual blurring between promotion/content corresponds with industrial blurring within and between the companies and occupations that actively produce promotional screen artefacts.

A key part of the argument in Part I is the fluidity of the promotional screen sector. We examine the intersection of client work and integration of skills between advertising and media agencies, film and television marketing compa-nies, and digital media design agencies. It remains the case, however, that even with the convergence of media aesthetics, economics and labour, companies still proffer expertise in relation to particular industries and forms. Accordingly, having established the contextual and conceptual frameworks that shape the book, Part II uses case studies to explore dynamics of contemporary screen promotion that focus on the respective, albeit connected, media of mobile communication, television, film and live events. Each chapter in Part II considers different kinds of *promotional screen intermediaries* (ad agencies, television promotion specialists, trailer houses, digital design agencies) and their relation to the promotional needs of clients in particular industry fields. This provides a means of examining indicative types of *promotional screen media* (ads, promos, apps, trailers, interactive web materials, bid videos, mascot films, digital venue animations) and the functions these serve as forms of content. Extending these concerns, the chapters also consider, more broadly, how promotional texts help navigate and imagine transformations reshaping media culture in the digital era. Critically, this final area overlays industrial and textual questions about *media promotion* (who does it? what are its creative forms? what role do these forms play?) with cultural and discursive questions about the *promotion of media* (how do promotional texts help define, explain and rationalize digital developments in particular media sectors?).

Chapter 3 provides the groundwork for analysing 'the new strategic imperatives of ubiquity, mobility and interactivity' that supply a theme in our analysis. We begin Part II with a case example that explicitly pursues, and dramatizes, these priorities on behalf of the mobile industry. Mobile and social networks have become a central site of change in the media environment, and have obliged established industries such as television and film to manage and respond to the digital possibilities and affordances that networks present. Chapter 3 examines how these possibilities have been framed within screen advertising. In specific terms we examine how an established advertising agency (Saatchi & Saatchi) developed promotional content strategies for the telecommunications firm T-Mobile in the late 2000s and early 2010s, and imagined new social relationships enabled by mobile technologies. Saatchi's 'Life's for Sharing' campaign, introduced in 2009, is emblematic of the way that screen advertising has sought in the last decade to blur status distinctions between promotion and content. In particular, the campaign's flashmob ads provide a critical vantage on the dynamics of 'spreadable marketing' (Jenkins, Ford and Green 2013) and promotional co-production that have developed within a world of networked communication.

Chapter 4 turns to television, where the new social behaviours afforded by digitalization have threatened established business models, challenging the relationship between the television industry and its audience. In this context, promotional screen intermediaries occupy an important position as navigators of media change for television broadcasters. Focusing on the work of Red Bee Media and the production of transmedia promotion and second screen apps, the chapter argues that promotional screen content offers a site through which to examine the ways in which the television industry attempts to manage the potentially unruly behaviours of the digital television viewer. In doing so it reveals how the demands of contemporary television promotion are troubling established professional boundaries between marketing and programme production.

If Chapter 4 explores the ways in which promotional screen texts, and the intermediaries that produce them, are helping the television industry to navigate transitions in the digital media environment, Chapter 5 extends these concerns to the film industry. Specifically, it examines the production and changing status of the trailer as a form of promotional screen content that has assumed a particular value online. Through an analysis of the marketing for blockbuster franchise *The Hunger Games* (2012–), the chapter explores the ways in which the trailer is situated within a larger promotional infrastructure that aims to construct an ongoing, targeted and participative relationship with viewers. Examining the role of the LA and London-based trailer house Create Advertising, and the wider function of film distributors in the marketing of Hollywood movies, Chapter 5 considers how promotional texts help position cinema as part of a broader digital social experience that is enacted online. More broadly, by drawing attention to the processes through which Hollywood products are positioned globally, the chapter suggests that promotional screen intermediaries are a potent site through which to examine the negotiations of control between Hollywood and local players in the global circulation of movies and film culture.

Finally, Chapter 6 opens out perspectives on the promotional screen industries by examining the digital short-forms and design work used for context-specific events and spaces. This moves our discussion beyond the world of ads, promos and trailers to content forms produced for, and on behalf of, the organizing committees of global media events. Taking the London 2012 Olympic and Paralympic Games as a point of departure, Chapter 6 examines China's largest digital design company, Crystal CG, and its role as official 'Digital Imaging Services Supplier' for the London Games. In this role Crystal produced digital promotional content including stadium visualizations, presentational media, mascot films and experiential pixel animations that appeared within the Olympic stadium. In case terms, Crystal demonstrates the global flows of promotional screen work. However, its digital work also moves the analysis of promotion beyond the content made for cinema, television, computer and mobile devices. Instead, it highlights the rich variety of screen media produced for 'out-of-home' and 'experiential' markets, including promotional screen forms used by corporate and organizational bodies.

In his insightful discussion of the 'popular imagination' of new media, William Boddy suggests that moments of transition within media history such as the arrival of digital audiovisual technologies are significant not only for what they reveal about 'technological innovation, market restructuring, and changes in traditional representational practices' (2004: 2) but also for what they produce in a vernacular sense. He argues that by looking at self-representations of media it is possible to uncover 'strategic fantasies of consumption' that shape ideas about media life and practice (ibid.). As artefacts of screen culture, promotional texts are especially suggestive self-representations, and are revealing, across Part II, of the way that media technologies, entertainment properties, and even nations, have sought to represent themselves and construct consumers, audiences, and publics. A thread that joins each case study is the relation of promotional screen forms to adjustments wrought by digitalization. This is examined in terms of professional and creative practice but also via the textual forms and self-representations that result. While the examples in each chapter may be specific in media, time and place – from T-Mobile's flashmob ads to the promotion of BBC's *Planet Earth Live* (2012), and from the blockbuster marketing of *The Hunger Games* franchise to the digital paratexts produced for the London Games – these all open out wider perspectives on screen promotion at the dawn of the twenty-first century.

Part of the fascination of researching this book was the opportunity we had to visit and explore the offices of the companies where our interviews and fieldwork took place. This often meant shuttling between different parts of London, arriving at headquarters that were sometimes sleek and spacious units within larger media complexes (Red Bee Media, Mindshare, Discovery) but were just as often anonymously marked buildings (JWT), townhouses (Thinkbox), and rented office spaces (Create Advertising, Crystal CG) in central London. Through regular trips to the White City office of Red Bee Media, we became familiar with a particular object that would be parked, sometimes in different places, on the floor of the Creative department. Amidst the desks, and positioned without ceremony, was a supermarket shopping trolley loaded with Promax Gold awards, similar to those won by 4Creative for 'Meet the Superhumans'. This was a clever piece of corporate messaging; it communicated that Red Bee was a company that had won so many awards in the field of television promotion that it could afford to pile them on top of each other; it implied that taking home gold statuettes was as common as shopping for groceries. And yet,

Figure 0.2 Red Bee Media's shopping trolley of Promax awards (2012). Courtesy of Red Bee Media.

there was also something about the trolley that felt discarded, as if the Promax awards were past their shelf life.

This whimsical form of award display captured, perhaps unwittingly, a prevailing view of promotion and its place within audiovisual culture and the media industries – as something ubiquitous but also commercial, disposable and apt to be disregarded. Rather than join laments about the influence of promotion and marketing in everyday life, *Promotional Screen Industries* takes seriously the work of a professional sector that is all too easily dismissed. Responding to Jonathan Gray's call for more study of the 'production cultures around paratexts' (2010: 221) – but significantly extending the focus to forms and intermediaries beyond the world of film and television – we examine promotion as a screen discipline with its own opportunities, challenges and systems of creative reward. When Promax commissioned the design of its Gold award statuette in 1995, it was titled 'the Muse of Creativity'. While our analysis stops short of such elevated claims of inspiration, we do make room for the art of promotion and for the significance of a creative industry sector that encapsulates the blurring boundary lines of contemporary screen practice.

Notes

1 Promax was established in the US in 1956 as a non-profit, membership-driven association for promotion and marketing professionals working in broadcast media. In 1997, it partnered with the Broadcast Design Association (BDA) to become PromaxBDA. Annual conferences take place in 'Europe, Arabia, United States, Asia, Australia, Africa, New Zealand, South America and the UK' (PromaxBDA 2014). Promax licenses two separate events in the European region, Promax Europe (held in March) and Promax UK (held in November).

2 The film depicted a bomb exploding, a car crash and a pregnant woman hearing the news that her child will be disabled. The film's director Tom Tagholm explains, 'we really didn't want to shoot around the particular physical attributes of these athletes and their disabilities. We wanted to absolutely embrace all of that – their stance, the ways they've adapted to their sport, the ways that they use their bodies' (Channel 4 2012). The trailer was not without its critics, however. In particular, the use of the word 'superhuman' became a source of debate within online discussion of the trailer's representation of disability, some observers feeling this an inappropriate tagline for the way it presented Paralympic athletes as other and freakish (Anon. 2012).

3 Idents are short graphic sequences used to depict television channels and are often referred to as 'IDs' in the US. The terminology for promotional screen forms can vary. In the television industry, for example, 'promo' and 'trailer' (or trail) are often used interchangeably, with 'spot' also used in the US market. While 'promo' can encompass the whole campaign, trailers are more often used to describe traditional 30-, 60- or 15-second spots (Hughes 2012).

4 In a discussion of the role of cities as the site of clusters, Terry Flew argues that 'London is the archetypal global city, sitting at the centre of international business and finance, politics and culture' (2012: 150). Indeed London dominates the creative industries in the UK with 35.5 percent of the UK's creative enterprises in 2011 being based in London, this figure rising to 52.7 percent when the area includes London and the South East (DCMS 2011: 30).

5 Chapter 6 offers a more detailed analysis of Crystal CG.

6 London is distinguished from the likes of Los Angeles in this respect. While LA is the home of film and television production, the major hubs of software and advertising are located elsewhere in the US, in Northern California (Silicon Valley) and New York respectively.

Bibliography

Albaredes, G. (2011) *Interview with authors*, 14 July.

Anon. (2012) 'Are They Superhuman?'. Online. Available: http://theinclusionclub.com/episodes/superhumans/ (accessed 8 July 2014).

Banks, M., Conor, B. and Mayer, V. (eds) (2015) *Production Studies, Volume II*, London and New York: Routledge.

Boddy, W. (2011) '"Is it TV Yet?" The Dislocated Screens of Television in a Mobile Digital Culture', in J. Bennett and N. Strange (eds) *Television as Digital Media*, Durham: Duke University Press.

——(2004) *New Media and Popular Imagination*, Oxford: Oxford University Press.

BOP Consulting, MIP C and NESTA (2006) *Creating Growth: How the UK Can Develop World Class Creative Businesses*, London: Nesta.

Caldwell, J. T. (2013) 'Para-Industry: Researching Hollywood's Backwaters', *Cinema Journal*, 52 (3): 157–65.

——(2009a) 'Screen Studies and Industrial Theorizing', *Screen*, 50 (1): 167–79.

——(2009b) 'Cultures of Production: Studying Industry's Deep Texts, Reflective Rituals and Managed Self-Disclosures', in J. Holt and A. Perren (eds) *Media Industries: History, Theory, and Method*, Oxford: Wiley-Blackwell.

——(2008) *Production Culture: Industrial Self-Reflexivity and Critical Practice in Film and Television*, Durham: Duke University Press.

Carter, S. (2009) *Digital Britain*, London: HM Government, Department of Business Innovation & Skills and Department for Culture, Media & Sport.

Channel 4 (2012) 'Decoding the Superhumans Trailer'. Online. Available: http://archive.today/NLVfA (accessed 4 January 2013).

Davis, A. (2013) *Promotional Cultures*, Cambridge: Polity.

Dawson, M. (2011) 'Television's Aesthetic of Efficiency: Convergence Television and the Digital Short', in J. Bennett and N. Strange (eds) *Television as Digital Media*, Durham: Duke University Press.

DCMS (2011) *Creative Industries Economic Estimates: Full Statistical Release*, London: DCMS, December.

Deuze, M. (2007) *Media Work*, Cambridge: Polity.

Deuze, M. and Steward, B. (2011) 'Managing Media Work', in M. Deuze (ed.) *Managing Media Work*, London: Sage.

Flew, T. (2012) *The Creative Industries: Culture and Policy*, London: Sage.

Freeman, A. (2011) 'London's Creative Industries 2011 Update', *Current Issues*, Note 33, London: GLA.

Gillan, J. (2015) *Television Brandcasting: The Return of the Content Promotion Hybrid*, London and New York: Routledge.

Grainge, P. (ed.) (2011) *Ephemeral Media: Transitory Screen Culture from Television to YouTube*, London: British Film Institute.

——(2008) *Brand Hollywood: Selling Entertainment in a Global Media Age*, London and New York: Routledge.

Grainge, P. and Johnson, C. (2015) '"Show Us Your Moves": Trade Rituals of Television Marketing', *Arts Marketing*, forthcoming.

Gray, J. (2010) *Show Sold Separately: Promos, Spoilers and Other Media Paratexts*, New York: New York University Press.

Hackley, C. (2010) *Advertising and Promotion: An Integrated Marketing Communications Approach*, 2nd edition, London: Sage.

Havens, T. and Lotz, A. (2011) *Understanding Media Industries*, Oxford: Oxford University Press.

Highfield, A. (2011) 'The Multi-Platform Market', paper presented at *The Future of Advertising*, Westminster Media Forum. London: 31 May. London: Westminster Media Forum.

Holt, J. and Perren, A. (eds) (2009) *Media Industries: History, Theory and Method*, Oxford: Wiley-Blackwell.

Holt. J. and Sanson, K. (eds) (2014) *Connected Viewing: Selling, Streaming and Sharing Media in the Digital Era*, London and New York: Routledge.

Hughes, T. (2012) *Interview with authors*, 25 October.

Jenkins, H., Ford, S. and Green, J. (2013) *Spreadable Media: Creating Value and Meaning in a Networked Culture*, New York: New York University Press.

Johnson, C. (2012) *Branding Television*, London and New York: Routledge.

Johnston, K. M. (2009) *Coming Soon: Film Trailers and the Selling of Hollywood Technology*, Jefferson: McFarland and Co.

Kernan, L. (2004) *Coming Attractions: Reading American Movie Trailers*, Austin: University of Texas Press.

Mayer, V. (2011) *Below the Line: Producers and Production Studies in the New Television Economy*, Durham: Duke University Press.

——(2008) 'Studying Up and F**cking Up: Ethnographic Interviewing in Production Studies', *Cinema Journal*, 47 (2): 141–48.

Mayer, V., Banks, M. and Caldwell, J.T. (eds) (2009) *Production Studies: Cultural Studies of Media*, London and New York: Routledge.

McAllister, M. P. and West, E. (eds) (2013) *The Routledge Companion to Advertising and Promotional Culture*, London and New York: Routledge.

Powell, H. (ed.) (2013a) *Promotional Culture and Convergence: Markets, Methods, Media*, London and New York: Routledge.

——(2013b) 'Introduction: Promotion in an Era of Convergence', in H. Powell (ed.) *Promotional Culture and Convergence*, London and New York: Routledge.

——(2013c) 'The Promotional Industries', in H. Powell (ed.) *Promotional Culture and Convergence*, London and New York: Routledge.

Pratt, A. and Gornostaeva, G. (2009) 'The Governance of Innovation in the Film and Television Industry: a Case Study of London, UK', in A. Pratt and P. Jeffcutt (eds) *Creativity, Innovation and the Cultural Economy*, London and New York: Routledge.

PromaxBDA (2014) 'About Promax BDA'. Online. Available: http://promaxbda.org/about (accessed 30 March 2014).

Red Bee Media (2012) 'Meet Red Bee Media'. Online. Available: http://www.redbee media.com/work/meet-red-bee-media (accessed 12 November 2012).

Spigel, L. (2008) *TV By Design: Modern Art and the Rise of Network Television*, Chicago: University of Chicago Press.

Strange, N. (2011) 'Multiplatforming Public Service: The BBC's "Bundled Project"', in J. Bennett and N. Strange (eds), *Television as New Media*, Durham: Duke University Press.

Szczepanik, P. and Vonderau, P. (eds) (2013) *Behind the Screen: Inside European Production Cultures*, New York: Palgrave Macmillan.

Walker, J. (2012) 'Show Us Your Moves', presentation delivered at Promax UK, London, 8 November.

Wang, J. (2008) *Brand New China: Advertising, Media and Commercial Culture*, Cambridge, MA: Harvard University Press.

Wernick, A. (1991) *Promotional Culture: Advertising, Ideology and Symbolic Expression*, London: Sage.

West, E. and McAllister, M. P. (2013) 'Introduction', in M.P. McAllister and E. West (eds) *The Routledge Companion to Advertising and Promotional Culture*, London and New York: Routledge.

Part I

The Blurring Boundaries of Promotion and Content

1 On Promotional Screen Content

> It's a problematic term really, I mean the term content ... you know it's just
> such a horrible word. We use it because there is no better alternative and it's
> becoming the industry descriptor of choice.
>
> (Andy Bryant, Director of Creative, Red Bee Media 2012)

Again and again in the interviews we conducted for this book with professionals
from the promotional screen industries, the word 'content' recurred. From references
to 'branded content', 'liquid content' and 'catalytic content' to 'content
platforms', the term has become pervasive in discussions across the media
industries. In November 2012 the UK branch of the media agency Mindshare
held one of its annual 'huddles' focused specifically on 'the future of content'.
The day-long event addressed the changing face of content across film, music,
television, news and technology, and included sessions called the 'creative content
lifecycle', 'the future of content is data', and 'is user-generated content the most
engaging content?' A year later, the Minnesota Interactive Marketing Association
held a sell-out event that examined 'what content really means' (MIMA 2013).
If, as these examples suggest, the status of content is up for grabs, so too are
questions about who gets to define the term in the world of digital media. As the
former founding editor of *Entertainment Weekly* noted in a blog titled 'What is
content, then?', 'We in media ... think we get to define what content is: It's what
we make. But Google, for one, doesn't define content that way. It sees content
everywhere' (Jarvis 2010). These definitional issues are equally felt within academic
debate. Paul McDonald, for instance, has argued that scholars in screen studies
have 'to face up to the unavoidable fact that film now exists as "content" in the
convergent media environment, alongside – and integrated with – consumer
video, games, music, and online video' (2013: 148). Although sometimes used in
begrudging ways by academics and industry executives alike – Mike Weise of
the ad agency JWT calling it 'the dreaded buzzword' (2011) – 'content' has
nevertheless become a ubiquitous designation that speaks to the unsettling of
established discourses and practices within contemporary media production.

In considering this designation, Simone Murray writes of a 'quintessentially
21st-century conceptualization of content as innately liquid and multipurposable'

(2005: 419). Like McDonald, she connects this with developments in entertainment media, and in particular, the ways in which 'content packages' are put together around anchor products such as movie blockbusters. Yet beyond Murray's discussions of cross-promotion, franchising and media branding are increasingly destabilized textual hierarchies between anchor products and promotional materials. As John Caldwell argues, promotional materials 'persistently migrate or travel towards "primary" textual status' within contemporary screen culture (2006: 103). Across our interviews, content was used not only to refer to films and television programmes, but also to a range of media paratexts and promotional forms that circulate between, beyond and below studio and network output. Indeed, the adoption of the term 'content' by the advertising industry in contemporary media discourse suggests that this blurring of promotion and content extends to more than the film and television industries and encompasses a broader cultural shift in screen media practice. On these terms, the liquidity of content not only describes the way that media brands transfer between platforms, it also suggests a loosening in the very parameters of what is defined as content and who produces that content.

In this chapter our intention is not to resolve these definitional difficulties, but rather to unpack the set of transitions within media culture that lie behind the reconceptualization of promotion as content. We address this in two ways. First, we examine the changes within media culture that have led to a blurring between 'promotion' and 'content' in a period when an increasing range of texts have come to circulate in more profuse ways across a greater range of screens and platforms. Second, we consider the specific case of branded entertainment. As Jennifer Gillan (2015) notes, branded entertainment is by no means new; 'content promotion hybrids' (sponsor entwinements, dramatized advertisements, product integrations) were utilized widely in mid-century American television programming. However, just as these strategies were a response to a period of media transition in the 1950s and 1960s – regarding the impact of new technologies on business models, fears about emergent viewing platforms, and anxieties about the behaviour of once dependence audiences – branded entertainment responded to an equivalent sense of transition in the first decades of the twenty-first century. As a site of discursive investment in the 2000s and 2010s, the term would come to denote the creation of promotion 'of such merit or interest that the audience actively seeks it out' (Lotz 2007: 172). In case terms, branded entertainment encapsulates the fluid boundaries of promotion and content within contemporary screen culture and reveals the shifting industrial configurations, and trade theorizations, that sit behind this change.

Blurred lines: the scope and status of promotional screen content

Promotional screen content can be broadly located within three areas that will be variously explored in this book: screen advertising, film and television marketing, and corporate and organizational promotion. These three areas have distinct histories, but each has undergone significant change as a consequence of broader shifts within the media landscape in the last two decades. While, as we shall go on to see, the precise nature of the change differs in relation to each area, they are similarly shaped by 'the new strategic imperatives of ubiquity, mobility and interactivity' (Boddy 2011: 76) that we outlined in the introduction to this book. These strategic imperatives offer a useful structuring device for mapping out the contexts within which the boundary lines between promotion and content have blurred in the contemporary media terrain.

The first decades of the twenty-first century have been characterized by a rapid increase in the number of sites where audiovisual forms can be viewed. These range from the development of new platforms for moving images, such as smartphones and tablets, to the growth of out-of-home media, such as digital billboards and interactive installations. In many senses, this increased *ubiquity* of audiovisual media can be traced back to developments in satellite, cable, fibre optics and broadband that have been expanding sites for accessing films, television programmes and advertising materials for decades. Yet the ubiquity of screen media has been accelerated by digitalization during the 2000s. This has facilitated the ease with which audiovisual texts can be reproduced and transferred across different platforms (Creeber and Martin 2009: 2). As such, the increased ubiquity of moving image media is intricately tied up with the increased *mobility* of such media. While, as Chuck Tryon (2013) argues, digital delivery has been technologically feasible since the late 1990s, it is only since the mid-2000s that it has begun to emerge as a dominant feature of the contemporary media landscape. This ranges from the expansion of digital cinema and television to the emergence of the internet as a platform for audiovisual material, notably in the burgeoning area of online video. More generally, the web has had a significant impact on the media terrain both in expanding the sites for moving image content and by facilitating the ways in which that content can be distributed and circulated (Tryon 2013). Beyond the emergence of digital cinema and television is what Tryon refers to as 'platform mobility' characterized by 'the ongoing shift towards ubiquitous, mobile access to a wide range of entertainment choices' (2013: 4).

The proliferation of sites for accessing audiovisual media and the ease with which that media can travel across platforms has led to increased audience fragmentation. Far from the mass audiences of the 'era of scarcity' (Ellis 2000), digital delivery addresses targeted or even individualized viewers through interfaces that purport to offer choice and control over media viewing (Tryon 2013). The increased ubiquity and mobility of media, therefore, is accompanied by a new dynamic of media consumption characterized by *interactivity*. Again, this can be understood as an extension of, rather than a radical break from, the past. With their roots in technologies such as the television remote control, new interfaces such as the personal video recorder or on-demand media services (such as Hulu and the BBC iPlayer) offer the contemporary viewer far greater choice and control over what, where and when to watch moving image content. This is what Philip Napoli refers to as 'audience autonomy', describing the extent to which audiences have control over their processes of media consumption (2011: 7). While alterations in the nature of viewer engagement are often discussed in relation to interactive forms of storytelling or participative forms of production (Jenkins 2006), Napoli argues that the key shift in audience autonomy lies not in the viewer's capacity to produce content, but to circulate it (2011: 81). Facilitated by video-sharing sites such as YouTube and social networking sites like Facebook and Twitter, this is what Jenkins, Ford and Green (2013) discuss as the new 'spreadability' of media. Epitomized in the concept of 'Web 2.0', the internet has become a participatory platform 'predicated on sharing, collaboration and content creation' (McStay 2010: 37). In this context, digital networks provide a space where content functions as part of the broader participatory culture of online social interaction. As such, ubiquity, mobility and interactivity should not be understood as distinct, but rather as interrelated phenomena tied to the expansion of networked digital sites that facilitate greater circulation of, and interaction with, audiovisual content.

These shifts in the media landscape are often positioned as a feature or consequence of convergence. Jonathan Hardy (2013) distinguishes between three areas of media convergence: technological, textual and industrial. Technological convergence is characterized by the emergence of networked systems that offer the potential for seamless digital interchangeability of media across platforms. This brings with it the potential for textual convergence where images and sounds can be experienced across a range of different media and can be recombined, unbundled and recomposed with ease. Meanwhile, industrial convergence describes the formation of giant media conglomerates that exploit this space by carrying, and controlling, the multiple media services that define contemporary communications systems. On these terms, media convergence describes a complex and uneven set of processes, practices, market conditions and power relations that centre on the 'coming together of different technologies and industries to create new ways of producing, distributing and using cultural goods and services' (Hardy 2013: 126, see also Meikle and Young 2012). In practice, convergence involves degrees of *divergence* in the way that different kinds of media are produced and consumed in relation to one another (Jenkins 2006). As Gerard Goggin argues, 'the process of achieving digital technologies and their convergence is actually a messy, complicated, politically loaded and historically contingent affair' (2012: 17). The rhetoric of convergence, therefore, can belie the continued institutional, technological and cultural barriers that constrain and shape the digital media landscape. Indeed Anja Bechmann Petersen (2006: 95) argues that the digital media environment is better understood as 'cross-media' rather than 'convergent', characterized by the coexistence of different media platforms and sites whereby the strategic imperatives of ubiquity, mobility and interactivity present possibilities and challenges to media organizations as something to be both exploited and controlled.

The shifts thus far outlined have fundamental ramifications for the traditional business models of the media industries, leading some to argue that the contemporary media scene is characterized by the development of a new 'attention economy' where the ubiquity and mobility of media has led to greater competition for audiences (Goldhaber 1997, Davenport and Beck 2001). While Max Dawson notes the pre-history of the attention economy thesis, dating back to the 1970s and theories of information overabundance, it was updated in the 1990s and 2000s to 'describe the ways in which digital technologies were transforming not only the global economy but also people's everyday experience of labour and leisure' (Dawson 2014: 231). One consequence for media producers of purported attention scarcity is that all forms of content have to work harder to stand out. This is not just because there is more audiovisual content. It also stems from the new possibilities of access and agency afforded to audiences *in relation to* content. While media and marketing companies still retain control over the ways in which films, television programmes and ad campaigns are released, they operate in a media environment where the 'plasticity' and 'malleability' of digital content more easily enables texts to be copied, edited, reshaped and recombined (Arvidsson 2006).

In the new economics of attention, it is not just the amount of time that people devote to media content that is at stake, but also the quality of that attention (Dovey 2011). Content is not simply about ratings and viewing hits, in this sense, but also the depth of involvement, interest and feeling (or affect) that audiovisual forms can inspire. This is not to argue that there has never been an attention economy around media. After all, the economics of the thirty-second advertising spot is predicated on the sale of viewer attention. As Ben Roberts argues, modern consumer capitalist economies have a history of attempting 'to organize attention through the agency of advertising and public relations' (2012: 4). Neither is it to argue that audience engagement with screen media has never been two-way before, as anyone who has ever written to a television programme or magazine would attest. However, digitalization does increase the possibilities for media producers to involve audiences in the process of making, creating and distributing content. From a promotional perspective, this is not benign. Adam Arvidsson argues that the rise of the internet has led to a shift in marketing theories in which consumers are understood to be 'empowered and interactive and should be invited to participate in the elaboration of the brand, as well as the product or service that they purchase' (2006: 101). However, he challenges accounts that see this as a shift of power from vendors to customers. Rather he relates such theories to the commodification of participation and to the development of corporate strategies 'that aim to put consumers to work in the production of forms of content that can be sold back to them' (2006: 104). In this case, the rhetoric of audience participation belies a tactical front in digital promotional culture where interactivity becomes a potential means of harnessing free labour and generating personalized data that can be mined and sold.

If the contemporary media landscape is characterized by a blurring of the categories of promotion and content, this blurring stems from the uncertainties that arise in the face of shifts within the media ecology that threaten to radically alter the relationship between audiences, producers and distributors of moving image content. The period since the early 2000s can be understood, then, as one of continued transition, in which change and stasis are being negotiated in complex ways. The next sections will examine these negotiations in relation to the specific challenges posed within the areas of screen advertising, film and television marketing, and organizational and corporate promotion.

Screen advertising

Traditionally, screen advertising has been typified by the thirty-second advertising spot.[1] Emerging as the dominant form of audiovisual advertising in the 1960s, the thirty-second spot separated advertising from the other forms of screen content (television programmes and movies) around which it sat. This separation was driven in part by regulatory concerns to maintain a distinction between 'commercial' and 'creative' speech (Schejter 2006: 98). The UK public service broadcasting system, for example, specifically adopted spot advertising as a model for the funding of commercial public service television in order to limit the influence of advertisers on content (Turnock 2007: 145, Murdock 1992). Even within the highly commercial system of television broadcasting in the US, spots emerged as the preferred model for television advertising in part in the wake of the quiz show scandals of the 1950s in which sponsors were found to be rigging televised quizzes in order to increase ratings (Lotz 2007: 152–92).[2]

The separation of screen advertising from film and television content extended into the production cultures for each industry. Although, as Hackley and Hackley argue, the creative revolution in the ad industry during the 1960s 'transformed advertising into a glamorous and lucrative creative industry aligned with movies and TV, rather than simply a business service' (2013: 75), screen advertising developed over this period as a specialism distinct from the production of movies and television shows. While there was movement of creative personnel between advertising and film and television (Spigel 2008: 213–50), there developed a discrete production culture for screen advertising. From the 1960s, the advertising industry would be driven by the TV spot as the primary form of screen promotion. In this context, ad agencies sold expertise in the craft of the commercial spot, forming the bedrock of advertising work for several decades.

At the turn of the twenty-first century, the increase in competition from cable, satellite, gaming, the internet and mobile platforms gave rise to a media environment that threatened the dominance of the traditional spot commercial. Television channels could no longer guarantee to deliver mass audiences to advertisers, and time-shifting technologies like the personal video recorder enabled viewers to avoid TV ads altogether. At the same time, new digital platforms provided opportunities to develop more interactive relationships with consumers, relationships that could be monitored to provide valuable consumer data. Amanda Lotz suggests that by the mid-2000s, through a combination of factors that included the effect of the economic downturn on the advertising market, the ad industry reached a 'tipping point' at which the risk of trying something beyond the thirty-second spot 'appeared less dangerous than blindly maintaining the status quo' (2007: 154).

Within advertising discourse the challenges posed by technological, economic and media change in the 2000s precipitated a shift in emphasis from 'interruptive' to 'engagement' advertising models. Dean Baker, a senior executive at the ad agency JWT London, provides a summary of this outlook:

> Everybody has always said that the thirty-second commercial is dead ... and whilst I don't think that is necessarily true, it is certainly the way it is heading ... It's changing from the interruptive model where you're renting someone else's audience and [saying] let's just interrupt what they were actually engaged with and put our thirty-second commercial out there, to one which is much more of an engagement model so that they [the viewer] would actually choose to spend time with whatever it is that you were producing with the brand.
>
> (Baker 2012b)

These ideas are reiterated in academic scholarship on promotional culture. Helen Powell argues that 'one of the fundamental changes experienced in the last twenty years is a shift in the nature of promotion from one based on interruption to one informed by engagement' (2013: 16). Emily West and Matthew McAllister concur, claiming that digital promotional culture challenges the previous assumption that 'advertising is necessarily unwelcome content imposed on audiences whose main priority is to avoid it' (2013: 7). The move from interruption to engagement speaks to a fundamental shift in the very conceptualization of marketing in the 2000s. For Powell, this is characterized by 'a marketing model that moves away from the "push" of messages onto a large mass target market, to the evolution of new, more personalized, customized approaches that "pull" the consumer in through what the brand has to offer' (2013: 2).

These industrial and academic discourses make a compelling case for promotional forms that actively engage the individuated consumer, necessary in an attention economy in which all content 'must now compete to get noticed' (ibid.: 16). Yet we need to be careful of buying into this rhetoric of transition too uncritically. To argue for a shift from interruption to engagement suggests that earlier forms of screen advertising were not attempting to engage consumers. Equally, it implies that contemporary advertising no longer interrupts. The nostalgia surrounding old spot commercials attests to the pleasures offered by traditional forms of screen advertising. As John Ellis argues,

> Commercials, and indeed interstitials more generally, are deeply concerned with the generation of a sense of beauty. This is the reason why they stand out from the TV that surrounds them, and why they have greater production values. It also enables viewers to watch and enjoy the most stylish commercials even when they have no intention of buying the products.
>
> (2011: 65)

It is useful to remember that anxieties about viewer resistance to advertising are not unique to the digital era and that advertising practitioners have long been occupied with how best to engage audiences to promote products and services (Hackley 2005). At the same time, the will to interrupt has not lessened. While the interruptive television spot remains a fixture of screen life and media business, the internet has ushered in new forms of interruption such as pop-ups and upfront advertising that must be endured to access certain forms of online content.[3] This does not mean that there has been no significant change to screen advertising in the digital era. Rather it is to argue that accounts of a move from 'interruptive' to 'engagement' advertising need to be understood – much as the debates about the definition of content – as part of a discursive shift whereby the advertising industry is attempting to make sense of the impact of the changes to promotional screen culture wrought by digitalization. As such, the rhetoric of a shift from push to pull, interruption to engagement, advertising to content, is part of the effort to adjust to a new media landscape that alters the assumptions upon which screen advertising has functioned since the 1950s and 1960s.

This new media landscape has had an impact on screen advertising in two related areas – the rise of search advertising and the development (or revival) of integrated advertising and content marketing. These both have implications for the articulation of promotion and content. The opportunities for tracking and monitoring consumer behaviour through data analytics has facilitated granular forms of targeted marketing achieved through search-based advertising (the practice of charging to connect brands with relevant search terms). Statistics from ZenithOptimedia (2013) claimed that globally 47 percent of online advertising spend in 2012 was on search ($41.3 billion out of $88.6 billion). This has benefitted new players such as Google whose business model is based on the sale of search-based advertising.[4] However, the rise of search advertising, with its emphasis on purchasing words, terms and links, should not be understood as indicative of a decline in the significance of audiovisual content to advertisers. Although Joseph Turow (2013) argues that online media buying to reach a targeted user is becoming more important than placing advertising around content, he also notes the rise of specialist content firms that produce materials such as web articles and online videos on subjects that are trending on sites like Google and around which online ads can be made to appear. For example, Demand Media created a YouTube video on how to make cornbread stuffing in 2009 that offered a site for targeted Christmas advertising (ibid.: 109).[5] Here search and content are combined in the recognition that content functions as a useful way of engaging audiences through, and in relation to, search activity.

The emergence of 'content firms' producing audiovisual material designed for advertisers to target consumers can be thought of in relation to a second development, in which marketers attempt to refigure the appeal of advertising *as content*. This is characterized both by extending existing practices such as advertiser-funded programming (AFP) and by developing new forms of screen advertising that exploit the affordances of digital culture. These practices have been associated with concepts such as 'integrated advertising' and 'content marketing'. For Christina Spurgeon, integrated advertising defines 'all types of advertising that do *not* assume the discrete form of interstitial spot advertising that is comparatively easily identified by media consumers as non-program content because it is placed in breaks between and within programs' (2013: 72).[6] While integrated advertising is long established, Spurgeon argues that key practices such as sponsorship, product placement, tie-ins and advertiser-funded programming have intensified in recent decades. This has been driven by the need for commercial media to remain attractive to advertisers in the face of multiplatform fragmentation. More specifically, it has been informed by theories of 'integrated marketing communications' (emphasizing the coordination of marketing messages across multiple media outlets) and by growing regulatory tolerance towards the merging of advertising and broadcast media. Since the early 2000s, integrated advertising has been accompanied by the related development of 'content marketing'. As we shall examine in the next section, this refers to ventures such as branded entertainment and describes 'a marketing technique of creating and distributing relevant and valuable content to attract, acquire, and engage a clearly defined and understood target audience – with the objective of driving profitable customer action' (CMI n.d.).

While search advertising might be seen as being at odds with integrated advertising and content marketing, in effect both are driven by the attempt to respond to the challenge that digitalization poses to the 'interruption' advertising model. Search advertising aims to deliver promotional messages in ways that are contextually relevant to whatever users are searching for, rather than interrupting audiences with potentially irrelevant ads. Meanwhile, integrated advertising and content marketing seek to engage audiences through promotional forms that have an entertainment or use value of their own. These are both linked to corporate manoeuvres in the wider media economy. While search advertising is underpinned by attempts by companies such as Google, YouTube and Yahoo to position themselves as conduits between viewers and content (circumventing the traditional function of broadcasters and studios), the rise of content marketing responds to the increasing role that consumer brands are assuming *as media owners and media suppliers*. Michael Reeves (Business Development Director, Red Bee Media) gives this last point a telling perspective:

> There's a rationale for why brands would want content, which is that audiences expect brands to be always on now. They expect to be able to interact with brands in different ways, 24/7, 365 days of the year, across every single platform. In preparing for that brands have actually invested in all sorts of different platforms, but actually don't have the content to fill those platforms. So in some ways they are media owners themselves now and some brands are bigger media owners than TV stations. If you think of Unilever – the amount of websites that they have for their brands, Twitter feeds, Facebook pages – they've probably got a bigger global presence than

some very well-known broadcasters. So they're media owners. They need
to start acting like media owners by supplying content.

(Reeves 2012)

The assumption that audiences online are searching for content has driven
brands like Unilever to create content that consumers might be interested in, as
well as situating advertising messages around content created by others (Spurgeon
2008: 49–54). Search advertising and content marketing should not be seen in
necessary opposition to the traditional spot commercial, however. In a fragmented media environment where people make choices about whether and where
to watch adverts, spot commercials have been inveighed with new directions.
Significantly, an increasing number of spot ads have been accompanied by
interactive multiplatform elements such as Facebook updates, tweets and blogs
or have otherwise been treated in much the same way as a film release with
'movie production values, targeted TV ad, connected social networking sites,
interactive feedback and clever launch day build up in the national press'
(Orlebar 2013: 205, see also Grainge 2008: 39–43). Far from redundant, the TV
ad has become a prospective launchpad for campaigns that exploit the ubiquity,
mobility and interactivity of digital media platforms.

Film and television marketing

Just as advertisers have adopted new promotional strategies in response to
shifts in the digital media environment, film studios and broadcasters have also
had to rethink the way they reach and engage audiences within a landscape of
'connected viewing' (Holt and Sanson 2014). Jennifer Holt and Kevin Sanson
relate this term to the integration of digital technology and socially networked
communication with the traditional screen practices of the media industries.
These developments, they suggest, 'have resulted in the migration of our media
and our attention from one screen to many, directed the flow of entertainment
content in new patterns, and upended traditional business models' (ibid.: 1).
Victoria Jaye (Head of TV Content, BBC iPlayer) relates this to the BBC,
observing:

> The biggest challenge we face is around content discovery – how are people
> going to find content? We focus a great deal on the production and quality
> of content. Is it brilliant? Will it be fabulously artful, truthful and dis-
> tinctive? Of course, we want our content to be all of those things, but how
> are audiences going to find it? In the past, we rather assumed audiences
> would find the content we made available online – 'stick something up, and
> they will come'. Well, we know they don't, so we've got to work really,
> really hard on a really noisy highway (the internet) to help people discover
> our content. What's become really important is to have a distribution
> strategy – we need to go to where our audience is, so syndication is really

important: for example our YouTube channels, our relationships with partners like Virgin and Sky.

(Jaye 2012)

Jaye points here to two crucial aspects of what she later referred to as the 'content ecosystem' within which the BBC is operating (see also Evans 2011b). This provides a different vantage on the blurring of promotion and content within the context of the increased ubiquity, mobility and interactivity of digital media. First is the need to help people to find content through multiple distribution sites and platforms. This has placed greater emphasis on transmedia marketing within the film and television industries and multiplied the promotional forms designed to help people navigate the 'noisy highway' that Jaye describes. According to the marketing director for Discovery Networks UK, 'a promo isn't necessarily a thirty-second spot, it's a 360 degree campaign' (Hughes 2012). Increasingly, as we shall examine in later chapters, movies and television programmes are being promoted not just with trailers, posters and publicity, but also with a wide range of promotional screen content that extend points of transmedia engagement. Second is the need for television programmes themselves to be adaptable, malleable and able to be re-versioned as they travel across platforms. Max Dawson terms this 'unbundling', the process through which television texts (and also films) are dismantled 'into fragmentary, yet self-contained, segments' (2007: 234). These segments act as discrete forms of content but also promote the textual whole from whence they came. Like other promotional short-forms, unbundling speaks to the proliferation of ephemeral media. As Paul Grainge argues,

> Not only has contemporary screen culture become more ephemeral in the durative shortness of many of its key audiovisual forms (idents, promos, abridgements, mobisodes, web dramas, user-generated content), it has become so in the voluminous plurality of clips and snippets that abound within moving image culture: the internet provides a platform where texts that might previously have been considered fleeting become more permanent and accessible by vastly increasing opportunities for their distribution and remediation.
>
> (2011: 3)

In this context, film and television marketers unbundle movies and television shows as a means of exploiting the online cultures and digital networks through which content is shared. This is linked to the production of paratexts such as teasers, trailers, websites, blogs and bonus features that surround and help construct film and television (Gray 2010).

As with screen advertising, new initiatives in film and television marketing have sought to respond to the participatory nature of digital media. While interactive trailers distributed online sometimes reward viewers with additional content – from behind-the-scenes extras to short narrative extensions of the films and television programmes themselves – viewers are also being used to co-produce promotional material. In the UK television market, for example, the digital youth channel BBC Three has run competitions since 2008 in which viewers are invited to send in their own continuity links for broadcast online and on-air. These forms of 'user-generated continuity' have functioned as peer-to-peer recommendations that connect with the interactive web presence developed as a feature of the BBC Three brand (Grainge 2011b: 93). In a different vein, British *Glee* (FOX, 2009–) fans were encouraged in 2012 to participate in sing-alongs and 'Gleemobbing' events specifically designed to form additional content for the release of the series on DVD (Vizeum n.d.). Meanwhile, Hollywood franchise films from *The Lord of the Rings* (2001–2003) to *The Hunger Games* (2012–) have harnessed fans' creative work within marketing plans and have even displayed user-generated trailers alongside 'official' marketing content on promotional websites (see Chapter 5). This world of user-generated content (UGC) suggests a rich field of promotional screen practice that can potentially intersect with the marketing campaigns built around films and television shows. Chuck Tryon argues that the popularization of video-sharing sites that allow users to upload, edit and share videos based on movies and television programmes (and significantly, their trailers) reinforces cultures of anticipation associated with studio and network releases. The user-generated trailers, mash-ups and movie remixes are often parodic and potentially critical, particularly of the conventions of film and television marketing. However, Tryon notes that 'these seemingly unruly texts also become part of a larger marketing chain, in which audiences become involved in the very processes of production for the studios themselves' (2010: 154). While the unruliness of user-generated content has caused anxieties about copyright within media corporations, studios and networks have increasingly, although not uniformly, recognized the marketing value of such material, seeing UGC as a prospective site of promotional interaction with audiences.

If developments in screen advertising have complicated once discernible boundaries between spot ads and broadcast media, new strategies of film and television marketing are blurring distinctions between 'primary' forms of film and television content and the 'secondary' or ancillary forms of media used to promote them. This speaks to a broader recognition inherent within attempts to redefine content itself. Indeed, what constitutes a movie or television programme can no longer be straightforwardly identified. Tryon argues that in the digital era there has been 'a potentially vast expansion of what constitutes a cinematic text' (2010: 3). This extends beyond the theatrical feature film (or equally the television series) to encompass the various paratextual forms that circulate around studio and network output. In the midst of this textual proliferation, traditional boundaries between 'content' and 'marketing' have become harder to maintain. As such, Jonathan Gray argues for the importance of moving beyond conceptualizations of film and television culture as constituting a primary 'source text' surrounded by peripheral 'paratexts'. Rather, he calls for an approach 'that focuses on paratexts' constitutive role in creating textuality, rather than simply consigning paratexts to the also-ran category of considering their importance only in promotional or monetary terms' (2010: 7). Like Gray, we want to move beyond the pejorative dismissal of promotional screen media. As he notes, seeing promotional texts as being informed solely by 'the realm of profits, business models, and accounting … may prove a barrier for us to conceive of them as creating meaning, and as being situated in the realms of enjoyment, interpretive work and play' (ibid.: 5–6). However, we also want to understand promotion on its own terms. Rather than emphasize the function of promotion as a component of larger units of entertainment, as in Gray's account, we want to allow for the possibility of promotional forms like trailers, interstitials and digital shorts having cultural meanings and aesthetic functions beyond their relation to discrete film and television franchises.

Corporate and organizational promotion

Beyond thirty-second spot advertisements and the trailers and promos of film and television marketing are a diverse range of promotional texts – from corporate videos to government films – that circulate across a more eclectic range of sites and screens. This speaks to the more nebulous area of corporate and organizational promotion, and to the rich variety of screen media produced for board meetings, corporate events, retail environments and other kinds of non-theatrical venue and semi-public space. Providing a third realm in which screen materials assume a promotional function, corporate and organizational promotion is produced for a range of audiences and purposes, and has a pre-history that connects with forms such as industrial promotional films.[7] Such texts can extend from commercial movies, instructional films, client pitches, company showreels and bid films, to corporate videos for staff, client testimonials, and the filming of business events such as conferences and product launches. Promotional screen content relates in this case to the ways in which companies and organizations communicate not only with public audiences but also with workers and other businesses. However, it can also refer to the way that workers themselves use screen media to promote skills, interests and identities (Caldwell 2011).

Aeron Davis suggests that 'as promotionally minded individuals and organizations increase their engagement with media, so they shift their cognitive processes, behaviours, relations and practices accordingly' (2013: 196). The production of screen content has become a feature of this 'engagement with media', central to the way that organizations communicate with their employees, shareholders and competitors, as well as with their consumers. This is perhaps most apparent in the ubiquity of the corporate website. However, it also extends to the production of audiovisual content for retail sites, corporate offices and organizational headquarters. Much as film and television marketers attempt to engage audiences in interactive ways, corporate and organizational promotions are also often designed with similar aims. The fashion brand Burberry, for instance, has positioned itself as a digital retail experience through its 'retail theatre' concept. Flagship stores in Chicago and London have been constructed with digital screens for synchronized broadcasts, while the launch of a new major store in Beijing in 2011 featured a catwalk show that seamlessly integrated holographic and real-life models. The integration of digital imagery also dominates the lobby of the brand's corporate offices in London where a giant screen projects footage of models such as Sienna Miller and Tom Sturridge cavorting in Burberry. In these examples, 'digital attractions' – Leon Gurevitch's (2010) term for audiovisual forms that use digital effects for promotional purposes – are deployed in site-specific contexts to engage consumers, employees and clients in an 'experiential' relationship with the brand.

If digital screen content has been used to extend brand messaging within physical locations, it has also become a feature of promotional communication in semi-public and business-to-business contexts. In its role as a specialist in computer-generated imagery and 3D animation, the digital media company Crystal CG (examined in Chapter 6) has produced promotional content for a wide range of clients. Beyond its work for consumer and media brands, this includes digital projects for countries exhibiting at global expos, national sports federations bidding to host major tournaments, and aerospace manufacturers and architectural companies pitching new project and construction ideas. Whether interactive content used to attract delegates at trade shows, or CG visualizations used to promote objects and constructions to investors before work has begun, promotional screen content describes more than simply ads, trailers and digital billboards designed for public consumption. Digital attractions also encompass moving image media made and displayed as pitches, corporate presentations and planning submissions – promotional sub-genres, in other words, that function within contexts of business-to-business transaction and organizational exchange.

At the same time, corporate and organizational promotion extends beyond screen content produced *by* corporations and organizations; it also includes audiovisual media created by workers to promote individual and collective interests. Within John Caldwell's analysis of 'worker-generated content' (WGC) in the contemporary film and television industry, output such as demo tapes, comp reels, unauthorized blogs and web videos provide a way for media workers to stand out in an oversupplied labour market. By the terms of his argument, WGC can be seen as 'the parallel to the "attention economy" that now defines the media markets that consumers face' (2011: 189–90). While advertisers, film and television companies and organizations may produce promotional screen content to engage audiences in brand terms, workers or craft groups have produced demos and spec projects to gain the attention of clients and producers in order to get contracts. According to Angela McRobbie, the nature of portfolio careers in the creative industries has brought about working conditions that are reliant on 'intense self-promotional strategies' (2002: 519). WGC is part of what Caldwell terms the 'insider's promotional surround' (2011) in this context; it describes audiovisual media designed to position individual and craft skills within media professional worlds. This represents a different facet of promotional screen culture, more 'ground-up' than 'top-down' in corporate and organizational terms.

According to Charles Acland, 'the integration of audiovisual screen formats – including television, cinema, mobile phones and massive outdoor spaces – with an array of everyday and aesthetic practices has multiplied the conditions and occasions for encountering moving images' (2009: 148–9). This multiplication has a bearing on promotional screen practice. Across the three categories of screen advertising, film and television marketing, and corporate and organizational promotion discussed in this section, changes have taken place in response to a shifting media landscape characterized by the rhetoric of a new attention economy. This is linked to the dispersal of screens and the fragmentation of audiences, a conjuncture that William Boddy associates with the 'expanding regimes of mobilized media consumption' (2011: 96). To a large extent, it is the perception within marketing and media industries that content needs to work harder to attract attention that has brought about transformations in promotional thinking. For Boddy, mobile digital culture has obliged media companies 'to devise appropriate programming and advertising forms for emerging applications and test the limits of public appetite for, and resistance to, the ever-greater penetration of advertising into public and domestic space' (2011: 77). One result, examined in this chapter, is that promotional forms have increasingly been conceptualized as content in themselves; that is to say, in working harder to engage audiences, promotional screen texts have been positioned as having value for that audience beyond their discrete marketing role.

Within contemporary audiovisual culture, promotional screen content is often designed to circulate and be circulated, to be repurposed across multiple sites and platforms, and to be interacted with or even co-created by audiences. As we have shown, the changes associated with the attention economy have played out in specific ways in the fields of screen advertising, film and television marketing, and corporate and organizational promotion. At the same time, however, changes to the media landscape have also challenged boundaries between these fields. This is particularly visible in the area of branded entertainment. The next section will therefore focus on this area as a means of exploring the fluidity between the sectors of advertising and entertainment media. Critically, branded entertainment provides this chapter with a means of anchoring the discussion of 'blurred lines' to a particular period (loosely bracketed by the years 2001 and 2012) and set of industrial and textual practices (the production of advertising content and the production of television and video content). As a case study, branded entertainment provides a situated example of the blurring of promotion and content within contemporary screen culture. At the same time, it provides a bridge to the more general concerns of Chapter 2, which asks to what extent blurring applies to the broader industrial configuration of the promotional screen sector and to working practices and production cultures within it.

Branded entertainment in the digital age

When [the column] Madison & Vine made its debut in 2004, branded entertainment was still somewhat of a novelty to many sectors of Hollywood and the ad community. Cut to 2010, and the connection between brands and entertainment is cemented, and a robust ecosystem has flourished.

(*Advertising Age* Hampp 2010a: 4)

During the 2000s, branded entertainment became a subject of extended trade discussion; it was a term that captured prospective shifts in the marketing and media environment. These discussions were especially prominent in the period between the launch of BMW's web video series *The Hire* in 2001 and the introduction of the first 'Branded Content & Entertainment' category at the Cannes Lion awards in 2012. This prize was designed to signal the 'proper kind of weight and credibility' the term and practice had assumed within the advertising industry (Dean Baker, Cannes judge, 2012b).[8] The extent to which branded entertainment differs from long-held advertising methods is open to debate. However, anxiety about the effectiveness of the thirty-second ad led to trade theorizing about the boundary lines of promotional media. Notably, *Advertising Age* inaugurated a weekly newsletter (in 2002), annual conference (2003), column (2004) and book-length treatise postulating the convergence of the advertising and entertainment industries, a phenomenon that it called 'Madison & Vine' (Donaton 2004). Responding to a fragmented media environment where audiences could evade television commercials, branded entertainment became a focal point for extending advertiser involvement in the production and circulation of content; it lay at the heart of the purported shift from 'interruptive' to 'engagement' advertising models.

Branded entertainment was a nascent practice in the 2000s. Analysis of the advertising and marketing trade press in this period reveals a recurring set of questions about how branded entertainment should be defined and what metrics should be used to measure success. On certain terms, of course, branded entertainment was a re-initiation of long-standing practices such as advertiser-funded programming and product placement. From the 1920s to the 1950s, a high proportion of radio and television programmes in the US were made by advertisers and advertising agencies, J. Walter Thompson producing more than thirty-three programmes (sixty hours of airtime) per week for radio by the 1930s (Kretchmer 2004: 41). In television, as in radio, this was typified by the sponsored programme where advertising messages were part of programme content. This ranged from the use of the sponsor's name in the title of the programme (in drama anthologies such as *Kraft Television Theatre*) to the integration of advertisements into the programme itself through 'host selling, product placement, on-set sponsor signage, and … spot advertisements' (McAllister 2010: 218, see also Gillan 2015). Similarly, product placement was an early feature of the Hollywood studio system, emerging before the First World War but intensifying in the 1930s when studios sent shot-by-shot breakdowns of scripts that indicated promotional opportunities to marketers (Galician and Bourdeau 2004: 16). In ways not lost on marketing practitioners, branded entertainment was hardly new in the 2000s. However, it was situated in a new promotional environment, becoming an elastic term for a diverse range of alternative, digital and content marketing initiatives.

Used to describe anything from event sponsorship and product placement to advergaming and mobisodes (Mahmud 2008), there was a certain definitional laxity to branded entertainment in the 2000s and early 2010s. Marketing practitioners were often themselves unsure what the term meant and equally uncertain about the so-called 'jurisdiction' of branded entertainment within and between agencies. Ad executive Mike Weise wrote in 2010:

> Who has the jurisdiction? Is it the creative agency, since they control the brand strategy? Is it the media agency that controls most of the budgets? And what about the PR agencies with their focus on earned media? This debate only gets more complicated when we add digital content to the mix.
>
> (Weise 2010)

This comment is redolent of a moment when companies were staking turf and competing for business in branded entertainment, a market that was up for grabs in every sense. Andy Bryant, Director of Creative at Red Bee Media, said of branded content in 2012: 'I think it's absolutely the Wild West at the moment, I really do, I think it's incredibly fragmented, and there are people trying to claim territory' (2012). Using the same metaphor, the president of the entertainment division of the media agency Mindshare remarked: 'In some ways it feels like the Wild, Wild West. We are constantly keeping up with what the new platforms are, whom they reach, when and how' (David Lang, cited in Graser 2007). It is this sense of unruliness and transition – of industrial and textual practices not fully settled – that makes branded entertainment indicative of the broader transitions outlined in the first part of this chapter. The definitional confusion, territory disputes and jurisdictional debates surrounding branded entertainment were in many ways born of a wider need in the ad industry to think about where promotional media should sit, how it should circulate and what it should do to engage audiences. If a 'robust ecosystem' of branded entertainment had flourished by 2010, this was driven in no small part by recognition among advertising professionals of the need to respond to the platform proliferation and audience fragmentation distinguishing the contemporary media landscape.

In 2011 the Chief Executive Officer of Ogilvy, Miles Young, pressed for the ad industry to find an agreed taxonomy for branded content. He asked, 'what's the difference between branded content and branded entertainment? Is product placement branded content or branding content? We must sort out these terms to be taken seriously' (cited in Anon. 2011: 11). Accordingly, he divided branded content into four categories: leveraged content, sponsored content, partnered content and originated content. Developing a different taxonomy, the Branded Content Marketing Association (BCMA) produced a white paper on 'the age of branded content' that proposed six variants, including branded entertainment, advertiser-funded programming, short- or long-form branded vignettes, brand storytelling, branded content partnerships and brand integration (Canter 2012).[9] If, as Christina Spurgeon suggests, 'branded content can be thought of as a continuum of creative advertising possibilities, with product placement, advertorial and infotainment located at one end, and full-blown content production at the other' (2008: 27), we want to focus on full-blown content production in the remainder of this chapter. This resonates most directly with the blurring of promotion and content that we have so far laid out. Unlike leveraged or sponsored content that affiliate brands with existing film and television properties, 'originated content' is funded by a brand's marketing strategy and developed in full by, or in partnership with, a media owner. For our purposes, this full-blown variety is revealing in two respects. First, it helps illustrate the contexts and conditions through which advertising and media agencies have moved into the entertainment sector. Second, it points to examples of content marketing that are tailored for the digital media era. This is especially marked in the case of online video, what *Advertising Age* called a 'breeding ground' of branded entertainment in the 2000s (Hampp 2010a: 4). If the objective of branded entertainment is to contextualize 'brand images in ways that are so appealing that consumers will seek them out for inclusion in their personalized media and entertainment flows' (Spurgeon 2008: 40), online video has become a means of connecting this objective to the particular goals of ubiquity, mobility and interactivity.

Emerging markets and agency manoeuvres

Sensing new market opportunities, there was a proliferation of companies in the 2000s specializing in the production of original content for brands. This ranged from the launch of small branded entertainment companies to the creation of divisions within major advertising agencies like Ogilvy Entertainment specializing in AFP. These companies and divisions were formed in response to the changes in the market for screen advertising examined in the last section. However, they were also motivated by particular regulatory shifts. According to Christina Spurgeon, the intensification of integrated advertising in the United States, United Kingdom and Australia at the turn of the twenty-first century was tied to the relaxation of the regulatory approaches to broadcast media in each country. This is borne out by the launch of the entertainment division of JWT London (JWTE) in January 2010. As managing director of the new division, Dean Baker noted that JWTE was a strategic response to two factors in the European market – the way that on-demand platforms and PVR technologies like Sky+ and TiVo were facilitating the avoidance of the thirty-second ad, and the implementation of European legislation designed to enable commercial broadcasters to access new revenue streams. Specifically, he told us in interview that JWTE was formed in anticipation of the relaxation of product placement rules by the UK media regulator Ofcom (Baker 2012b). Taking effect in February 2011, these rules gave greater licence for brands to appear in programmes, and enabled advertisers to exert more influence in the co-creation of multiplatform and off-air content.[10]

JWTE was set up precisely to capitalize on what Spurgeon calls the 'international trend to increased regulatory tolerance of integrated advertising' (2013: 80).

This accompanied developments in major markets beyond the West, demonstrating the extent to which advertising companies were moving into the entertainment industry across regional territories. In 2012, WPP, the parent company of JWT, bought a controlling stake in Filmworks China Entertainment Marketing, the official agent in China representing the Hollywood majors and gaming companies (including Dreamworks Animation, Warner Bros., Universal Pictures, 20th Century Fox, Electronic Arts and Bruce Lee Enterprises). Subsequently, in 2012, JWT Shanghai launched a new entertainment division in partnership with Filmworks China designed to exploit opportunities for product placement, tie-in promotion, in-game advertising and branded content in the Chinese advertising and entertainment market. In regulatory terms, this partnership was born of the liberalization of Chinese creative industry policy in the 2000s, as well as trade agreements between China and the US that relaxed restrictions on the distribution of Hollywood films in the Chinese market (Keane 2013). These policies opened the door for commercial relations between Chinese companies and Hollywood blockbusters, and saw the placement of brands such as Lenovo and Yili Milk in franchise movies like *Transformers 3* (2011).

The creation of entertainment divisions within major advertising agencies was not uniform or unproblematic in organizational terms. JWT's global entertainment divisions were all slightly different in 2012. For instance, while JWTE New York had an in-house team of experts with backgrounds from the marketing and entertainment industries, JWTE London used a co-production model, building collaborative relations with external production companies like Endemol and Hat Trick. In this model, fee structures could vary and were in each case different from traditional advertising billing systems used by JWT as a global company. This could present challenges for entertainment divisions in producing the kind of revenues expected at major agencies. While ad agencies generate revenue by billing for the time of the teams who produce commercials (account handlers, planners, creatives), branded entertainment often requires money to be used for media investment, artist fees, production fees and the like. Although branded entertainment has the capacity to generate valuable intellectual property, questions often remain about who owns the property – the brand, the agency or the production partner? It is in this context that Baker remarked that the greatest challenge for JWTE London was, quite simply, 'making enough money' (Baker 2012b).

To compound these issues, for all the industry talk about branded entertainment in the 2000s and early 2010s, clients were often more concerned to learn about the practice than actually pursue it as a strategy. Indeed there remained hesitancy amongst clients, agencies, studios and networks about the business models involved, and what fusion of entertainment and branded content might alienate, or be accepted by, audiences. Within agencies themselves, Dean Baker comments:

> I would be lying if I said that everybody 100 percent thinks that [branded entertainment] is the way because there's a lot of people here that are very

traditional about how they see everything and, whilst it's always good to push things, they get afraid that you're jeopardizing traditional revenues.

(Baker 2012b)

Equally, from a client perspective, marketing budgets are often structured in conventional ways, and this can make ventures in branded entertainment appear risky without tangible measurements of success. Given these factors, the companies most likely to invest in branded entertainment in the 2000s and early 2010s were those that either positioned themselves as media brands (like Nike or Red Bull) or that had marketing budgets large enough to explore new promotional strategies (like Unilever). Surveying the market in 2012, Michael Reeves at Red Bee Media surmised that the brands most disposed to (online) content strategies were those 'willing to have a go at a new area, experiment in what's seen as unchartered territory and, in my view, usually have a total marketing spend of above £5 million' (Reeves 2012). This budget estimate is less to do with the prospective costs of branded entertainment – digital shorts and web series being a fraction of the cost of spot commercials[11] – than with the willingness of brands to commit money to promotional forms that focus less on consumer selling than building brand reputation.

Although branded entertainment was an uncertain practice, it nevertheless took hold in the mid to late 2000s and became part of the promotional offer of advertising and media agencies. For Dean Baker (2012b), there is always a lead platform for branded entertainment and he differentiates between 'broadcast-led', 'event-led' and 'digital-led' approaches. While AFP is 'broadcast-led' and is the main focus of JWTE's output, the global media agency Mindshare (a sibling of JWT also owned by WPP) was one of the first major agencies to develop web series for brands, a 'digital-led' approach par excellence. Such ventures have been steered by Mindshare's content division, 'Invention', which is located in the agency's media planning department. Invention provides creative and production services and works with partners ranging from large television production companies to small digital and content creation agencies. This has resulted in projects such as the MSN web series *In the Motherhood* (2007) made for Sprint and Unilever, the online popularity of which led to a short-lived, and much less successful, sitcom on ABC (2009). Made as a comedy series about the daily perils of maternal parenthood starring Leah Remini, Jenny McCarthy and Chelsea Handler, *In the Motherhood* developed storylines submitted to 'inthemother.com' by viewers themselves. Digital ventures such as this have distinct promotional opportunities. Not only are web series relatively inexpensive and low risk, they also provide a means of targeting niche audiences and tracking their engagement in terms of views, dwell times and social media circulation. In short, web series increase opportunities for engagement and surveillance which, as we have seen, is central to contemporary promotional screen practice.

Branded entertainment was mainly spoken of as an 'alternative' marketing strategy when Cannes launched its inaugural award in 2012. However, the 'Branded Content & Entertainment' category was suggestive of the growing development and legitimacy of the practice (Baker 2012a). With twelve prize categories (from best 'integrated content campaign' to 'best non-fiction programme, series or film where a client has successfully created a reality, documentary or light entertainment show around a product or brand'), the Grand Prix went to an integrated campaign for the American fast-food brand Chipotle. Devised by the marketing arm of the Hollywood talent agency Creative Artists Agency (CAA), this was a digital-led campaign built around a short animated video called *Back to the Start* on the state of the food industry. Depicting a farmer who industrializes his farm and then opts for a more sustainable future, the stop-motion animation was accompanied by a Willie Nelson cover of the Coldplay hit 'The Scientist' (which CAA commissioned and which was sold on iTunes to raise funds for Chipotle's Cultivate Foundation and Nelson's charity FarmAid). Launched on YouTube and through social media channels, *Back to the Start* also ran on 10,000 theatre screens in the US and was broadcast on television during the 2011 Grammy Awards. According to CAA's submission to the Cannes award, the video was watched six million times and earned eleven million impressions via Twitter in its first nine days (Cannes Lion 2012).

Rather than produce a high-end commercial campaign (such as the computer-generated polar bear ads that CAA produced for Coca-Cola in 1993), the agency created a 'content platform' for Chipotle. By its own account *Back to the Start* helped 'ignite a conversation in pop-culture' (ibid.) about sustainable farming. This was achieved through the video's circulation through formal and informal media channels and via its relation to Cultivate food and music festivals held across the US. In business terms, the Cultivate Campaign demonstrates the movement of entertainment industry companies like CAA into the advertising sector. The award of the Grand Prix also highlights the importance of online video to the development of *digital* content promotion hybrids. Indeed, *Back to the Start* would prefigure the four-part webisode comedy series *Farmed and Dangerous*, a satire of agribusiness that Chipotle launched on Hulu in 2014 in partnership with the production company Piro. Although, in many ways, *Back to the Start* played like a traditional advert or music video – and there was disagreement on the Cannes prize committee about whether it should win the top prize for branded entertainment for this reason – it catalyzed a broader content strategy by starting out as a digital short on YouTube. This invites closer inspection of the relation between online video and content marketing.

Online video as content marketing

As we have seen, the new strategic imperatives of ubiquity, mobility and inter-activity are intertwined with the rise of sites such as YouTube that make screen content more sharable and easier to repurpose. In business terms, YouTube has sought to capitalize on the promotional/content opportunities that result. From the point of its acquisition by Google in 2006, YouTube signed deals with major copyright holders to create branded channels within the main YouTube site, part of the attempt to monetize the platform's high volume of viewing traffic through e-commerce initiatives (McDonald 2009, see also Kim 2012). While these channels were initially built around the content of partners like NBC, CBS, Disney, Warner Music, BBC and HBO, marketers would also create channels for an increasing number of corporate brands. This would dovetail with Google's 'branded entertainment' programme, a service that allows content providers to distribute material through a 'hub' (namely a YouTube channel) and through the 'spokes' of the Google Content Network, a digital ad system that embeds video on demographically targeted web pages (Wallenstein 2008).

Although branded entertainment involves a range of practices, online video has emerged as a strategic means through which consumer brands such as Unilever, Proctor & Gamble, Coca-Cola, IKEA, Toyota, Sprint and Kraft have experimented with content marketing. As a nascent area, a range of communications agencies, media companies and digital boutiques have jostled for position in this burgeoning market, with digital production companies (Generate, Electric Farm, Vuguru, Katalyst), media agencies (Invention, Drum PHD) and independent television production companies (Endemol, Fremantle) all competing for work. Identifying web video as a new industry trend, *Advertising Age* wrote in 2010:

> Today, brands are increasingly seeking to develop proprietary content and in some cases are becoming media producers on their own. This innovation is taking place on the web, and the key players producing original branded content come largely from outside of Hollywood's circle of A-Listers.
>
> (Hampp 2010a, see also Hampp 2010b)

In one sense, branded entertainment points to the movement of advertising agencies into areas of content production traditionally seen as the purview of film and television companies. However, online video has emerged as a territory in which companies from various sectors have staked a claim. This is illustrated by the movement of Red Bee Media in the early 2010s into a market space which it coined 'on-brand TV'. As a digital and communication company whose major clients are television broadcasters, Red Bee proposed to consumer brands that its deep-rooted television 'know-how' could be applied to web video (informing the repositioning of Red Bee's Creative division as an 'entertainment and content marketing agency' in 2014). It is worth briefly considering the concept of on-brand TV as it provides a basis for examining the fluid boundaries of promotion and content in a specific digital case.

According to Red Bee's glossy 'on-brand TV' prospectus, the digital media world 'is becoming a more televisual place'. In 2012 the company argued that the future will require brands to make 'TV-quality content that's shareable and consumable across any screen platform' (Red Bee Media 2012). In accordance with this logic, Red Bee adapted principles from broadcasting to video-based content strategies. In suggesting that consumer brands would need to start behaving like media brands to communicate with audiences, it proposed that practices drawn from television could inform, and improve, the promotional use of online video. This included various lessons in televisual remediation: how to give video content dramatically gripping narrative structures; how to recognize the value of scheduling and the function of editorial calendars such as seasons; how to position and package the online 'channel brand' through idents; and how to increase audience interactivity through live events and second screens (Hipwell 2012). These lessons were consistent with attempts by You-Tube to model itself on the flow-like viewing experience of television. According to Josh Jackson (2014), YouTube changed production incentives and redesigned its interface in the late 2000s to encourage viewers to 'stay tuned' for longer periods with fewer clicks. In business terms, YouTube sought to remediate the experience of television as a means of appealing to national brand advertisers. By aspiring to be more like TV, YouTube hoped that television advertisers would overcome their reluctance to commit to the platform and increasingly pay for pre-roll and spot ads to appear in video content. Like YouTube, Red Bee drew equivalence between online video and television. In this case, however, Red Bee argued that advertisers should actually *provide* content. As an example of trade theorizing, the concept of on-brand TV provides a formulation of content marketing strategies that were becoming widely explored by consumer brands and their agencies in the late 2000s. However, the case of Red Bee also reveals uncertainty about how branded entertainment might function online and the extent to which online video needs to behave like other media forms to capture and engage audience attention. This can be examined in the particular case of Foster's Funny (2010–12), an applied example of the attempt to combine the televisual with online in the creation of branded entertainment.

Foster's Funny was a web venture devised for the UK market by the entertainment marketing company Upfront in conjunction with the digital content agency Hypernaked. Foster's is an Australian brand of lager licensed and distributed in the UK by Heineken. With its core market described as 'tribal drinkers' – what one Heineken account director defined as '18- to 34-year-old males with a mental age of 21' (cited in McElhatton and Charles 2011) – the Foster's brand has developed a historical connection with comedy. This ranges from associations with comedians like Paul Hogan in the 1970s to overt 'lad' humour within contemporary advertising campaigns. In 2010, Foster's extended its sponsorship and advertising initiatives by creating what it called an 'engagement platform' for comedy (Bacon 2012). At the time, Foster's sponsored the comedy output of the UK terrestrial broadcaster Channel 4 and both the British and Edinburgh Comedy Awards. It also had partnership deals with a range of comedy venues. Foster's Funny was a means of amplifying these forms of brand communication through a content strategy that involved commissioning new British comedy for the web. According to Gayle Harrison, brand director at Heineken UK,

> We knew our customers were watching a lot of content online generally and doing a lot of dual screening, which is why we looked at working online. In terms of the content itself, we decided to work with big names in

the comedy world because we were just starting out and it was important for us to really associate ourselves with really good quality content.

(cited in Bacon 2012)

In pursuing this online strategy, Foster's commissioned new episodes of classic UK comedy television series from the 1990s and produced three web series. These included *Mid Morning Matters with Alan Partridge*, a Steve Coogan comedy series that was later acquired and shown on the digital television channel Sky Atlantic, *Vic & Bob's Afternoon Delights*, a twenty-part daily sketch series featuring Vic Reeves and Bob Mortimer, and the ensemble sketch show *The Fast Show – Faster*.

Each web series was made up of episodes curated in short bites of between three and ten minutes. The comedians were given creative freedom and did not have to tie the comedy to the product in any way. As a media owner, Foster's maintained what David Hesmondhalgh calls 'loose' control of its 'symbol creators'. Much like a major studio or network, however, it exerted 'tight' control over distribution and marketing (2013: 32–3). For each series, Foster's negotiated exclusive ownership and content rights for the first eighteen months. During this period, the episodes were distributed exclusively through Foster's branded website, the Foster's YouTube channel, and via an app tied to Facebook.

Rather than simply sponsor comedy, Foster's Funny sought to originate and aggregate British comedy, becoming a hub for comedy online. Foster's website and YouTube channel demonstrated some key principles of Red Bee's 'on-brand TV' proposition in this respect. Not only did Foster's use its 'brand essence' as a springboard for content and channel positioning, but episodes of each web series were also scheduled in a weekly slot. For example *The Fast Show – Faster* appeared on Thursdays at 1 pm for a period of twelve weeks, conveniently placed to coincide with the online surfing and multitasking propensities of the workday lunch break.[12] While Foster's stopped short of devising full editorial calendars around its programming, the Foster's Funny website paralleled initiatives by other consumer brands in the creation/curation of online content. To take a different case, Proctor & Gamble's shaving brand Gillette launched Gillette Football Club as a YouTube branded channel in 2012 (Bacon 2012). This was devised as a hub for football videos across YouTube, Gillette moving beyond traditional television sponsorships to become a host for videos from the 150 football broadcasters with whom YouTube already had deals. In addition, the channel showed exclusive content (entertainment and analysis programmes made by the production company Big Balls) and incorporated an interactive statistics tool and social gaming platform to facilitate greater user participation. In purpose, Foster's Funny, like Gillette Football Club, acted as a destination where viewers could find content that was entertaining or useful to them. This can be seen as part of a broader response by the advertising industry to digital search culture. Rather than produce a campaign every eighteen months based around television and print ads that could be easily avoided, Foster's (and Gillette) produced content that people would want to watch, that was always available and that could be easily shared.

The status of branded entertainment as an experimental marketing strategy was ultimately borne out in the case of Foster's Funny. In November 2012 Foster's took the decision to move back to traditional television advertising and sponsorship. This was typical of the periodic marketing shifts and agency splits (in this case between Foster's and Hypernaked) that surround corporate branding efforts. However, Foster's Funny, like branded entertainment more generally, challenges us to reconsider not only *what* counts as promotional content in contemporary screen culture, but also *who* counts as a professional broadcaster and content producer in the digital media era. The significance of branded entertainment within marketing practice should not be overstated. However, neither should it be regarded simply as an old method with a new name. Through its foray into online content marketing, Foster's positioned itself as a broadcaster rather than simply a sponsor of content. As a result, the company *became* a broadcast channel for a period of two years.

While many companies were still experimenting when the new Cannes award launched in 2012, branded entertainment was a strategic response to a digital media economy that had unsettled promotional methods and economic models based on commercial spot advertising. Emily West and Matthew McAllister note that developments in digital promotional culture at the dawn of the twenty-first century have challenged, or at least complicated, the view that advertising is unwelcome content 'in light of what appears to be a wide-scale openness, and at times even enthusiasm, on the part of some audiences to new promotional forms' (2013: 13). Online forms like *The Hire*, *In the Motherhood* and *Back to the Start*, and content hubs such as Foster's Funny, provide examples. Producing and hosting digital shorts with their own creative and circulatory value, branded entertainment in these and other examples are dually encoded as promotion *and* content.

Conclusion

This chapter has shown how shifts in the digital media environment have unsettled distinctions, categories and definitions of screen content. The strategic priorities of ubiquity, mobility and interactivity, driven by the perception of a new attention economy, have led to an acute blurring of boundaries between 'promotion' and 'content'. The case of branded entertainment points to the ways in which this blurring is accompanied by a broader set of industrial reconfigurations within and between advertising and entertainment companies. Both textually and industrially, the blurring of boundaries presents critical challenges to scholars of film, television and advertising. Not least, it makes textual and analytic hierarchies much less clear. If promotion is now content, it becomes more difficult in screen studies to judge what counts as an object of analysis and what doesn't, what is thought of as creative work and what isn't, what is deemed meaningful as primary screen media and what is dismissed as secondary hype. Within advertising practice and its study, the fluid boundaries of promotion and content present different challenges. Notably, distinctions between agency disciplines and skill-sets have been called into question, as have traditional ways of charging for, managing and understanding promotional work.

This blurring of industrial and textual boundaries is neither complete nor uniform. As we shall go on to see in the next chapter, blurring sits alongside continued industrial practices that maintain distinctions between advertising and film and television, even as companies within these sectors stake claims to emergent areas that challenge their traditional working practices and business models. While our focus has thus far been contextual – examining the status of promotional screen content and a case example where the industrial and textual logics of blurring have played out – the next chapter deepens our analysis of the companies and creative labour involved in promotional work. It is to the make-up and management of the burgeoning, and appropriately fluid, sector that we call the promotional screen industries that we now turn.

Notes

1 Screen advertising is used here to refer specifically to moving image advertising and does not encompass non-audiovisual forms of advertising, such as billboards.
2 The quiz show scandals were not the only reason why spot advertising became dominant in US television. The shift of television production to Hollywood led to an increase in budgets (partly as a consequence of the move from live to filmed production) which made programme production a riskier investment for sponsors. The networks were also keen to gain more control over production, particularly in order to benefit from the emerging syndication and overseas exports markets for television programmes (see Hilmes 2007, Meyers 2009, Spurgeon 2013).
3 Across the European Union, the Audiovisual Media Services (AVMS) Directive limits the amount of advertising that may be shown on television in one hour to twelve minutes. In the UK, this is an increase from an initial limit of an average of six minutes an hour when commercial television was established in 1955 (Turnock 2007: 145). In economic terms, the UK advertising industry spent £4,480 million on television (including video-on-demand) and £5,420 million online (excluding video-on-demand and digital newspapers/magazines) in 2012 (Advertising Association/WARC 2013). In the same year, however, advertising spend on broadcast television ($39.6 billion) exceeded online ($36.6 billion) in the US. When combined with the advertising spend on cable, the overall advertising spend on television in the US in 2012 was $72.1 billion (IAB and PricewaterhouseCoopers 2013: 19).
4 According to the Internet Advertising Bureau (IAB and PricewaterhouseCoopers 2013: 12), 46 percent of online advertising spend in the US in 2012 was on search, worth $16.9 billion. Meanwhile European advertising expenditure on search advertising grew by 15.5 percent, worth €11.9 billion (IAB Europe 2013). By the account of eMarketer (2013), Google took 31.46 percent of the net digital advertising share worldwide in this particular year.
5 Turow points to the complaints by users about the usefulness of such placed video content, which led Google to add ratings for the usefulness of content into their algorithms and has arguably led to a decline in content produced by content firms (2013: 109). However, this need not undermine the value of online content as a marketing strategy, but rather points to the need for high quality content, arguably intensifying the advertising industry's turn towards the expertise of film and television production, which will be explored in more detail in Chapter 2.

6 Spurgeon argues that the intensification of integrated advertising in the digital era developed in part as an attempt 'to re-assert the intellectual leadership of the advertising discipline in the field of marketing communication at a time when advertising has been de-centred' by media planning and buying (2013: 75).

7 As illustrative examples, these industrial films range from the 'tractor films' made for US rural communities in the 1930s to the variety of promotional shorts made in the same decade by the GPO (General Post Office) film unit in the UK (Waller 2007, Anthony and Mansell 2011).

8 Responding to the possibilities and challenges presented by new digital distribution technologies, *The Hire* (developed by the advertising agency Fallon and produced by David Fincher's production company Anonymous Content) was the first venture in branded entertainment to make concerted use of mobile video technology. Costing $10 million to produce, the series included eight digital short films based on car chases, each helmed by a major film director. Encouraging audiences to actively seek out the films on the web, *The Hire* demonstrated marketing attempts to co-link entertainment content with new technological infrastructures to give brands greater credibility, interactivity and depth of appeal. Fusing the boundary between art and commerce, the series was viewed an estimated sixty million times on the internet, spawned a comic strip, and was subsequently incorporated into the Museum of Modern Art's cinema collection (Kennedy 2009: 147–83).

9 The BCMA originated in the UK in 2003 and additional regional chapters were launched in Russia and North America in 2012.

10 Ofcom relaxed guidelines about 'undue prominence' of products in response to concerns about the viability of the UK TV production industry under existing funding arrangements. However, conditions about the types (and transparency) of product placement were still strictly controlled. Hackley and Hackley note that 'paid-for product placement did not take off in the UK in anything like the volume that was expected, partly because the regulations are so tight that the free prop supply system is easier, cheaper and more convenient for brand clients' (2013: 83).

11 While *Advertising Age* estimated in 2010 that a typical web series consisting of six (five-minute) episodes would cost an average of $100,000 to $1 million to create (Hampp 2010b), *Brandweek* put the costs at between $5,000 and $50,000 per episode (Stanley 2009). In each case, these figures were seen as modest compared to the $1 million sums involved in producing high-end TV commercials.

12 According to Hypernaked, Foster's Funny attracted eight million views at an average dwell time of ten minutes in its first eighteen months (Bacon 2012).

Bibliography

Acland, C. R. (2009) 'Curtains, Carts and the Mobile Screen', *Screen*, 50 (1): 148–66.

Advertising Association/WARC (2013) 'Advertising Association/WARC Expenditure Report: Q4 2012 Results'. Online. Available: http://expenditurereport.warc.com/Free TopLineData.aspx (accessed 20 November 2014).

Anon. (2011) 'Broadcasters Aren't the Only Channel Choice for Branded Content Moves', *New Media Age*, 14 April: 11.

Anthony, S. and Mansell, J. (eds) (2011) *The Projection of Britain: A History of the GPO Film Unit*, London: British Film Institute.

Arvidsson, A. (2006) *Brands: Meaning and Value in Media Culture*, London and New York: Routledge.

Bachman, K. (2010) 'Branded Entertainment Set to Surge', *Adweek*, 29 June: n.p.

Bacon, J. (2012) 'A Series of Online Broadcasting Events', *Marketing Week*, 4 October: 14.

Baker, D. (2012a) 'And the Grand Prix Goes to', *Campaign*, 29 June: 12.

——(2012b) *Interview with authors*, 17 July.

Bechmann Petersen, A. (2006) 'Internet and Cross Media Productions: Case Studies in Two Major Danish Media Organizations', *Australian Journal of Emerging Technologies and Society*, 4 (2): 94–107.

Bilton, C. (2009) 'Relocating Creativity in Advertising: From Aesthetic Specialisation to Strategic Integration', in A. C. Pratt and P. Jeffcutt (eds) *Creativity, Innovation and the Cultural Economy*, London and New York: Routledge.

Boddy, W. (2011) '"Is it TV Yet?" The Dislocated Screens of Television in a Mobile Digital Culture', in J. Bennett and N. Strange (eds) *Television as Digital Media*, Durham: Duke University Press.

Bryant, A. (2012) *Interview with authors*, 2 July.

Burgess, J. and Green, J. (2009) *YouTube*, Cambridge: Polity Press.

Caldwell, J. T. (2011) 'Corporate and Worker Ephemera: The Industrial Promotional Surround, Paratexts and Worker Blowback', in P. Grainge (ed.) *Ephemeral Media: Transitory Screen Culture from Television to YouTube*, London: British Film Institute.

——(2008) *Production Culture: Industrial Self-Reflexivity and Critical Practice in Film and Television*, Durham: Duke University Press.

——(2006) 'Critical Industrial Practice: Branding, Repurposing, and the Migratory Patterns of Industrial Texts', *Television & New Media*, 7 (2): 99–134.

Cannes Lions (2012) 'Inspiration'. Online. Available: http://www.canneslions.com/inspiration/past_grands_prix_advert.cfm?sub_channel_id=305 (accessed 12 May 2013).

Canter, A. (2012) 'The Age of Branded Content'. Online. Available: http://www.thebcma.info/ (accessed 12 May 2012).

CMI (n.d.) 'What is Content Marketing?', *Content Marketing Institute*. Online. Available: http://www.contentmarketinginstitute.com/what-is-content-marketing/ (accessed 9 September 2013).

Creeber, G. and Martin, R. (eds) (2009) *Digital Cultures*, Maidenhead: Open University Press.

Davenport, T. H. and Beck, J. C. (2001) *The Attention Economy: Understanding the New Currency of Business*, Cambridge, MA: Harvard University Press.

Davis, A. (2013) *Promotional Cultures*, Cambridge: Polity.

Dawson, M. (2014) 'Rationalizing Television in the USA: Neoliberalism, the Attention Economy and the Digital Video Recorder', *Screen*, 55 (2): 221–37.

——(2007) 'Little Player, Big Shows: Format, Narration, and Style on Television's New Smaller Screens', *Convergence*, 13 (3): 231–50.

Donaton, S. (2004) *Madison & Vine: Why the Entertainment and Advertising Industries Must Converge to Survive*, New York: McGraw-Hill.

Dovey, J. (2011) 'Time Slice: Web Drama and the Attention Economy', in P. Grainge (ed.) *Ephemeral Media: Transitory Screen Culture from Television to YouTube*, London: British Film Institute.

Ellis, J. (2011) 'Interstitials: How the "Bits in Between" Define the Programmes', in P. Grainge (ed.) *Ephemeral Media: Transitory Screen Culture from Television to YouTube*, London: British Film Institute.

——(2000) *Seeing Things: Television in the Age of Uncertainty*, London: I.B. Tauris.

eMarketer (2013) 'Google Takes Home Half of Worldwide Mobile Internet Ad Revenues', June 2013. Online. Available: http://www.emarketer.com/Article/Google-Takes-Home-Half-of-Worldwide-Mobile-Internet-Ad-Revenues/1009966 (accessed 6 August 2013).

EMF (2012) 'We're Living in an Event-Centric Content Created World', *Experiential Marketing Forum*, 5 March. Online. Available: http://www.experientialforum.com/content/view/363/48/ (accessed 9 September 2013).

Evans, E. J. (2011a) *Transmedia Television: Audiences, New Media and Daily Life*, London and New York: Routledge.

——(2011b) 'The Evolving Media Ecosystem: An Interview with Victoria Jaye, BBC', in P. Grainge (ed.) *Ephemeral Media: Transitory Screen Culture from Television to YouTube*, London: British Film Institute.

Galician, M. and Bourdeau, P.G. (2004) 'The Evolution of Product Placements in Hollywood Cinema: Embedding High-Involvement "Heroic" Brand Images', in M. Galician (ed.) *Handbook of Product Placement in the Mass Media: New Strategies in Marketing Theory, Practice, Trends, and Ethics*, Binghamton, NY: Haworth Press.

Gillan, J. (2015) *Television Brandcasting: The Return of the Content Promotion Hybrid*, London and New York: Routledge.

Goggin, G. (2012) *New Technologies and the Media*, Basingstoke: Palgrave Macmillan.

Goldhaber, M. H. (1997) 'The Attention Economy and the Net', *First Monday*, 2 (4), April 1997. Online. Available: http://firstmonday.org/article/view/519/440 (accessed 6 August 2013).

Grainge, P. (2011) 'Introduction: Ephemeral Media', in P. Grainge (ed.) *Ephemeral Media: Transitory Screen Culture from Television to YouTube*, London: British Film Institute.

——(2011b) 'TV Promotion and Broadcast Design: An Interview with Charlie Mawer, Red Bee Media', in P. Grainge (ed.) *Ephemeral Media: Transitory Screen Culture from Television to YouTube*, London: British Film Institute.

——(2010) 'Elvis sings for the BBC: Broadcast Branding and Digital Media Design', *Media, Culture & Society*, 32 (1): 45–61.

——(2008) *Brand Hollywood: Selling Entertainment in a Global Media Age*, London and New York: Routledge.

Graser, M. (2007) 'Killer Content', *Advertising Age*, 5 February: 1.

Gray, J. (2010) *Show Sold Separately: Promos, Spoilers and Other Media Paratexts*, New York: New York University Press.

Gurevitch, L. (2010) 'The Cinema of Transactions: The Exchangeable Currency of the Digital Attraction', *Television & New Media*, 11 (5): 367–85.

Hackley, C. (2005) *Advertising and Promotion: Communicating Brands*, London: Sage.

Hackley, C. and Hackley née Tiwsakul, R. A. (2013) 'From Integration to Convergence: The Management of Marketing Communications in Promotional Culture' in H. Powell (ed.) *Promotional Culture and Convergence: Markets, Methods, Media*, London and New York: Routledge.

Hampp, A. (2010a) 'How Madison & Vine Moved to Silicon Valley', *Advertising Age*, 15 March: 4.

——(2010b) 'If You Build a Web Series Around It, Will They Come?' *Advertising Age*, 9 August: 13.

Hardy, J. (2013) 'The Changing Relationship Between Media and Marketing', in H. Powell (ed.) *Promotional Culture and Convergence*, London and New York: Routledge.

Hesmondhalgh, D. (2013) *The Cultural Industries*, 3rd edition, London: Sage.

Hilmes, M. (2007) *Only Connect: A Cultural History of Broadcasting in the United States*, 2nd edition, Belmont, California: Thomson Wadsworth.

Hipwell, K. (2012) *Red Bee Media On-brand Workshop*, 15 May.

Holt, J. and Sanson, K. (2014) 'Mapping Connections', in J. Holt and K. Sanson (eds) *Connected Viewing: Selling, Streaming and Sharing Media in the Digital Era*, London and New York: Routledge.

Hughes, T. (2012) *Interview with authors*, 25 October.

IAB and PricewaterhouseCoopers (2013) 'IAB Internet Advertising Revenue Report: 2012 Full Year Results', April. Online. Available: http://www.iab.net/media/file/IABInternetAdvertisingRevenueReportFY2012POSTED.pdf (accessed 9 September 2013).

IAB Europe (2013) 'European Online Advertising Market Surpasses €24.3b in Value', 23 May. Online. Available: http://www.iabeurope.eu/news/european-online-advertising-market-surpasses-243bn-value (accessed 9 September 2013).

Jackson, J. (2014) 'Streaming the Small Screen: YouTube and the Experience of Television'. Paper presented at the Society for Cinema and Media Studies conference, Seattle, 19 March.

Jarvis, J. (2010) 'What is Content, Then?' *Buzz Machine*, 7 April. Online. Available: http://buzzmachine.com/2010/04/07/what-is-content-then/ (accessed 9 September 2013).

Jaye, V. (2012) *Interview with authors*, 1 June.

Jenkins, H. (2006) *Convergence Culture: Where Old and New Media Collide*, New York: New York University Press.

Jenkins, H., Ford, S. and Green, J. (2013) *Spreadable Media: Creating Value and Meaning in a Networked Culture*, New York: New York University Press.

Johnson, C. (2013a) 'The Continuity of "Continuity": Flow and the Changing Experience of Watching Broadcast Television', *Key Words: Journal of the Raymond Williams Society*, 11: 23–39.

——(2012) *Branding Television*, London and New York: Routledge.

Johnson, D. (2013) *Media Franchising: Creative License and Collaboration in the Culture Industries*, New York: New York University Press.

Johnston, K. M. (2009) *Coming Soon: Film Trailers and the Selling of Hollywood Technology*, Jefferson: McFarland and Co.

Keane, M. (2013) *Creative Industries in China*, Cambridge: Polity.

Kennedy, A. J. (2009) *Branded Art*. Unpublished PhD dissertation, University of Kingston, UK.

Kernan, L. (2004) *Coming Attractions: Reading American Movie Trailers*, Austin: University of Texas Press.

Kim, J. (2012) 'The Institutionalization of YouTube: From User-Generated Content to Professionally Generated Content', *Media, Culture & Society*, 34 (1): 53–67.

Kretchmer, S. B. (2004) 'Advertainment: The Evolution of Product Placement as a Mass Media Marketing Strategy', in M. Galician (ed.) *Handbook of Product Placement in the Mass Media: New Strategies in Marketing Theory, Practice, Trends, and Ethics*, Binghamton, NY: Haworth Press.

Lotz, A. (2007) *The Television Will Be Revolutionized*, New York: New York University Press.

McAllister, M. P. (2010) 'Television Advertising as Textual and Economic System', in J. Wasko (ed.) *A Companion to Television*, Oxford: Wiley-Blackwell.

McDonald, P. (2013) 'Introduction: In Focus: Media Industries Studies', *Cinema Journal*, 52 (3): 145–49.

——(2009) 'Digital Discords in the Online Media Economy: Advertising Versus Content Versus Copyright', in P. Snickars and P. Vonderau (eds) *The YouTube Reader*, Stockholm: National Library of Sweden.

McElhatton, N. and Charles, G. (2011) 'Brands Bring it All Together', *Marketing*, 20 July: 14.

McRobbie, A. (2002) 'Clubs to Companies: Notes on the Decline of Political Culture in Speeded Up Creative Worlds', *Cultural Studies*, 16 (4): 516–31.

McStay, A. (2010) *Digital Advertising*, Basingstoke: Palgrave Macmillan.

Mahmud, S. (2008) 'PQ: Branded Entertainment to Surge', *Adweek*, 12 February: np.

Meikle, G. and Young, S. (2012) *Media Convergence: Networked Digital Media in Everyday Life*, Basingstoke: Palgrave Macmillan.

Meyers, C. B. (2009) 'From Sponsorship to Spots: Advertising and the Development of Electronic Media', in J. Holt and A. Perren (eds) *Media Industries: History, Theory and Method*, Oxford: Wiley-Blackwell.

MIMA (2013) 'Sold Out – The Future of Content – Sold Out', *Minnesota Interactive Marketing Association*. Online. Available: http://www.mima.org/?page=pe_13_future_content (accessed 20 November 2014).

Murdock, G. (1992) 'Embedded Persuasions: The Fall and Rise of Integrated Advertising', in D. Strinati and S. Wagg (eds) *Come On Down? Popular Media Culture in Post-War Britain*, London and New York: Routledge.

Murray, S. (2005) 'Brand Loyalties: Rethinking Content Within Global Corporate Media', *Media, Culture & Society*, 27 (3): 415–35.

Napoli, P. M. (2011) *Audience Evolution: New Technologies and the Transformation of Media Audiences*, New York: Columbia University Press.

Orlebar, J. (2013) 'The TV Ad and its Afterlife', in H. Powell (ed.) *Promotional Culture and Convergence*, London and New York: Routledge.

Perren, A. (2011) 'Producing Filmed Entertainment', in M. Deuze (ed.) *Managing Media Work*, London: Sage.

Powell, H. (2013) 'Introduction: Promotion in an Era of Convergence', in H. Powell (ed.) *Promotional Culture and Convergence: Markets, Methods, Media*, London and New York: Routledge.

Red Bee Media (2012) 'On-Brand TV', corporate prospectus.

Reeves, M. (2012) *Interview with authors*, 30 March.

Roberts, B. (2012) 'Attention Seeking: Technics, Publics and Free Software Individuation', *Culture Machine*, 13. Online. Available: http://www.culturemachine.net/index.php/cm/issue/view/24 (accessed 9 September 2013).

Schejter, A. M. (2006) 'Art Thou for Us, or for Our Adversaries? Communicative Action and the Regulation of Product Placement: A Comparative Study and a Tool for Analysis', *Tulane Journal of International and Comparative Law*, 15 (89): 90–119.

Spigel, L. (2008) *TV By Design: Modern Art and the Rise of Network Television*, Chicago: University of Chicago Press.

Spurgeon, C. (2013) 'Regulating Integrated Advertising', in M. P. McAllister and E. West (eds) *The Routledge Companion to Advertising and Promotional Culture*, London and New York: Routledge.

——(2008) *Advertising and New Media*, London and New York: Routledge.

Stanley, T.L. (2009) 'Amid Upfronts, Brand Experiments with Web', *Brandweek*, 4 July: np.

Tryon, C. (2013) *On-Demand Culture: Digital Delivery and the Future of Movies*, New Brunswick: Rutgers University Press.

——(2010) *Reinventing Cinema: Movies in the Age of Media Convergence*, New Brunswick: Rutgers University Press.

Turnock, R. (2007) *Television and Consumer Culture: Britain and the Transformation of Modernity*, London: I.B. Tauris.

Turow, J. (2013) 'Media Buying: The New Power of Advertising', in M. P. McAllister and E. West (eds) *The Routledge Companion to Advertising and Promotional Culture*, London and New York: Routledge.

Vizeum (n.d.) '20th Century Fox: *Glee* – Using Superfans to Add to Boxset Sales'. Online. Available: http://vizeum.co.uk/p/case-study/20th-century-fox-glee-using-superfans-to-add-to-boxset-sales/ (accessed 9 September 2013).

Wallenstein, A. (2008) 'Google Hopes to Make a Splash with Poptub', *Adweek*, 15 October: np.

Waller, G. A. (2007) 'Free Talking Pictures – Every Farmer is Welcome: Non-theatrical Film and Everyday Life in Rural America During the 1930s', in R. Maltby, M. Stokes and R. Allen (eds) *Going to the Movies*, Exeter: Exeter University Press.

Weise, M. (2011) 'The Evolution of Branded Entertainment', *Forbes*, 22 August. Online. Available: http://www.forbes.com/sites/onmarketing/2011/08/22/the-evolution-of-branded-entertainment/ (accessed 9 September 2013).

——(2010) 'Going Hollywood', *Adweek*, 20 September: np.

West, E. and McAllister, M. P. (2013) 'Introduction', in M. P. McAllister and E. West (eds) *The Routledge Companion to Advertising and Promotional Culture*, London and New York: Routledge.

ZenithOptimedia (2013) *Advertising Expenditure Forecasts*, April. Online. Available: http://www.zenithoptimedia.com/zenith/wp-content/uploads/2013/04/ZO-Adspend-Forecast-April-2013-executive-summary.pdf (accessed 6 August 2013).

2 On the Promotional Screen Industries

On Sunday 29 April 2012, Channel 4 dedicated the whole of its first ad break during the hit US drama *Homeland* (Showtime, 2011–) to a world exclusive broadcast of the new trailer for *Prometheus* (2012), Ridley Scott's much anticipated return to the *Alien* franchise.[1] The trailer itself was advertised in Sunday newspapers in the UK as a television event. When broadcast at 9:10 pm, it was introduced by Channel 4's continuity announcer who invited viewers to share their thoughts on Twitter using the hashtag #areyouseeingthis, a key line in the promotional campaign for the film. In what Channel 4 claimed was a world first, viewers' tweets were then broadcast during the second ad break (Channel 4 2010). The campaign was extended beyond television and Twitter through Zeebox, a free app that facilitates the use of social media while watching television.[2] When the *Prometheus* trailer aired on television, Zeebox alerted viewers and offered them the opportunity to win free tickets to the film. Channel 4's broadcast of the trailer and the social activities surrounding it were part of a much larger promotional campaign for the film, including theatrical trailers, TV spots, online and broadcast featurettes, viral videos and a website for Weyland Industries, the fictional company within the movie (Pomerantz 2012).[3]

The case of *Prometheus* is indicative of changes in contemporary film and television marketing, specifically the way that digital media technologies are used to amplify promotional campaigns. As the digital strategy director at Vizeum (the media agency responsible for the Channel 4 trailer strategy) commented:

> *Prometheus* gives us the perfect opportunity to harness second-screen innovation. By synchronising our TV spots with Zeebox, we are moving beyond the bounds of TV ad lengths and extending users' experience to allow for further exploration of the campaign.
>
> (Caroline Clancy, cited in McCabe 2012)

In attempting to enhance viewer engagement, the *Prometheus* campaign illustrates the blurring boundaries of promotion and content examined in Chapter 1. Indeed, Ofcom investigated whether the Channel 4 campaign contravened the broadcasting code by positioning promotional material *as* editorial content (Ofcom 2012: 36–7).[4] Yet this campaign also demonstrates the complex set of industrial structures that lie behind the production and circulation of promotional screen content. The promotion of *Prometheus* involved a number of different companies, including the film studio 20th Century Fox, the media agency Vizeum, the broadcasters Channel 4 and Sky Media, the digital technology start-up Zeebox, and a range of trailer houses and creative agencies, including Ignition, Wild Card, Jamestown Productions, Skip Film and The Cimarron Group. While film studios and television broadcasters are increasingly partnering with new media start-ups to harness the power of social media to promote movies and television programmes, trailer houses such as Skip Film are creating promotional content in a range of formats, from traditional theatrical trailers and TV spots to online teasers and featurettes. Meanwhile, media agencies like Vizeum are selling analysis of 'the consumer decision making journey' across the digital landscape and developing strategies for media producers based on these insights (Vizeum 2014). If, as Mark Deuze and Brian Steward suggest, 'content about content is the fastest-growing sector of content creation, including any and all advertising, marketing, and promotions' (2011: 7), this involves a complex network of promotional intermediaries.

Within the study of media industries, the term 'intermediaries' is often used to describe companies that remain relatively unknown to audiences but that provide a service or function that supports an aspect of the contemporary media ecosystem. Intermediaries are often business-to-business firms or internal departments that develop and trade specialist kinds of technical or creative expertise. In one example, Joshua Braun describes the 'transparent intermediaries' that support the software infrastructures that enable the distribution of video online; he examines little known tech companies like Nexidia, Ooyala or YuMe and the way these impact 'not just who sees video content online, but what sort of content is delivered' (2014: 127). In a different invocation of the term Aeron Davis uses 'promotional intermediaries' to describe those who work in the occupations of 'public relations, lobbying, advertising, marketing and branding, as well as those in related fields (e.g. pollsters, publicists, speech writers and agents)' (2013: 2). In both examples, intermediaries are seen to act upon the media world in which we live – helping to facilitate technological and symbolic systems – but in ways that are less likely to be publicly known or noticed. They represent, in other words, firms and occupational fields that sell technical/communication expertise in the transactional markets that surround media industries.

Taking an occupational focus, Davis uses the term promotional intermediaries to designate specific professions, describing those centred on 'active promotional practices' and involving individuals working 'either for a promotional company, in-house for an organization, or as an independent consultant' (2013: 2). While Davis relates his account to established promotional professions like advertising and public relations, we would argue that the intermediaries of the promotional screen industries can be understood as companies and occupations that function within and between three main areas: advertising, film and television, and digital media design. This includes companies and occupations that specialize in the creation and/or circulation of promotional screen materials, namely the content divisions of advertising, media and communications agencies, the internal marketing departments of film studios and television broadcasters, and a wide range of firms and freelancers with specialist production skills or strategic market expertise in promotional screen forms such as trailers, online videos, commercial films, experiential media and digital content of various kinds.

Although closely intertwined, advertising, film and television, and digital media design are often seen as distinct. This is especially the case within creative industry policy discourse. In a well-cited example, the UK Department of Culture, Media and Sport's (DCMS) Standard Industrial Classification for the creative industries divides the creative industries into twelve sectors, with separate classifications for 'advertising', 'design', 'video, film and photography', 'digital and media entertainment', and 'radio and TV'.[5] Although typologically neat, such categories belie the deep intermedial relations between industrial sectors. Writing of the screen industries, John Caldwell suggests that the 'dense interaction of film, television and marketing today makes the aggregate industry "a mess" for scholars to research' (2013: 163). The idea of mess, he suggests, is not a denigrating concept but an affirmation of the complexity of cultural industry systems and networks, specifically as this applies to 'the institutional logic of multiplatform texts and the cultural logic and complex labor arrangements that produce them' (ibid.). This sense of mess can be applied to the production and circulation of promotional screen content. Within our account, the promotional screen industries are not a clearly discerned sector, but rather exist as a fluid, fast-moving and ill-defined area of the creative industries with many players coming in and out and with the boundaries of work changing and varying across different companies. In examining this sector our intention is not to produce a singular definition of the promotional screen industries. Neither are we claiming that there are no significant differences between the working practices of, say, an advertising agency on the one hand and a digital design company on the other. Rather we wish to illuminate the increasing fluidity between different types of promotional intermediary as companies and occupations within the fields of advertising, film and television, and digital media design move into each other's territory.

In what follows, our aim is to account for, rather than resolve, the potential messiness of the promotional screen industries. This chapter starts by examining the composition of the promotional screen industries by tracing the ways in which advertising and media agencies, film and television marketing companies, and digital media design specialists are adapting to the contemporary promotional environment. We examine how the opportunities and challenges of the digital media landscape – and the strategic priorities of ubiquity, mobility and interactivity discussed in Chapter 1 – are serving to blur industrial boundaries in the way that different companies are operating and staking out territory. We then go on to consider how this blurring reveals itself within the organization of work within one company – Red Bee Media. Red Bee is a useful example because it sits between the professional worlds of advertising, broadcasting and digital media and is indicative of the negotiation of working practices occurring at the intersection of these sectors. In its hybridity, Red Bee provides a snapshot of the cultural and operational management of promotional screen work. The final section of the chapter reveals the importance of discourses of creativity to promotional work, often dismissed as a form of creative labour. Despite the fluid nature of the promotional screen industries, creative hierarchies and distinctions are still often maintained across a range of discursive sites, from industry awards to labour disputes. These distinctions (especially the notion that 'marketing' and 'creativity' are distinct) belie the creative challenges of promotional screen work and the need, in the multiplatform environment, for promotional labour that is flexible, adaptable and multiskilled. If media life and work has become increasingly 'liquid', as Mark Deuze (2007) suggests, the promotional screen sector offers a particularly rich site for re-assessing what is understood as creative practice. In examining the promotional screen industries, we draw attention to an emergent, if nebulous, area of screen production and the intermediaries, working practices and creative labour that make it up.

The intermediaries of the promotional screen industries

Within contemporary media culture, screen promotion is increasingly designed for multiple sites and platforms, as the case of *Prometheus* above demonstrates. This requires a range of strategic, creative and technical skills. Promotional intermediaries operating in the markets of advertising, film and television, and digital media design bring particular kinds of specialism to this work, from the expertise in strategy and media buying offered by media agencies to the craft skills in short-form editing provided by trailer houses. However, as we shall go on to see, the complexities of promotional screen practice are challenging established ways of working within the contemporary promotional screen industries, as intermediaries from advertising, film and television, and digital media design find themselves competing for and collaborating in the production of the same work. In this section, we trace the ways in which the three sectors that make up the promotional screen industries are adapting to the contemporary media ecology outlined in Chapter 1, examining the specific demands facing these sectors while drawing out similarities in the challenges and responses that each encounters.

Advertising and media agencies

As many critics have observed, the fragmentation of the media landscape and changes brought about by technological convergence have altered the structure of the advertising industry (McAllister and West 2013, Powell 2013). Not least, the traditional division between ad agencies (selling creative solutions) and media agencies (providing services in media buying) began to erode in the 1990s and 2000s when the rise of digital media made the practice of media planning and buying a more significant dimension of any marketing campaign. As Chris Bilton argues, 'Digital media are part of a more complex, targeted and inter-active media system where customer needs are more varied and individualised, and where customer relationships have replaced one-off transactions as the most valued commodity' (2009: 33). Bilton suggests that this complex media system is redefining the work of advertising; rather than a business focused on the development of ad campaigns, advertising is recast as a 'form of strategic consultancy' in which 'the "product" of the agency becomes a creative com-munication strategy rather than a creative execution' (2009: 33).

The importance of communication strategy has led contemporary advertising agencies to expand their expertise into a host of new areas. For instance, the rise of social media has seen customer relationship management (CRM) become more central to the work of traditional ad agencies (Willott 2012).[6] At the same time, the development of new media technologies and platforms has led many agencies to move into growth areas like website design, apps and mobile advertising (Hackley 2010: 103). In 2012, JWT London produced a diagram of its core expertise. Around a central circle containing the name of the agency were eighteen smaller circles, presenting a seamless colour spectrum that went from 'advertising' at the top, clockwise to 'brand strategy' and 'branded content', through to 'CRM', 'digital' and 'experiential', and back up through 'mobile', 'social media', 'sponsorship' and 'website build and e-commerce'. If, as has been suggested, 'traditional advertising agencies are buying in specialists in digital, print, viral, mobile and other disciplines to broaden their planning scope and make good their claim to be "full service"' (Hackley and Hackley 2013: 79), JWT's diagram is a projection of this tendency. Concurrently, however, media agencies have also broadened their scope, launching creative divisions that sell insight and skills in the development of multimedia campaigns.

Advertising and media agencies also face competition from new players stepping into promotional markets. This varies from Hollywood talent agencies like CAA, mentioned in the last chapter, to digital agencies offering expertise in digital creativity, search marketing and interactive services. One consequence of this proliferation of expertise has been a shift in the intermediary function of advertising and media agencies. While agencies like JWT and Mindshare would once handle all the creative and planning work stemming from a client brief, major clients such as Unilever are now turning to a number of different com-panies to realize their promotional needs. As such, developing a communication strategy often involves advertising and media agencies managing a network of specialists and brokering partnerships with other companies (see Nixon 2011: 199, Hackley 2010: 103–104). Mindshare's content division, Invention, is indicative here. Although, like other media agencies, Mindshare is very data driven – it uses algorithms, data analytics and audience intelligence to devise, develop and manage marketing campaigns at a micro level – Invention builds relationships with partners ranging from large television production companies to small digital and creative agencies to deliver content to clients. Matt Andrews, Chief Strategy Officer of Mindshare UK, states, 'We have a pool of talent that we can go and talk to, whether it's TV production companies, or content creation companies, or digital agencies ... we can just bring those agencies and collaborate with them and create stuff for clients' (2012).

Collaboration is sometimes aimed at maximizing a promotional campaign through identifying cross-promotional opportunities. However, it can also stem from the need by agencies to bolster expertise to create platform elements that can't be delivered in-house. This involves new working practices. As Hackley and Tiwsakul suggest,

> advertising professionals are under pressure to devise content solutions that fit the convergence landscape. This demands not only creative and strategic ability but also digital literacy across a range of media platforms. Therefore, professional networks have to range beyond their immediate discipline so individuals can, when required, supplement their own skills by calling on those of other specialists. In turn, this is pushing more agencies into project-based working since it is harder than ever to maintain the creative and technical skills in-house that are needed to deliver integrated, multiplatform campaigns.
>
> (Hackley and Tiwsakul 2011: 210)

The need to call on specialists is common within the marketing and media sector; ad agencies, media agencies, and film and television marketing departments all routinely work with freelance and contract staff and outsource aspects of production and post-production. However, the digital media landscape has amplified the range of creative skills and technological competences required to deliver multiplatform promotional campaigns. According to Rei Inamoto, Chief Creative Officer of the digital ad agency AKQA, 'There are more players in the mix when it comes to working with a client, not just a client and an agency. Agencies need to learn to collaborate' (cited in Anon. 2008: 29). This can affect production processes but can also bear on fee structures, big agencies sometimes finding themselves priced against nimbler rivals with lower overheads and leaner billing systems.

While major global ad agencies invariably oversee client relationships with big-spending advertisers, these agencies must nevertheless compete with, and sub-contract, other promotional intermediaries to meet client demands. This is exemplified by a client workshop for the concept of 'on-brand TV', introduced in the last chapter, held at Red Bee Media's London headquarters in 2012. The purpose was to discuss the ways in which a high profile hair-care brand, owned by a multinational consumer goods company, might develop a content strategy. In the room were representatives from a number of different companies responsible for the promotional strategy of the brand. The Head of Mobile and a range of account planners from JWT sat alongside the global planning team from Mindshare. Meanwhile, social media experts from the global social agency Edelman Digital shared ideas with the brand directors for the hair-care range, while creatives, strategic planners, account managers and business directors from

Red Bee set the agenda and steered the activities. This type of meeting illustrates the ways in which global brands work with multiple companies to achieve their goals. More broadly, it points to the way that promotional intermediaries like Red Bee can potentially undercut traditional advertising agencies by adopting a different production model (in this case combining the role of writer/director/producer to make online video) to cut down layers of billable work.[7]

The range of companies that advertising and media agencies collaborate with extends beyond creative and digital agencies and includes film studios, production companies and television broadcasters. As branded entertainment has developed as an advertising industry strategy (explored in Chapter 1), advertising and media agencies have forged strategic relationships with studios, broadcasters and production companies to develop movies and television programmes that are funded by consumer brands (Hackley and Hackley 2013: 83). Indeed, ad agencies and their clients are looking towards the film and television industries not just for their expertise in the production of long-form content, but also for their ability to create compelling content across a range of platforms. Television production companies like Twofour, Endemol, Fremantle, and Maverick Television are diversifying into the production of digital video content, games, apps and branded events for the film, television and advertising industries.[8] Equally, television broadcasters have translated their knowledge of digital television viewing behaviours into consumer and media planning insight that can be sold to commercial advertisers.[9] As such, advertising and media agencies are collaborating and competing with companies from across the advertising, film and television, and digital sectors in the creation of promotional screen content.

Film and television marketing companies

If media and advertising agencies are increasingly managing a network of specialists and brokering partnerships, then film studios, distributors and broadcasters are also working with an expanding range of companies in the marketing and promotion of movies and television programmes. Indeed, film studios and broadcasters often turn to media agencies to help plan high-end strategic projects such as channel re-brands, new service launches, and the promotion of movie and television blockbusters (as with Vizeum's work on *Prometheus*). As the media landscape has become more complex and the data for tracking media use and consumer behaviour has become more extensive, media agencies sell valuable expertise in data analysis and consumer insight (alongside their more traditional expertise in media buying). In 2012, the top five Nielsen-ranked media agencies in the UK all had major film and television companies as clients (*Campaign* 2013). This included MediaCom (BSkyB), Carat (Disney), OMD (Virgin Media and Sony Pictures Home Entertainment), Mindshare (ITV and ITV Studios) and ZenithOptimedia (BBC Worldwide). The role of media agency PHD in promoting Warner Bros.' *The Lego Movie* (2014) is indicative of the changing work of media agencies for the film and television industries. PHD conceived a promotional campaign for the movie in which an entire advertising break in the middle of ITV's light entertainment series *Dancing on Ice* (transmitted on 9 February 2014) was recreated in Lego. The campaign was created in partnership with broadcaster ITV, PHD's content agency Drum, and production partners ITN Productions and Bricksports (PHD 2014). PHD's role here extended beyond the media agency's traditional expertise in media buying. In addition, it devised the campaign strategy and managed the complex networks of partners (including its own content division) needed to realize the campaign. As this example suggests, media agencies are selling consumer, media and creative insight to, and brokering partnerships for, film and television clients looking for novel ways to engage audiences with their products.

The increased complexity of the digital media landscape has also altered the work of in-house marketing departments in film and television, as well as the external agencies that service them. Within the film industry, promotional campaigns for movies are run by the marketing departments of distributors (typically divided into theatrical and non-theatrical teams), but the majority of the creative work is outsourced to trailer houses and print agencies (Marich 2013: 16–18). While trailer houses remain the primary providers of audiovisual promotional content for movies, the fact that most trailers now launch online has required trailer houses to adjust to the digital landscape. Not only have trailer houses such as Create Advertising (examined in Chapter 5) expanded their client base to include trailer work for entertainment technology companies, many have extended their work promoting movies across new media platforms, offering screen expertise in viral videos and apps, 3D, websites, mobile games, banners and broadcast programmes as well as trailers and TV spots.[10] In addition, the rise of DVD and specialist broadcast and online film channels has increased the need for content about films. In this market, boutique companies such as Special Treats Production Company have emerged to provide content and programming about individual films – from electronic press kits and web blogs to half-hour specials, bonus features and commentaries for DVDs. While specialist companies remain, there has also been consolidation in the sub-sector responsible for the production of film and television paratexts. For example, the trailer house Trailer Park merged with marketing company Creative Domain in 2005 and with design firm Art Machine in 2007 to create a 'one-stop shop' for the promotional needs of companies in the film, television and home entertainment business (Lake Capital n.d.).

Unlike film marketing that is based on extended promotional campaigns over many months (or even years), the television industry requires the production of a large number of high-turnover promos for its programmes and channels. Beyond high-profile campaigns such as channel re-brands, most of this work is created in-house and outsourcing is typically limited to freelancers and digital design agencies that offer specific creative and technical skills in areas such as graphics and finishing.[11] The marketing departments within broadcasters, however, have also had to respond to the rise of digital media, repositioning themselves as experts in multiplatform and digital promotion. As the digital era alters the business models for media companies, the film and television industries have a wider range of products and services to promote, from digital channels to on-demand distribution and interactive delivery services. Accordingly, in-house marketing divisions have broadened their scope of promotional expertise. It is no longer simply the case that television programmes are made, passed to a marketing department, and a trailer is cut. Such departments are increasingly involved in transmedia marketing, producing content and paratextual media that anticipate, surround and support programmes and channels. These new practices have, in some instances, upset the boundaries between marketing and programme production and, as we shall see in Chapter 4, there remains uncertainty about who is best placed to create paratextual and transmedia content and whether this work should come from marketing or production budgets. Despite this, although much of the work of marketing departments within broadcasters involves high-turnaround on-air and off-air campaigns, these departments are also developing experience in how to navigate and produce content for the multiplatform environment.

In this multiplatform context, film and television marketing departments and their creative agencies are often having to navigate more complex production processes that demand the involvement of external specialists. Stephen Jeffery-Poulter suggests that 'it is impossible for any one company or organization to handle large-scale multiplatform projects in-house' (2003: 163). In the film and television industries, as in the advertising industry, multiplatform strategies involve creating a range of content forms (ads, apps, websites, trailers, mobisodes, online videos) that can require different kinds of creative and technical skills to produce. As Jeffery-Poulter argues, multiplatform projects 'can only be achieved by creatives, programmers and technologists from across the entire traditional and digital media spectrum, working in new collaborative arrangements' (2003: 159). The pressures on the production of promotional work come not only, then, from the need to create a range of content across multiple platforms, but also from the need to understand the specific demands of digital production. As digital media design has become an increasingly necessary component of promotional screen content, promotional intermediaries in advertising and film and television are having to compete and collaborate with new players from digital agencies and this, as we shall go on to see, can challenge the working practices of ad agencies and film and television marketers.

Digital media design agencies

One of the challenges of devising content strategies for the contemporary media market is the rise of digital. This demands a range of disciplinary skills based on understanding the specificities and languages of digital media. Although ad and media agencies and film and television marketing specialists have expanded their expertise into the digital field, this brings its own challenges. Within traditional ad agencies, for example, it can mean educating co-workers about *what* is digitally possible and educating clients about *why* digital strategies are necessary in the first place (Hackley and Hackley 2013: 80). It is in this context that digital media specialists have emerged. These work directly with clients but also sub-contract their services to ad agencies and film and television marketing companies/departments who do not possess the technical skills, organizational infrastructures or production pipelines to deliver digital projects.

While some digital media specialists are small start-ups made up of a handful of staff, others are larger enterprises that have pre-histories in the business of graphics and visual effects. For instance, a number of companies in the US and UK specializing in visual effects (VFX) refashioned themselves in the 1990s and 2000s as interactive digital agencies (Caldwell: 2008: 253–6). The New York-based company R/GA and the London-based MPC (Moving Picture Company) provide examples in kind. Beginning as a motion graphics company in 1977 producing effects for television commercials and film titles, R/GA relaunched as an interactive agency in 1993 and currently has offices in London, Singapore, São Paulo, Stockholm, Sydney and Buenos Aires. Describing itself as 'the agency for the digital age', R/GA specializes in digital, interactive, social and mobile advertising, e-commerce, data visualization, live events, platform applications and systematic design. With its own in-house digital production studio, this involves an organizational model that integrates 'planning, analytics and the reintegration of media planning as a strategic and creative discipline' alongside interaction design, copywriting and visual design (R/GA 2014). While R/GA is a full service agency, MPC is a post-production facility offering a range of services in graphics, animation and CG design for the film, advertising, television and digital industries. Originally owned by the British television network ITV, MPC was purchased by Technicolor in 2002 and currently has offices in London, Los Angeles, Vancouver, New York and Bangalore. While R/GA and MPC have different organizational structures, they are indicative of the movement of digital companies into promotional screen markets; they both service the needs of advertising and media clients in the design and production of digital assets and effects. Offering skills in 3D animation, visual effects (VFX) and user-experience design (UXD), companies like R/GA and MPC produce digital content for a range of media platforms. This includes effects work for ads, promos, trailers and corporate videos and, as we shall see in Chapter 6 with the example of Crystal CG, the production of bespoke digital content for live events. Such digital specialists, therefore, are a key component of the promotional screen industries and play an important part in the production of multimedia and interactive screen content.

Paul Springer argues that the graphic flexibility required of multimedia projects tends to increase the creative role of designers in promotional work (2009: 132–3). Meanwhile, in a report on multiplatform production in the UK, James Bennett et al. found that specialist digital production companies were valued by broadcasters not only for their technical skills but also for their insight into (online) audience behaviour and new business models (2012: 32). This does not mean to say that such expertise is always seamlessly integrated into the planning and production of multiplatform digital projects. In exploring the challenges of 'creating and producing digital content across multiple platforms' (2003: 159),

Jeffery-Poulter stressed the need to overcome differences between traditions of film and television production (rooted to models of producer, director and writer) and digital media production (associated with models of client, account manager and project manager). Digital content often needs to be produced well in advance of release in order to allow for user testing and iterative development, and this conflicts with the linear tendency within film and television (and advertising) for production changes to be made up to a fixed transmission or release date (Bennett et al. 2012: 34). In a special edition on the role of production companies in contemporary advertising in the trade magazine *Creativity*, executives from across the ad industry expressed the need for specialist digital providers and traditional production companies to collaborate early on in the creative process of multiplatform projects. These examples point to the differences in production routines between 'content' and 'digital' teams and highlight the importance of communication and knowledge sharing on multiplatform projects. Describing the development of promotional ad campaigns that combine television and digital elements, Nadia Blake (Head of Broadcast at advertising agency Publicis) stated,

> The ideal solution is when we shoot web content alongside the TV spots. It would be so helpful if the production companies could partner us to deliver this work. Some do, but others have not been excited to work with us on this.
>
> (cited in Anon. 2008: 29)

In work terms, these differences in practice can create clashes of culture, vocabulary and understanding. James Bennett observes that boundaries between the production cultures of television (tied to transmission (TX) schedules) and digital media (focused on user-experience (UX) design) are redrawn discursively around a failure to understand each other's processes and languages, resulting in ritualized accusations of not 'getting it' (Bennett 2013). This discourse of not getting it recurs across the three sectors examined here.

In a similar vein, Bennett et al. found that within the television industry the primacy placed on television programming in the commissioning process often meant digital companies were brought into projects at a late stage and 'placed at the end of the value chain' (2012: 34). Digital specialists are frequently employed on a project-by-project basis, leaving little time to pitch their own ideas to clients. Their work, in this sense, risks being 'bolted-on' rather than fully integrated into the development of content strategies. However, digital agencies have shifted from project-based to client-based work in a number of cases. Benjamin Palmer, CEO of interactive marketing company The Barbarian Group, noted in 2008 that clients were beginning to use and pay his company 'for a creative concepting phase before we begin production, and in some cases we are doing some brand strategy for the project, or media strategy' (cited in Anon. 2008: 29). As Palmer suggests, bringing digital media specialists into the creative process earlier points to a potential shift in the nature of work for such companies, requiring digital agencies and design shops to build teams with a range of creative, planning and technical skills, as can be seen in the case of R/GA.

If the boundaries of 'promotion' and 'content' have become more fluid in contemporary media culture, so too have the structures of the promotional screen industries and the working practices of the departments, companies and agencies that make it up. Within and between the worlds of advertising, film and television, and digital media design, incumbent companies are expanding their expertise into new areas (consumer insight, media planning, content production and digital design) at the same time that new specialist companies are emerging. The increased complexity of multiplatform promotional content requires a wider skill-set, with more emphasis on strategic planning at the point of conception and a broader range of creative and technical skills at the stages of production and post-production. In describing the contemporary screen industry as 'a mess', John Caldwell makes a broader point about the nature of the industry's 'rhizomatic' composition. He suggests that 'film and television comprise constantly reaffiliating entities, briefly aligned by contract in fleeting, opportunistic postures of willed affinity, postures that quickly evaporate when revenues do' (2013: 161). These fluxing industry connections can be applied to the promotional screen industries and the willed affinities that underlie the production of promotional screen content. This involves advertising and media agencies, film and television marketing companies, and digital specialists competing *and* joining together to realize projects. As a result of this, while there remain distinctive characteristics in the disciplinary work worlds of each area, a sense of blurring has taken place between promotional screen intermediaries at the level of occupational practices, production processes and business models. The next section extends this analysis to consider the management and organization of promotional work through the specific case of Red Bee Media. Within the terms of this chapter, Red Bee offers a means of examining the divisions, roles and agency routines that inform promotional screen practice in a company that sits in the blurred space between the sectors of advertising, broadcasting and digital design.

Promotional screen work

In researching this book, we visited a number of companies that operate in the promotional sector. This involved degrees of time waiting in corporate reception areas. These are often carefully designed spaces that project a sense of creative and business identity to potential clients. The Knightsbridge office of advertising agency JWT London and the headquarters of Red Bee Media in London's White City offer a point of comparison. Sitting in the sleek reception of JWT – a mixture of polished wood, glass and brushed steel – one's eyes are drawn to the large photographic illustrations of ad campaigns for Shell, Unilever, Diesel and DeBeers, and the 6 ft pencil leaning behind an oval reception desk. At Red Bee Media, having passed through the imposing glass lobby of the BBC-owned building where the company rents office space, one ascends to a

Figure 2.1 Props in Red Bee Media's office, BBC Broadcast Centre (2012). Photo by authors.

floor of open-plan desks, meeting rooms and atria lined with pictures of client work for the BBC, UKTV, Discovery and FOX. Rather than a giant pencil, one's gaze in the Creative department is drawn to oversized props such as a decorated '2' used in idents for the BBC's second terrestrial television channel. While JWT uses the symbolic instrument of the advertising copywriter to signal the company's prominence in the ad agency market, Red Bee combines images and artefacts from television's interstitial space to reinforce its creative pedigree in the area of broadcast design.

JWT and Red Bee Media sell different kinds of promotional expertise to consumer and media brands. However, as we have suggested, there is considerable overlap in the way that promotional intermediaries operate and the expertise they offer to clients. This extends to structures and practices in the orchestration of work. Following studies that explore the management of media work (Julier and Moor 2009, Deuze 2011) Red Bee helps move our analysis in this chapter from a broad picture of the promotional screen sector to a specific consideration of organizational practice at the level of the firm. Although somewhat unusual in its history and identity, Red Bee brings together within one company roles, skills and ideas developed from television, advertising and digital. It thereby offers a suggestive site from which to outline the organization and blurring of work found across the promotional screen industries thus far surveyed. Focusing on Red Bee allows us to examine common disciplinary divisions found within promotional companies. At the same time it provides a vantage on the management of work culture, physical space and creative routine in a company straddling industry sectors.

Red Bee grew from BBC Broadcast, a commercial subsidiary of the BBC that comprised a range of services from the Corporation's technical, engineering and editorial arms. In June 2005, BBC Broadcast was sold for £166 million to the Australian investment fund bank Macquarie Capital Alliance Group.[12] The company was renamed Red Bee Media three months later. Red Bee is, at the time of writing, one of the largest digital and communications companies of its kind, with regional offices in France, Spain, Germany and Australia. Employing 1500 staff and selling both technological and creative expertise to broadcasters and brand owners around the world, Red Bee made annual revenues of £130 million in 2012. As a company, Red Bee is made up of three divisions: 'Creative' – responsible for the promotional design of TV interstitials (idents, promos) and interfaces (electronic programme guides, content discovery systems); 'Access Services' – responsible for subtitling and audio descriptions; and 'Media Delivery' – responsible for the 'playout' and digital management of the output of broadcast and cable operators like the BBC, Channel 4 and Virgin Media. Whilst the majority of Red Bee's work is in the technical domain of media delivery, in 2012 Red Bee's Creative division accounted for a quarter of the company's annual revenue, approximately £35 million, and comprised 150 staff. Red Bee's Creative department has established a dominant position in the European promotional broadcast market and a reputation that extends internationally, winning PromaxBDA 'European Agency of the Year' in 2012, 2013 and 2014. Between 2005 and 2015 Red Bee produced the majority of the BBC's promotional content which, alongside similar high-churn promotional content for its other major client UKTV, amounted to around 5000 television promos each year. Beyond this, Red Bee has produced channel identities and complete network rebrands for terrestrial broadcasters like BBC One and ITV, as well as digital channels such as Dave, Blighty, Virgin One, Living, SyFy Channel and Discovery International. In addition, the company has carried out a wide variety of promotional work for television networks in Europe, America and East Asia, including Disney and FOX, as well as CCTV's entire Olympic branding for the Beijing Games.

Although emerging out of the broadcast market, Red Bee has also sought to 'fish in a different pond' by selling its television and online video expertise to advertisers (Clare Phillips, former Head of Strategic Planning at Red Bee, 2012). As we saw with the example of 'on-brand TV' in the last chapter, Red Bee is one of a number of companies generating knowledge claims about the digital media environment. In a period when, in its own words, 'organisations are being forced to find new ways of reaching and engaging increasingly fragmented audiences', Red Bee offers promotional strategies to broadcasters and advertisers that promise to find 'new ways of talking to audiences' (Red Bee Media 2007, see also Grainge 2010). By 2014, Red Bee Creative was describing itself as 'an entertainment and content marketing agency that specialises in the creation and production of promos, campaigns, brand identity, UX design and apps for broadcasters' (Red Bee Media 2014). This rhetorical move can be seen as part of a broader effort on the part of the company to focus and project its media marketing nous. When BBC Broadcast was formed in 2002, it hired an experienced advertising executive, Andy Bryant, to 'lead it towards a commercial future' (Bryant 2012). Bryant had worked on television accounts for brands such as Heinz and Mars and he immediately introduced strategic planning into the operations of BBC Broadcast. This is a fundamental ad agency discipline. According to Bryant, 'Everything starts with planning; everything starts with consumer understanding, consumer insight, or in our terms, understanding the audience' (ibid.). The shift in vocabulary from 'consumer' to 'audience' is telling and marks a perceived difference in the kind of media (as opposed to advertising) expertise that Red Bee sells. While Red Bee distinguishes itself from the world of advertising, the Creative department is nevertheless organized in ways similar to an ad agency; it is structured around five interconnecting divisions with discrete management reporting lines. While the first four (mapped below) are also commonly found in ad agency structures, the final area relates more specifically to Red Bee's historical origins in broadcasting. Outlining these divisions helps demonstrate the organization of work across different teams and disciplines within a promotional company.[13]

Client services (account management) – At Red Bee, this involves a team of eleven business and account directors who liaise between the client (such as the BBC) and the creative teams, and who manage the personalities and tasks to ensure that work generates revenue. The number of account directors at Red Bee is much smaller than at traditional ad agencies, meaning that account directors tend to be involved in five projects at a time and in more parts of the process. According to Emma James, account director for BBC One and the children's channels CBeebies and CBBC, this can range from 'high-end strategy thinking down to writing the minutes' (2012). However, the craft skills of account management are largely the same as at major advertising agencies, specifically relationship management, project management, planning and coordination. In organizational terms, business and account directors act as the 'pivot-point' between clients and creative teams, helping to 'find a way through projects without either side feeling they have conceded anything' (Victoria Findlay, former Business Director for UKTV at Red Bee, 2012).

Strategic planning – This includes a team of six planners who are responsible for the 'insight generation' that provides focus and guidance for the work of Red Bee's creative and technical teams. This involves commissioning research or using data to transform a client brief (e.g. 'appeal to 16–24 year olds' or 'drive viewing for x programme') into what Tim Whirledge (former Strategic Planner at Red Bee, 2012) calls an 'actionable creative proposition'. As in ad agencies, strategic planning provides the 'road map' or 'revelation' that fuels the creative process, translating an understanding of the audience and 'what is likely to resonate and what is likely to be effective' into ideas that both creative personnel and clients can understand. In the context of Red Bee, planners do not simply pass over a brief to a creative team who then execute a project. Instead, planners often collaborate throughout, especially on digital projects like companion television apps where different craft skills combine, and where a planner can take a step back from specific coding or design issues to 'wrap a project in a language which is going to actually make it happen' (ibid.).

Creative – Together with planners, creative directors will be involved in writing internal briefs that go to one of Red Bee's creative teams. These teams are made up of between three and six creatives/designers who will look after a portfolio of brands. In some cases, this may be a single brand like BBC One, and in other cases several brands may be grouped together such as the digital channels Dave, Alibi and Watch. Creative teams will stay together for approximately six months before being mixed to keep the talent core fresh. Each team has a creative head who reports to one of six creative directors who, in turn, report to the Executive Creative Director, Charlie Mawer. Unlike staff in client services and strategic planning who often come from ad agency backgrounds, staff in the creative structure tend to have backgrounds in programme production, editing, animation, graphic design and even music and theatre, many previously employed by the BBC. Accordingly, the major professional award for creatives at Red Bee would not be a Cannes Lions, as in the advertising industry, but would instead be a BAFTA or a Promax Gold. Also within the creative division are teams that specialize in user-interface design. These teams have technical backgrounds in new media design and help develop the front-end 'experience' of media players and connected TV services.

Operations – Alongside Creative is an operational and technical structure which oversees the management of production, support, finances, technology and resourcing. Mandy Combes, Head of Operations, calls this the department's 'engine room' (2012). This includes roles such as the 'production traffic manager' who coordinates the work flow and runs the budgets for the teams that produce the fast turnaround promos that make up half of Red Bee Creative's revenue. Auditing and tracking procedures are routine within creative/design agencies and Red Bee is no different (Springer 2009, Dorland 2009). The production traffic manager reports to an operations manager who makes sure that a team is hitting the correct cost for a bundle of deliverables. This might be a certain number of trailers for a television channel for which a client will have been given a unit price. According to Combes, 'all the time we're talking in terms of what percentages you hit, what staff percentages you hit, what freelance percentage you hit, what production facilities you used, how that related to the income and therefore what profit dropped out of the bottom, and they [the creative teams] must hit those targets' (2012).

Production – Together with quick turnaround promos, trailers and voice-overs, Red Bee has a production unit for 'high-end' promotional work, often involving off-site shoots. The Head of Production, Laura Gould, was previously a

TV commercial producer and was recruited by BBC Broadcast in 2002 to give more 'commercial rigour' to the BBC's promo department, 'creating the best value on screen with the money available' (Gould 2012). Within production, there are two lead producers (overseeing television and multiplatform), seven producers and a number of production managers, researchers, assistants and runners. Maintaining an in-house production department was a contractual obligation when BBC Broadcast was sold in 2005 and this is where the structure of Red Bee departs from many ad agencies. While some agencies have opened up divisions that produce viral, digital and web-based content, the majority of large television campaigns are still contracted out to production companies. Red Bee, on the other hand, takes control of all parts of the production process and delivery of television promo work. While there is a core team of permanent in-house directors and production staff at Red Bee, freelance directors are used for specific campaigns and freelance workers form the basis of the on-shoot crews.

As a digital and communications company, Red Bee Media has sought to a large extent to model itself on the professional organization and craft disciplines of the advertising industry while maintaining an identity and client base distinct from the ad sector. This creates a work culture shaped by the 'media logic' of the advertising *and* broadcast businesses, involving a certain blurring of the institutional, technological, organizational and cultural features of these media professions (Deuze 2007: 110–12). Red Bee is located in the heart of one of the world's major television production centres and is still shaped in geographic and business terms by its relationship with the BBC.[14] However, in seeking to become more commercial in its operations (a dedicated 'Commercial' division cultivates non-media clients) and more competitive in the market for promotional communication, the company has developed a structure and pose closer to the advertising industry.

In many ways Red Bee is suggestive of a space in between the media professional worlds of advertising and marketing, film and television production, and digital management and design. This relates not only to its structural organization but also to its work culture. According to critics like Deuze (2007: 124) and Hackley and Tiwsakul (2011: 211), the advertising, PR and marketing industries are defined by a highly competitive work culture where the main disciplines (account management, planning, creative) exist in a state of creative tension and where departments and agencies are often involved in ongoing power struggles within larger holding companies. Deuze acknowledges that work can differ from agency to agency, and from region to region. However, he also identifies characteristics of the way that people in these industries 'collectively work together, relate to each other and outsiders (clients, consumers, critics) and give meaning to these competences' (ibid.: 138). This includes the influence of agency 'stars' and founders that often codify ways of doing things at the level of the firm, the crystallization of professional 'creeds' within core advertising teams, and the importance of personal and professional networks on such issues as career mobility. In the daily routine of the ad agency, competitiveness is arguably the key motif, with individuals and departments frequently pitted against each other as 'frenemies' or outright foes.

This creates some interesting differences with a company like Red Bee. While adopting the organizational principles of advertising and with staff coming from similar social and educational backgrounds (young, well resourced, university-educated and often with a background in the advertising industry), the company has developed a work culture distinguishable from the ad agency. This has been shaped in part by Red Bee's ties with the BBC – its contract with the Corporation in its first ten years of operation cushioning it from the high turbulence of the advertising market – but also by managerial attempts to apply 'lessons learnt in advertising about how *not* to do things' (Bryant 2012). Not least, this includes the development of a stable management team with a strong gender balance. While the employment practices and occupational cultures of advertising tend to privilege men, four of Red Bee's senior management team at the time of our field research were women (from a total of six, this included the heads of client services, operations, planning and production). Across all divisions, there is a 'heavy amount of female influence' (ibid.), including at the creative level, which has often been seen as a male domain in British ad agency culture (Nixon 2003, see also Spurgeon 2008: 46–62). According to one female planner, working in the world of television promotion 'is more laid back and family friendly than the kind of cut and thrust of Soho' (Hipwell 2012). While the public service legacy of the BBC has a residual influence here, Red Bee's general work culture is shaped by a 'relatively flat structure' compared with that of many ad agencies. According to Bryant, this creates an environment where 'there aren't too many egos, there aren't too many prima donnas, you don't get a lot of hissy fits, and tantrums and people throwing their weight around' (2012). In striving to create a 'supportive, safe culture within which hopefully people can do their best work' (ibid.), Red Bee is shaped by a self-identified language of collaboration, a term frequently noted in interviews with staff who often compare their experience at Red Bee with the more regimented and pressurized nature of work in ad agencies. The language of collaboration in the television promotion industry is reinforced more generally at trade conferences such as Promax, with a plenary event at Promax UK in 2012 pairing 'marketers' and 'creatives' from major networks (Sky, ITV, Discovery and UKTV) to reflect on the way that disciplinary practice could (and should) move beyond 'outdated, old-school advertising ideas of us and them' (Reemah Sakaan, Network Marketing Director of ITV, 2012).

This is not to laud Red Bee at the expense of advertising agencies. Many agencies have themselves moved beyond 'old-school advertising ideas'. As we saw in the last section, the work of media and advertising agencies is increasingly characterized by collaboration, and some agencies have deliberately positioned themselves as '3-D marketing consultants' (Nixon 2011) or as specialists in 'communication design' (Springer 2009). Equally, many agencies depend for their success on the fostering of volatile creative cultures. This leads Andy Bryant to

Figure 2.2 Competition and collaboration: creative Lego-building at Promax UK (2012). Photo by authors.

affirm that collaboration should never become too cosy. He says: 'dynamic creative cultures thrive on a degree of creative ambition and competitiveness and it's great to get that combustion ... but you don't want it to be all the time, that burns people out' (2012). This reflects the tenor of the aforementioned Promax conference which, through formal talks and zones focused on creativity and play (from knitting classes and Scalectrix racing to Lego-building competitions), encouraged collaboration *and* competition as central to creative success (Johnson 2012b).[15]

The underlying question for Bryant is how to foster a 'coherent creative culture' that is fertile, big enough to be sustainable, yet also flexible enough to reduce costs to a minimum. This balancing act shapes decisions about the management of promotional work, specifically how to reconcile business demands (i.e. making revenue for owners and shareholders) with an effective creative process. On these terms, Red Bee has had to learn from agency culture and develop a more determined commercial mentality loosened from the 'media logic' of the public service broadcast business from which it sprang. As part of the BBC, carving out profit margins and winning clients was not ingrained. These have become imperative for Red Bee as the company has sought to compete in an open market. This has involved a series of management decisions about the way that the company's organization of work – including its physical space – fosters both creativity *and* cost efficiency.

The workspace of Red Bee is another point where the company's blending of media professional worlds becomes apparent. Based at BBC Broadcast Centre, the ground floor of Red Bee's White City office is where 92 percent of UK linear television plays out; in function and design, it is the equivalent of mission control for British television. Behind secure glass rooms in a bomb-proof building, banks of monitors play out the BBC's terrestrial and digital channels (alongside other major networks) with continuity announcers ready to voice links within the linear flow.[16] Red Bee Creative uses three atria around these playout suites and occupies the entire floor above. The atria have been designed to facilitate different kinds of activity, self-described as 'making', 'meeting' and 'working'. The 'making' atrium has thirty-two desks with pens and tablets for creatives to produce and edit in groups or with their creative heads, 'meeting' provides a space with soft seating and desks for discussion of projects, and 'working' is for quiet work such as scriptwriting. The main office floor has additional meeting and presentation rooms, a kitchen (with table football for staff breaks) and a floor layout where management and production support coordinators have fixed desks, and where teams of account managers, planners and creatives hot-desk to maximize their flexibility within and between projects.

According to former Group Creative Director for the BBC Frazer Jelleyman, Red Bee's workspace is designed from a creative point of view to facilitate 'happy accidents where you bump into someone or something that you weren't quite expecting' (2012). He continues, 'we tend to be very fluid in how we work, we don't work in silos; it's about getting the best brains in the room'. However, this sense of fluidity is carefully overseen from an operational perspective;

Figure 2.3 Red Bee Media's atrium workspace (2012). Courtesy of Red Bee Media.

flexibility is also a management strategy for maximizing staff efficiency (enabling people to work on several things at once) and monitoring 'what client perception is of a team and how well that team is working together' (Combes 2012). These spatial and operational strategies relate to what Guy Julier and Liz Moor call the 'management of design'. They argue that creativity in design is linked to the development of 'repertoires of action' that organize the way that an agency or design studio functions. These repertoires translate into schemas for 'helping clients understand the process and value of what they get from different design consultancies' (2009: 6).

As a company specializing in broadcast design, Red Bee has developed repertoires of action that structure and make sense of the high turnaround nature of the company's promotional work. One might think here of the way that a vocabulary of 'scrums' and 'sprints' has been incorporated into daily work routines. Adapted from the software industry, these refer to 'agile' work practices that are designed to be adaptive rather than governed by rigid, long-term planning cycles.[17] 'Scrums' describe short (15–30 minute) meetings between team members to assess a project on a daily or weekly basis, and 'sprints' are goal-focused schedules around a project (involving anything from a day to six weeks). These terms provide a language for organizing workflow but they can be set alongside a more expansive set of metaphors used in the promotional screen industries to describe creative thinking and process. From issue-based 'hothouses' to client-facing 'huddles', promotional intermediaries are especially apt to theorize disciplinary practice. This has a promotional value of its own and can be parsed (via blogs, white papers and summits) in ways meant to establish a company's 'thought leadership' in addressing a particular market or media issue. However, trade theorizing of this kind can also, in John Caldwell's terms, provide a space where 'media workers make critical sense of their own screen practices to themselves' (2009: 168). It is here, again, that Red Bee occupies a place between the advertising, broadcast and digital markets, its underlying claim and sales pitch 'we know television' adapting to a digital media environment where, as we saw in Chapter 1, content and platform boundaries have become more fluid.

The example of Red Bee is case specific but it points to nuances in the structure and management of promotional work. This section has focused on what Deuze and Steward call the 'meso' level of media management (2011: 6). Examining some of the methods, cultures and strategies that lie behind promotional screen work at the level of the firm, we have sought to convey how a company at the interstice of advertising, broadcasting and digital communication operates. Red Bee captures a sense of industrial blurring but also provides a vantage on the more general way that promotional work is operationalized within agency practice. This organizational focus does not try to explain specific labour practices among the various planners, account handlers, creatives, production assistants, designers, software developers, runners, support staff and freelancers that work in the promotional sector and at companies like Red Bee. Indeed, a different approach to promotional work might look in detail at how issues of pay, hours, training, job security, self-fulfilment, union activity (or lack thereof) relate to the sector. If, as Mark Deuze suggests, the 'workstyles of contemporary media professionals are consistent with a portfolio worklife' (2007: 100) – one that involves a relentless emphasis on networking and the acquisition of on-the-job skills to stay competitive – the promotional sector is defined by these occupational traits in what remains a highly flexible labour market. This invites more entrepreneurial strategies of 'personal branding' (Perren 2011: 162) undertaken by workers seeking to build a career within an employment market that is chronically oversupplied. From a production studies perspective, there is scope for further research on the life and conditions of workers in the promotional screen industries. While such an account is beyond the purview of this book, we do wish to situate promotion *as a form of creative labour*. This is often overlooked in critical accounts that regard promotion as a nefarious influence in cultural life. Rather than an industry driven solely by business calculation and market imperatives, as some would have it, the promotional screen sector is a complex field of practice with its own systems of professional recognition and expectations and understandings of skill and creativity. We address these issues in the last section.

Promotion as creative labour

Reflecting on the job of making promotional short-forms for television since first starting in the BBC promotions department in 1994, the Executive Creative Director of Red Bee Media, Charlie Mawer, said in 2010:

> What has changed fundamentally I think is the recognition of the importance of marketing and the importance of getting viewers to a show. What's not necessarily changed as dramatically is the recognition that there are people who have that as their skill set and are ruthlessly professional at doing it versus many programme-makers who still think they can sell their show.
>
> (cited in Grainge 2011: 89)

This highlights the potential tension that can exist between the makers of films and television shows and those whose professional business it is to create the promotional forms that surround 'primary' screen content. This tension is often reflected in critical studies of the media industries. For example, in their discussion of creative labour in the television, music and magazine business, David Hesmondhalgh and Sarah Baker discuss marketing in largely negative terms, highlighting the costs it can bring to television producers, including a potential 'loss of control over the "framing" of their products' (2011: 104–105). Similarly, in her seminal study of the BBC in the 1990s, Georgina Born argues that the introduction of marketing to the Corporation over the period offered a potential threat to creativity, particularly when used 'to batten down and curtail the particular and expansive imaginative engagement required by good programme-making' (2004: 301). In these accounts, marketing is seen as a pressure on the creative autonomy of media producers. However, these positions belie the centrality of creativity to promotional screen practice; they construct hierarchies of creative labour that value the imaginative work of the programme-maker but that overlook the creative acumen and imaginative engagement of the marketer.

Although promotional screen forms are sometimes crudely conceived and badly produced, they can also, just as often, be a site of originality, entertainment and poetic invention. Indeed, rather than stand in opposition to creative thinking, the discourse of creativity is central across the promotional screen industries. According to Andrew McStay 'creativity is the lingua franca with which advertising agencies operate … [it] flows through all its tendrils, its output and its internal goings-on' (2013: 22). This can create hierarchies of its own between promotional screen intermediaries of different kinds. For example, according to several Red Bee staff who worked formerly in the advertising sector, ad agencies and trade magazines like *Campaign* have a tendency to perceive cut promos and television idents as lesser creative forms than spot commercials (Findlay 2012). In contradistinction, Charlie Mawer (who began his career at J. Walter Thompson) describes the design of television idents as 'the single hardest bit of creative work you'll ever be asked to do' owing both to the complex role that idents serve within television junctions and the number of times they will be repeat-viewed (cited in Grainge 2011: 91). As these comments suggest, hierarchies of value are often felt and debated within socio-professional fields. Despite the increasing fluidity of the promotional screen industries, lines of distinction are still often maintained when it comes to valuations of promotional creativity.

Central to these valuations are industry awards. The professional fields of advertising, television marketing and movie promotion each have their own trade awards, represented by the Cannes Lions, Promax and Key Art Awards, to name three of the most prominent in each area. Industry awards are important to career progression and are a way that practitioners gain recognition and peer approval (McStay 2013: 27). However, these awards also mark out distinctions within promotional screen disciplines. For Tim Hughes, co-chair of Promax UK, the purpose of the Promax awards is precisely to reward the skills of *television* marketing. Although the prize categories of Promax overlap with those of other awards, Hughes spoke frankly to us about his discomfort with the 'Best Game or App' Promax category, commenting that 'best game or app is not something that is particularly a TV skill'. He went on: 'Generally you go out and commission that from an outside source for your campaign. There are other people who award, or reward, that as far as I'm concerned' (2012). As revealed here, the prize categories within professional awards maintain boundaries within industry practice. However, they can also function as markers of change and debate, raising questions about the creative parameters of particular disciplinary fields.

Although advertising, television marketing and film promotion maintain their own awards, all three have introduced categories that reflect the rise of integrated and multiplatform promotion. Together with awards for traditional television marketing disciplines – including prize categories for 'best promo' in various television genres as well as awards for specific craft skills and campaign executions[18] – Promax UK has categories that address the emergence of new marketing strategies such as 'Best Use of Digital Media' and the previously mentioned 'Best Game or App'. Meanwhile, the Cannes Lions has introduced awards for 'Branded Content & Entertainment' (discussed in Chapter 1) as well as its own category for 'Best Use of Digital Media'. Similarly, the Key Art Awards for the promotion and marketing of movies includes categories for 'apps', 'games' and 'social media', together with an award for best 'integrated campaign' consisting of three different promotions across at least three different media. If, as Hackley and Hackley suggest, 'technological convergence is highlighting, heightening and facilitating the interdependence of marketing and media' (2013: 80), these fluid lines are evidenced in no small part by the changing taxonomy of industry award categories.

Despite attempts through industry awards to raise the professional and creative status of advertising and entertainment marketing, promotional screen work is still often cast low within hierarchies of artistic value. To its critics, promotion is creative labour of the worst kind, serving the instrumental needs of marketing and commerce. As we hope to suggest, this view risks underplaying the skills involved in making promotional screen media. However, such views also threaten to ignore the traffic of personnel *between* the creative worlds of marketing and media, design and visual art. This goes beyond the long-established tendency for film directors to make commercials. Interconnections also bear on institutional histories of cultural production. Lynn Spigel points to the influence of art movements on television design in the 1950s and the particular way that on-air title and promotional art was informed by trends in modern graphic design. Focusing on the creative talent of the in-house advertising and art department of CBS in the fifties and sixties, as well as the major networks' hiring of leading artists, designers and photographers to create on-air/publicity art, Spigel draws attention to the 'social networks and labor relations among painters, graphic designers, architects, educators, museum curators, television producers, network executives, broadcasters and advertisers who worked together in relations of mutual support' (2008: 8). Spigel interrogates distinctions between 'art' and 'commerce' as it bears on promotional practice, complicating the boundaries that separate these categories in conceptual terms. And yet, distinctions are still routinely drawn between 'creative' and 'promotional' work, something that has taken on political significance within contemporary labour disputes such as the Writers Guild of America (WGA) strike in 2007–2008.

The WGA strike threw into relief the particular way that workers in Hollywood film and television production were labelled as 'creatives' or 'marketers'. The strike focused on the issue of DVD and online royalty payments for writers. However, this became linked to writers' involvement in creating paratextual forms such as webisodes, mobisodes, alternate reality games and digital shorts.

Within Hollywood, writers have not traditionally been paid for work that is regarded as promotional and the strike contested the location of the boundary between content and promotion. Jonathan Gray suggests that 'while audiences may be just as if not more captivated by paratextual creativity, Hollywood still tends not to count this as creativity' (2010: 215). At the end of the dispute, terms of credit and compensation were set for writers (at least those who belonged to the WGA) who made short-form material for digital platforms (Dawson 2011: 228, n. 31). However, these negotiations *maintained* a boundary between content and promotion, belying the increasing fluidity of these categories within production culture. Indeed, the transmedia tendencies of film and television place demands on workers to produce a proliferating range of paratexts and this can have a bearing, as we saw earlier, on traditional creative roles and production routines. While these demands have been seen to bear negatively on television writers and showrunners – writers and directors facing increasing pressure to create content for websites, social media pages and so on (Mann 2009) – they have, at the same time, given those associated with 'marketing' more influence over the paratexts that surround films and television shows. The loosened creative jurisdiction in the production of spin-offs, digital content and promotions for the web points to a broader set of changes in the skill-sets and expectations of workers in the crosshatches of the promotional/screen industries.

These changes are not specific to film and television production but extend more widely, especially as advertising and media agencies have become more deeply involved in digital content as part of transmedia marketing campaigns. Notably, multiplatform film, television and advertising projects have given new importance to what Yates Buckley (Technical Director of the production company Unit9) terms 'crossover people who can take on responsibility for a job and enable communication between roles that have completely different views on a production' (cited in Anon. 2008: 29). The demand for crossover skills and people can be seen in different areas of promotional practice, from the rise of the hybrid media producer and the emergence of the 'preditor' (producer/editor) to the multiskilled ad executive that can move between strategic and editorial roles. Describing the process of coordinating cross-media projects, media executive Justin Wilkes outlined the changing role of the producer at the creative content agency Radical Media, a company that makes branded entertainment, commercials, music videos, digital content, and studio and network entertainment. As the agency's President of Media and Entertainment, Wilkes commented:

> it's really in the role of the producer, as the project's flight controller from start to finish, where the greatest change has occurred. More often than not our producers are creatively and logistically collaborating with agencies, clients and networks long before a project is greenlit and a director is assigned. That puts an incredible amount of responsibility on this type of talent, and finding people with these multiple skill sets is always a challenge.
>
> (cited in Anon. 2008: 29)

These comments bear out Stephen Jeffery-Poulter's view that multiplatform projects require 'a very talented facilitator/connector figure' that can oversee and align the technological, creative and commercial facets of the production process (2003: 163). While producers are often required to handle a range of relationships with external contractors, suppliers and freelancers, the need for talented facilitators is matched by increasing demands for multiskilled film, television and video practitioners. For example, the 'preditor' describes a new kind of filmmaker, combining the roles of producer and editor, who can assume more than one duty in the production process (Christine Beardsell, cited in Anon. 2008: 29). More broadly within the advertising industry, multiskilled ad executives are sought to mediate between a wider range of creative, production and client needs. As the Deputy Creative Director of Drum (the content division of the ad agency PHD) argues: 'Agencies that develop content for brands need people who understand the advertising and editorial worlds, and are part-creative, part-strategist, part-entrepreneur' (Mark Rivers, cited in Anon. 2013: online).

The demand for 'crossover people' within film, television, advertising and digital media highlights the need for workers to operate across platforms and technologies and to occupy a range of roles. Equally, however, it emphasizes the professional need for practitioners to communicate across disciplinary boundaries. According to Hackley and Hackley, the rise of digital content strategies within marketing communication has engendered a 'blurring of the promotional mix hierarchy' that has led to 'greater career mobility between the channels for media and marketing communication professionals' (2013: 80). Some agencies have seized upon this mobility as a selling point in generating work. Take this description from Drum's website:

> Our creatives weren't born in ad land. Their background is technology and entertainment. They're from the worlds of gaming, website and app production, TV, film and radio. They know from experience how to generate ideas that work and they're trained in keeping people engaged.
>
> (Drum n.d.)

Here, the craft disciplines of advertising are downplayed in favour of skills relating to technology and content. As this quote and the aforementioned comments about multiskilling suggest, the blurring of promotion and content in contemporary media culture has placed value on a particular kind of labour force: one that is flexible to the changing media terrain, responsive to the increased variability of multiplatform work and adaptable to the demands of clients across a range of businesses.

These changes have had a bearing on the very definition of creativity within the promotional screen industries. The growing importance of the cultural industries to Western (and, increasingly, global) economies has led to a wide-ranging literature examining the nature of creative practice (Flew 2012, Hesmondhalgh and Baker 2011, Davies and Sigthorsson 2013). While it is beyond the scope of this book to examine this literature in depth, some of the central concerns that emerge are particularly salient to discourses of creativity within the promotional screen industries. This is marked, for example, in discussions about the relationship between creative labour and the bureaucratic forms of organization which enable and restrain it. As Andrew McStay notes, there is a long-standing debate within advertising (and advertising studies) about the role of creativity within agency structures. This often depicts a fault-line between creatives who believe in 'the power of novel and unique ideas' and account executives that centre 'on the brand and product' (2013: 23). In discursive terms, this corresponds with traditional notions of creativity as being defined by autonomy and non-conformity (Flew 2012: 103). By this account, creativity can only flourish outside of the formal control of organizations and managers. It is this understanding of creativity as being uncircumscribed that is often central to critical dismissals of promotion, seen as a prescribed form of creativity operating to briefs set by clients. Such theorizations position creativity in opposition to strategic thinking and problem solving, the growth of strategic planning within agency structures seen to place limits and measures on the creative process. However, McStay and Chris Bilton (2009) argue that some advertising agencies (like Mother and St Luke's) have sought to reduce the division between 'creatives' and 'account managers' and apply a greater emphasis to creativity throughout the different areas of agency work. Indeed, Bilton argues that creativity in ad agencies is being redefined as central to the management process, with strategic insight seen as inherently creative (2009: 30). This repositioning of creativity is framed as a key selling point, 'a brand value which managers and non-managers seek to promote to their clients' (ibid.: 24). Paul Springer presents a similar argument, claiming that 'producing a "big idea" is central to the creative process' leading to the research and development stages being promoted by agencies *as* creative labour (2009: 133).

The redefinition of creativity within ad agencies chimes with Dominic Power's discussion of creativity in design. Again, in contrast to the traditional positioning of the creative process as distinct from problem solving, Power argues that 'design combines an aesthetic (even artistic) dimension with a problem solving dimension (for instance, increasing usability, bettering ergonomics, rationalizing production routines, etc.)' (2009: 204). Within the design industry, knowledge-based interaction with the client is seen as central to competitive practice rather than as limiting to creativity. This emphasis on creativity as a dimension of problem-solving echoes Bilton's account of the repositioning of strategic insight as a creative discipline within advertising. These views challenge models of creative labour that see pre-set goals and problem-solving as running contrary to the creative process.

If, as we have seen, promotional screen content requires practitioners from a range of backgrounds and production environments to work more closely together, definitions of creative labour, and decisions about how this labour should be managed, have become a site of negotiation and debate among professionals within advertising, film and television marketing, and digital design. Work changes can, of course, be read negatively. Multiskilling can be seen to place increasing pressure on workers in already unstable labour markets and the blurring of 'promotion' and 'content' has undoubtedly created greater expectations about the volume and variety of output required to be produced for transmedia campaigns. We do not wish to gloss over the workaday realities of those faced with producing and circulating the '*huge* amounts of paratextual material needed for multichannel and multiplatform promotion' in the contemporary mediascape (Caldwell 2011: 181–2). In many ways, work routines and skill expectations are being upended by changes brought about by the demands of multiplatform digital media. At the same time, however, ideas of creative labour are also changing. While the discourse of creativity may flow through the tendrils of advertising agencies, marketing departments and promotional companies, the shifting borders and definitions of creativity levelled within trade awards, industry disputes and disciplinary skill-sets suggest that the promotional screen sector is ripe for a critical re-examination of what might *constitute* creative labour within the contemporary creative industries.

Conclusion

At the opening of this chapter we pointed to the 'messiness' of the promotional screen industries. This chapter has endeavoured to capture aspects of this 'mess' not only as it relates to the composition of the promotional screen industries, but also to characteristics and complexities in the management and creativity of promotional screen work. The production of promotional screen content can present logistical difficulties in the way that different companies, practitioners and disciplinary skills collaborate and compete on project work. This can also present analytic challenges, however. In planning this chapter, our initial intention was to 'map' the promotional screen industries. And yet, it became evident that the fast-moving nature of the sector and the complex range of promotional intermediaries involved made this map too intricate to be legible. How, indeed, do you map industrial mess? What *can* be drawn out is the nature of blurring and fluidity in a creative industry field that cuts across advertising, film and television, and digital media design. While these sectors retain distinct characteristics, they also overlap in ways that present challenges to existing working practices, business models and production processes. In industrial terms, blurring has seen a loosening of the 'media logic' (Deuze 2007) that separates the professional fields of advertising, film and television, and digital design, giving rise to greater levels of flow, mobility and exchange (institutional, organizational, creative) between them.

Within Part I of this book we have examined the concept of promotional screen content and the configuration of the hybridized industrial sector that produces it. Rather than make general claims about the nature of promotional communication, we have traced indicative forces, discourses, structures and practices that inform promotional screen production in the 2000s and 2010s. While promotion and marketing professionals fall within creative categories – they are not 'invisible' screen producers such as those described by Vicki Mayer (2011) in her account of 'below the line' creative labour – it remains the case that promotional screen work is still poorly understood. As such, having established a broad sense of the industrial field, we move in Part II to case-specific examples of media promotion. Drawing upon trade research, institutional fieldwork and textual analysis, we focus on the work of different promotional screen intermediaries in the early twenty-first century, and consider the relation of indicative promotional screen forms to the cultural and market needs of clients in the connected fields of mobile communication, television, film and live events. As we shall see, this provides a means of considering industrial and textual practice as promotional screen content has been produced to navigate, and imagine, transformations reshaping media culture in the digital era.

Notes

1 'World exclusive' is the industry term used to refer to the first non-US screening of a trailer.
2 Zeebox has since been rebranded as Beamly (see Chapter 4).
3 Featurettes are short documentaries providing insight into a film or television programme, such as interviews with directors and stars or behind-the-scenes footage.
4 The Broadcasting Code states that 'Broadcasters must ensure that television advertising and teleshopping is readily recognisable and distinguishable from editorial content and kept distinct from other parts of the programme service' (cited in Ofcom 2012: 34). Channel 4 resolved the complaint by agreeing to clearly signal 'Channel 4 advertising premieres' in the future (Ofcom 2012: 36).
5 In 2006, the UK's National Endowment for Science, Technology and the Arts (NESTA) introduced a different taxonomy for the creative industries. Focusing more on styles of creativity than end-products, NESTA distinguished between 'creative content producers', 'creative service providers', 'creative originals producers' and 'creative experience providers'. While acknowledging overlaps between these types, the categories of this model still draw attention away from the flows between content, service and experience producers/providers (see Flew 2012: 9–32).
6 CRM is a business strategy focused on managing a company's interactions with current and future customers, using technology to create more memorable and satisfying customer experiences for brands.
7 In another example, big auto brands like Ford and Audi have used AKQA to develop campaigns and web elements around particular car launches. However, they have also turned separately to smaller digital agencies like Rubber Republic (a start-up based in Bristol and London with a core staff of six people) to develop viral video content, an area in which Rubber Republic has developed a specific auto-focused niche. Thanks to James Lyons for drawing attention to the case of Rubber Republic.
8 Indeed, Twofour describes itself as a production company *and* a 'content agency' with a client base that includes HSBC, Levi's and the British Heart Foundation as well as Channel 4, BSkyB and ITV.
9 For example, UK commercial broadcaster ITV operates a commercial research department that has developed its 'ITV Lives' tool, selling viewer insight based around ten key product categories, such as travel, motoring and finance.
10 To take one case, trailer house Picture Production Company created an interactive trailer for *Avatar* (2009), and a 'fan kit' that included wallpapers, animated screensavers, printable downloads and a suite of games for *Despicable Me* (2010).
11 The BBC has been a notable exception to this. Between 2005 and 2015 the majority of its audiovisual promotional work was produced by Red Bee Media, with additional

work from ad agencies RKCR/Y&R and Karmarama. However, from 2016 the BBC will be taking most of its clip-based promotional work in-house, while retaining a roster of companies for the rest of its promotional work.

12 In July 2013, Swedish mobile communications giant Ericsson revealed its intention to buy Red Bee Media. This was given regulatory approval in March 2014.

13 As we discuss in Chapter 5, this organization is different within trailer houses, where client service responsibilities are generally taken on by producers and creative roles are assumed by trailer editors.

14 Red Bee's location in White City places it in the heart of the BBC's White City complex which, despite the sale of TV Centre in 2012, remains the home of the BBC's television and multiplatform operations. Whether this structure and identity will remain given Red Bee's purchase by Ericsson in 2014 and loss of the BBC contract for creative work from 2016 is not clear at the time of writing.

15 Given that the costs of attending Promax UK tend to come from companies' training budgets, the emphasis on collaboration, creativity and competition at the conference could be seen as indicative of a broader professional work ethos being communicated to junior staff starting out in the profession.

16 Red Bee's contract with the BBC to provide playout, metadata and interactive services was extended in 2013 from December 2015 to March 2017.

17 Some advocates see 'agile marketing' as a necessary means for the advertising and marketing industry to cope, tactically, with the rapid pace of change in the digital media environment. This involves moving away from business models based around long-cycle campaigns and occasional brand bursts to more responsive promotional methods (see Perkins 2010, Ewel 2011).

18 In 2012, the awards for best promo included 'originated' and 'clip-based' categories within the genres of drama, entertainment, factual, news and current affairs, film, sports, children's, leisure and lifestyle, as well as an award for season or stunt. The awards for craft skills included categories for production, directing, graphic design or animation, script or copy, sound design, music and editing. Meanwhile those for campaign execution included awards for print or digital outdoor, cross-media, launch, sponsorship, idents and on-air planning.

Bibliography

Adbrands.net (2012) 'Leading Digital Agencies'. Online. Available: http://www.adbrands. net/top_interactive_agencies.htm (accessed 22 September 2013).

Andrews, M. (2012) *Interview with authors*, 1 November.

Anon. (2013) 'Double Standards – Why You Need Cojones to Crack Branded Content', *Campaign*, 24 January. Online. Available: http://www.campaignlive.co.uk/news/11677 29/Double-standards—Why-need-cojones-crack-branded-content/?DCMP=ILC-SEARCH (accessed 22 September 2013).

——(2008) 'The Changing Game', *Creativity*, 1 August: 29.

Bennett, J. (2013) 'Getting It: Understanding Television as Digital Media', paper delivered at the University of Nottingham, 27 November.

Bennett, J., Strange, N., Kerr, P. and Medrado, A. (2012) *Multiplatforming Public Service Broadcasting: The Economic and Cultural Role of UK Digital and TV Independents*. London: Royal Holloway, University of London. Online. Available: http://cowboysor indies.files.wordpress.com/2012/09/bennett-strange-kerr-medrado-2012-multiplatforming-psb-industry-report.pdf (accessed 22 September 2013).

Bilton, C. (2009) 'Relocating Creativity in Advertising: From Aesthetic Specialisation to Strategic Integration', in A. Pratt and P. Jeffcutt (eds) *Creativity, Innovation and the Cultural Economy*, London and New York: Routledge.

Born, G. (2004) *Uncertain Vision: Birt, Dyke and the Reinvention of the BBC*, London: Secker and Warburg.

Braun, J. (2014) 'Transparent Intermediaries: Building the Infrastructures of Connected Viewing', in J. Holt and K. Sanson (eds) *Connected Viewing: Selling, Streaming and Sharing Media in the Digital Era*, London and New York: Routledge.

Bryant, A. (2012) *Interview with authors*, 2 July.

Budden, R. (2013) 'Yahoo Hires UK television Veteran as Europe Head', *Financial Times*, 20 August. Online. Available: http://www.ft.com/cms/s/0/a62a7c12-0985-11e3-8b32-001 44feabdc0.html#axzz2fQJ3C0CV (accessed 22 September 2013).

Caldwell, J. T. (2013) 'Para-Industry: Researching Hollywood's Backwaters', *Cinema Journal*, 52 (3): 157–65.

——(2011) 'Corporate and Worker Ephemera: The Industrial Promotional Surround, Paratexts and Worker Blowback', in P. Grainge (ed.) *Ephemeral Media: Transitory Screen Culture from Television to YouTube*, London: British Film Institute.

——(2009) 'Screen Studies and Industrial Theorizing', *Screen*, 50 (1): 167–79.

——(2008) *Production Culture: Industrial Self-Reflexivity and Critical Practice in Film and Television*, Durham: Duke University Press.

Campaign (2013) 'Top 50 Media Agencies 2013', *Campaign*, 8 April. Online. Available: http://www.campaignlive.co.uk/news/1175162/Top-50-media-agencies-2013/ (accessed 20 June 2013).

Channel 4 (2010) 'Channel 4 to Air New Prometheus Trailer in World Exclusive', 26 April. Online. Available: http://www.channel4.com/info/press/news/channel-4-to-air-new-prometheus-trailer-in-world-exclusive (accessed 4 May 2012).

Combes, M. (2012) *Interview with authors*, 29 May.

Davies, R. and Sigthorsson, G. (2013) *Introducing the Creative Industries*, London: Sage.

Davis, A. (2013) *Promotional Cultures*, Cambridge: Polity.

Dawson, M. (2011) 'Television's Aesthetic of Efficiency: Convergence Television and the Digital Short', in J. Bennett and N. Strange (eds) *Television as Digital Media*, Durham: Duke University Press.

Deuze, M. (ed.) (2011) *Managing Media Work*, London: Sage.

——(2007) *Media Work*, Cambridge: Polity.

Deuze, M. and Steward, B. (2011) 'Managing Media Work', in M. Deuze (ed.) *Managing Media Work*, London: Sage.

Dorland, A. (2009) 'Routinized Labour in the Graphic Design Studio', in G. Julier and L. Moor (eds) *Design and Creativity: Policy, Management and Practice*, Oxford: Berg.

Drum (n.d.) 'About Drum'. Online. Available: http://www.phdww.com/United-Kingdom/About-PHD-%281%29/About-PHD-Drum.aspx (accessed 22 September 2013).

Ewel, J. (2011) 'Getting Started with Agile Marketing'. Online. Available: http://www.agilemarketing.net/GettingStartedWithAgileMarketing.pdf (accessed 4 January 2012).

Flew, T. (2012) *The Creative Industries: Culture and Policy*, London: Sage.

Findlay, V. (2012) *Interview with authors*, 1 March.

Gould, L. (2012) *Interview with authors*, 29 May.

Grainge, P. (2011) 'TV Promotion and Broadcast Design: An Interview with Charlie Mawer, Red Bee Media', in P. Grainge (ed.) *Ephemeral Media: Transitory Screen Culture from Television to YouTube*, London: British Film Institute.

——(2010) 'Elvis sings for the BBC: Broadcast Branding and Digital Media Design', *Media Culture & Society*, 32 (1): 45–61.

——(2008) *Brand Hollywood: Selling Entertainment in a Global Media Age*, London and New York: Routledge.

Gray, J. (2010) *Show Sold Separately: Promos, Spoilers and Other Media Paratexts*, New York: New York University Press.

Hackley, C. (2010) *Advertising and Promotion: An Integrated Marketing Communications Approach*, 2nd edition, London: Sage.

——(2005) *Advertising and Promotion: Communicating Brands*, London: Sage.

Hackley, C. and Hackley, A. R. (2013) 'From Integration to Convergence: The Management of Marketing Communications in Promotional Culture', in H. Powell (ed.) *Promotional Culture and Convergence*, London and New York: Routledge.

Hackley, C. and Tiwsakul, A. R. (2011) 'Advertising Management and Professional Identity in the Digital Age', in M. Deuze (ed.) *Managing Media Work*, London: Sage.

Hardy, J. (2013) 'Cross-Media Promotion and Media Synergy: Practices, Problems, and Policy Responses', in M. P. McAllister and E. West (eds) *The Routledge Companion to Advertising and Promotional Culture*, London and New York: Routledge.

Hesmondhalgh, D. (2013) *The Cultural Industries*, 3rd edition, London: Sage.

Hesmondhalgh, D. and Baker, S. (2011) *Creative Labour: Media Work in Three Cultural Industries*, London and New York: Routledge.

Hipwell, K. (2012) *Interview with authors*, 14 May.

Holt, J. and Perren, A. (eds) (2009) *Media Industries: History, Theory and Method*, Oxford: Wiley-Blackwell.

Hughes, T. (2012) *Interview with authors*, 25 October.

James, E. (2012) *Interview with authors*, 12 May.

Jeffery-Poulter, S. (2003) 'Creating and Producing Digital Content Across Multiple Platforms', *Journal of Media Practice*, 3 (3): 155–64.

Jelleyman, F. (2012) *Interview with authors*, 30 March.

Johnson, C. (2012a) *Branding Television*, London and New York: Routledge.

——(2012b) 'Creativity, Collaboration and Competition – What an Industry Conference Might Tell Us About Industrial Self-Reflexivity', *CST Online*, 16 November. Online. Available: http://cstonline.tv/creativity-collaboration (accessed 22 September 2013).

Julier, G. and Moor, L. (eds) (2009) *Design and Creativity: Policy, Management and Practice*, Oxford: Berg.

Lake Capital (n.d.) 'Trailer Park, Hollywood, CA'. Online. Available: http://www.lake capital.com/trailerCS.asp (accessed 22 September 2013).

McAllister, M. P. and West, E. (eds) (2013) *The Routledge Companion to Advertising and Promotional Culture*, London and New York: Routledge.

McCabe, M. (2012) 'Ridley Scott's *Prometheus* to Air First Synchronised Ad on Zeebox', *Media Week*, 27 April. Online. Available: http://mediaweek.co.uk/news/1129255/ Ridley-Scotts-Prometheus-air-first-synchronised-ad-Zeebox/ (accessed 22 September 2013).

McStay, A. (2013) *Creativity and Advertising*, London and New York: Routledge.

Mann, D. (2009) 'It's Not TV, It's Brand Management TV: The Collective Author(s) of the *Lost* Franchise', in V. Mayer, M. Banks and J. T. Caldwell (eds) *Production Studies: Cultural Studies of Media Industries*, London and New York: Routledge.

Marich, R. (2013) *Marketing to Moviegoers: A Handbook of Strategies and Tactics*, 3rd edition, Carbondale and Edwardsville: Southern Illinois Press.

Mayer, V. (2011) *Below the Line: Producers and Production Studies in the New Television Economy*, Durham: Duke University Press.

Nixon, S. (2011) 'From Full-Service Agency to 3-D Marketing Consultants: "Creativity and Organizational Change in Advertising"', in M. Deuze (ed.) *Managing Media Work*, London: Sage.

——(2003) *Advertising Cultures: Gender, Commerce, Creativity*, London: Sage.

Ofcom (2012) *Ofcom Broadcast Bulletin*, Issue 216, 22 October. Online. Available: http://stakeholders.ofcom.org.uk/binaries/enforcement/broadcast-bulletins/obb216/obb 216.pdf (accessed 22 September 2013).

Ogilvy (2013) 'Ogilvy Entertainment'. Online. Available: http://www.ogilvy.com/About/ Network/OgilvyEntertainment.aspx (accessed 9 May 2012).

Perkins, N. (2010) 'Agile Marketing'. Online. Available: http://neilperkin.typepad.com/ only_dead_fish/2010/10/agile-marketing.html (accessed 15 January 2012).

Perren, A. (2011) 'Producing Filmed Entertainment', in M. Deuze (ed.) *Managing Media Work*, London: Sage.

PHD (2014) 'The Making of The Lego Movie Ad Break', A Cup of Tea with PHD: Thoughts on Media from the Folk at PHD UK. Online. Available: https://acupof teawithphd.wordpress.com/2014/02/20/the-making-of-the-lego-movie-ad-break/ (accessed 14 November 2014).

Phillips, C. (2012) *Interview with authors*, 29 May.

Pomerantz, D. (2012) '"Prometheus": When Movie Marketing Goes Very Right', *Forbes*, 18 April. Online. Available: http://www.forbes.com/sites/dorothypomerantz/2012/04/ 18/prometheus-when-movie-marketing-goes-very-right/ (accessed 12 June 2013).

Powell, H. (2013) 'The Promotional Industries', in H. Powell (ed.) *Promotional Culture and Convergence*, London and New York: Routledge.

Power, D. (2009) 'Creativity and Innovation in the Scandinavian Design Industry: Designed in Stockholm', in A. Pratt and P. Jeffcutt (eds) *Creativity, Innovation and the Cultural Economy*, London and New York: Routledge.

Pratt, A. and P. Jeffcutt (eds) (2009) *Creativity, Innovation and the Cultural Economy*, London and New York: Routledge.

PromaxBDA (2014) 'About Promax BDA'. Online. Available: http://promaxbda.org/ about (accessed 30 March 2014).

Red Bee Media (2014) 'Red Bee Creative'. Online. Available: http://www.redbeemedia. com/creative (accessed 9 July 2014).

——(2012) 'Content Marketing: Start with the Audience'. Online. Available: http://www. redbeemedia.com/blog/content-marketing-start-audience (accessed 22 October 2012).

——(2007) 'Interactive Design'. Online. Available: http://www.redbeemedia.com/interactive/ index.shtml (accessed 22 October 2007).

——(2005) 'We are Pleased to Announce our New Name', *M2 Presswire*, 27 October.

R/GA (2014) 'What We Do'. Online. Available: http://www.rga.com/about/featured/what-we-do (accessed 7 April 2014).

Sakaan, R. (2012) 'Let's Stay Together', presentation delivered at Promax UK, 9 November.

Solman, G. (2007) 'Q&a: Deutsch/LA's Dunlap', *Adweek*, 17 September. Online. Available: http://www.adweek.com/news/advertising/qa-deutschlas-dunlap-90306 (accessed 22 September 2013).

Spigel, L. (2008) *TV By Design: Modern Art and the Rise of Network Television*, Chicago: University of Chicago Press.

Springer, P. (2009) 'Auditing in Communication Design', in G. Julier and L. Moor (eds) *Design and Creativity: Policy, Management and Practice*, Oxford: Berg.

Spurgeon, C. (2008) *Advertising and New Media*, London and New York: Routledge.

Vizeum (2014) 'Our Approach'. Online. Available: http://vizeum.co.uk/our-approach/ (accessed 7 April 2014).

Wasko, J. (2003) *How Hollywood Works*, London: Sage.

Weise, M. (2011) 'The Evolution of Branded Entertainment', *Forbes*, 22 August. Online. Available: http://www.forbes.com/sites/onmarketing/2011/08/22/the-evolution-of-bran ded-entertainment/ (accessed 9 September 2013).

Whirledge, T. (2012) *Interview with authors*, 13 March.

Willott, B. (2012) 'Top 100 Creative Agencies 2012', *Brand Republic*, 26 March. Online. Available: http://www.brandrepublic.com/league_tables/1122212/top-100-crea tive-agencies-2012/ (accessed 22 September 2013).

Part II
Media Promotion

3 Mobile Communication

Screen Advertising and Shareable Media

From our experience with the T-Mobile's 'Life's for Sharing' campaign, a new shift is taking place. We are entering the age of the Participation Economy. When watching or approving anything we make, my rule of thumb used to be: Do I want to see it again? But increasingly that's given way to: Do I want to share this?

(Kevin Roberts, Worldwide Chief Executive of Saatchi & Saatchi, 2009)

In 2003 the *New York Times* took notice of a trend occurring in various North American and European cities that year – the fad or phenomenon of 'flashmobs' (Walker 2003: SM11). Describing groups of 'well-wired folks who gather suddenly, perform some specific but innocuous act, then promptly scatter', the feature pondered the significance of these idiosyncratic public happenings, in particular their coordination through websites and mobile phones. Fending off those who dismissed the trend as the 'technological equivalent of streaking', the feature borrowed from Howard Rheingold (2002) in making a case for their cultural significance, specifically the way that flashmobs 'make networks tangible'. Regarded as a new expression of connectivity, the article also described the fear among bloggers that 'flashmobs are going to be hijacked, most likely by consumer companies' (Walker 2003: SM11). In the UK, this moment can be dated precisely and came in the form of a brand campaign for the mobile phone operator T-Mobile, owned by Europe's second largest telecommunications company Deutsche Telekom.[1] On 16 January 2009, T-Mobile launched a promotional campaign on television and YouTube that performed the company's brand slogan 'Life's for Sharing'. This took the form of a spontaneous dance routine in the main concourse of Liverpool Street Station in London. Staged during the previous day's rush hour and shot through ten hidden cameras, the routine began with the movement of a single disguised commuter, and would build to include 350 dancers all performing in sync to a medley of classic and contemporary chart hits before suddenly stopping and dissolving into the assembled crowd. Spectacular in its display of rhythmic synchronization and impromptu sociality – the advert dwelling on those moments where unsuspecting members of the public joined in the performance – the dance became an immediate television talking point and YouTube hit. In brand terms, the flashmob was the first of several choreographed public events by T-Mobile designed to animate everyday relationships in a world of mobile social media.

In her account of the promotional industries, Helen Powell suggests that 'one of the most significant changes in terms of the dynamic nature of promotional culture in the first decades of the twenty-first century has been the embedding of digital mobile devices within everyday life' (2013: 55). Since the mid-2000s, the rise of mobile and social networks has led to new forms of personalization and interactivity within marketing practice, as discussed in Chapter 1. These drivers were borne out in the T-Mobile campaign. In a series of ways, the campaign literalized the 'new strategic imperatives of ubiquity, mobility, and interactivity' that have developed in response to audience fragmentation and platform proliferation in the digital media landscape. Indeed, 'Life's for Sharing' was explicit in pursuing these strategic aims – it strove for *ubiquity* in the way that advertising content could be circulated and reproduced, it thematized *mobility* as a principle of social and digital behaviour, and it developed *interactivity* as a mode of consumer address.

Together with the Liverpool Street flashmob in 2009, the campaign would involve a mass karaoke event in Trafalgar Square, a further flashmob called 'Welcome Home' staged in London's Heathrow airport, and a series of multimedia ads following an aspiring musician, Josh Ward, in his attempt to put together a band using free texts and internet through his mobile phone. The ongoing promotion of 'Josh's band' included TV ads and web content showing Josh recruiting members of the public at gigs in various British cities. This culminated in a three-minute advertisement featuring the song 'Come With Me', performed by 1,107 band volunteers. With neat marketing shape, the ad premiered exactly a year after the Liverpool Street flashmob. According to Adam Arvidsson, 'one of the most important and fundamental trends in contemporary consumer society is the progressive inclusion of consumers in the processes where value is produced around products and brands' (2008: 326). This trend was clearly demonstrated by T-Mobile in its ambition to connect mobile users; it developed an integrated media campaign that used television and new media to facilitate the work of brand community-building. According to Saatchi & Saatchi, the agency responsible, the aim of the campaign across its various articulations was 'to create an event that people would want to take part in and then share with each other' (Saatchi & Saatchi 2009).

Although devised for the UK market, 'Life's for Sharing' is emblematic of wider promotional tendencies in the digital media ecology. Like other multinational companies, T-Mobile develops marketing strategies for specific regional territories. However, the capacity for media to circulate informally through social networks gave videos in the 'Life's for Sharing' campaign a presence across national borders. While the Liverpool Street flashmob received 38 million YouTube views globally in its first four years, a royal wedding dance spoof also staged by T-Mobile as part of the 'Life's for Sharing' campaign (released shortly before the marriage of Prince William and Kate Middleton in 2011) received

27 million views within two years. The flashmob's familiarity was such that T-Mobile even received a backhanded reference in a Hollywood film, the romantic comedy *Friends with Benefits* (2011) lamenting the use of flashmobs by corporations, mentioning T-Mobile explicitly in the course of the movie. As a promotional text, 'Life's for Sharing' captures a 'cultural moment' in the development and marketing of mobile social media (Hjorth, Burgess and Richardson 2013).

According to Charles Acland (2009), moving images in contemporary screen culture are marked by a growing 'informality'. This describes the variability of situations where audiovisual content is viewed and the ease with which it can be reproduced, miniaturized, personalized and transferred between media formats. The flashmob campaign tapped into this regime of informality; it was designed to imagine the world of mobile and social networks but also to be dispersed and shared *through* these networks. As a case study, the campaign is significant not only by virtue of its accumulation of advertising awards ('Dance' received six Cannes Lions in 2009), and the fact that it has been widely shared as a form of content, but also because it highlights the growing centrality of mobile and social networks within promotional screen practice. The campaign demonstrates how a promotional intermediary (the ad agency Saatchi & Saatchi) serviced the brand needs of a major client (T-Mobile) by developing a multiplatform ad campaign that generated shareable media and that enlisted consumers in the promotional process.

Within his reference to 'the participation economy' that begins this chapter, Kevin Roberts describes how advertising content should not only capture attention ('do I want to see it again?') but also engage audiences in such ways that consumers become co-creators and distributors of that content ('do I want to share this?'). This chapter explores this rhetorical 'shift' in advertising approach, examining the manner in which marketers have 'designed for spreadability' within television and new media initiatives (Jenkins, Ford and Green 2013: 195–228). This extends the discussion of branded entertainment in Chapter 1 and the purported move from 'interruptive' to 'engagement' advertising models in the 2000s and 2010s. In critical terms, 'Life's for Sharing' provides a platform for analysing the dynamics of spreadable marketing and consumer co-production that have shaped, and are continuing to shape, promotional screen practice. At the same time, in a discursive sense, the campaign demonstrates how forms emblematic of mobile connectivity – in this case flashmobs – have been used by mobile brands to promote social and media fantasies of digital living.

Mobile promotion, spreadable marketing and the case of Saatchi & Saatchi

Before analysing the genesis of 'Life's for Sharing' as a campaign, it is necessary to situate the growth of mobile and social network advertising in the 2000s and 2010s, and the context of what Jenkins, Ford and Green term 'spreadable marketing'. In terms of revenue, online and mobile advertising has high financial stakes, part and parcel of the wider, and well-documented, shift in advertising expenditure from traditional media to the internet in the last twenty years (Hardy 2013: 134–7). In 2011, online advertising spending in the US reached $36.6 billion, second only to broadcast television at $39.6 billion (IAB 2012). In 2012, Facebook posted ad revenues of $1.33 billion, representing 84 percent of the site's total revenue (IAB 2012, Facebook 2012). With increasing amounts of leisure time spent online, sites like YouTube, Facebook and Twitter have all developed practices to maximize advertising revenue. Although wary not to commodify their sites too overtly, each company has developed advertising initiatives tied to its core identity as a platform. This has ranged from YouTube's introduction of 'sponsored videos' (2008) that enable users to promote videos through self-selected keywords, to the syndication of Facebook's 'like' button to third-party websites (2010) and the development of 'sponsored stories' (2011) where ads knit with users' profiles and appear on friends' pages. For Twitter, these initiatives include the launch of 'promoted trends', 'promoted tweets' and 'promoted accounts' (2011), allowing advertisers to pay for placement atop a list of topics or have tweets inserted into users' Twitter feeds (McDonald 2009, Cohen 2013). Combined with major developments in search advertising by Google, which controls over 50 percent of online advertising in the US (largely based on 'cost-per-click' fees where advertisers pay when users click through to an ad), the internet has had a profound effect on models of advertising finance and, with it, expectations about tracking, measurement, performance and pricing (Hardy 2013, Turow 2013).

In the burgeoning field of online advertising, mobile advertising was still a relatively small market in the early 2010s. While search advertising accounted for 46.4 percent of online advertising revenues in the US in 2011 (worth $16.9 billion), display-related advertising such as banner ads, rich media ads, digital video and sponsorship made up a further 33 percent ($12 billion). Mobile advertising, describing the placement of ads on mobile websites or applications, accounted for just 9 percent of total revenues ($3.4 billion) (IAB 2012). However, mobile advertising had the highest proportional growth of any media channel by 2012, accelerating as users of social networking sites began to gravitate towards mobile devices. This was true across regional markets. In Europe, for example, while search advertising grew by 15.5 percent in 2012 (worth €11.9 billion), mobile advertising grew by 78.3 percent (€392 million) in the same year (IAB Europe 2013). The penetration of mobile phones using third-generation (3G) networks and the development of smartphones using fourth-generation (4G) networks provided, and continues to provide, new ways of assembling and delivering audiences to advertisers. In particular, the rise of mobile apps and touch-screen phones has allowed marketers to deliver high-end audiovisual materials, as well as more personalized content that can speak to a specific user.[2] More broadly, mobile and smartphones have become central to a culture where screen texts, images, clips and content, promotional and otherwise, can be shared in newly prolific ways. According to Jenkins, Ford and Green, mobile and social networks have facilitated new business models where 'the media industries and marketing worlds are moving towards a model of circulation based on the logic of spreadability' (2013: 44).

It is helpful to expand on this logic to draw out some of the implications for promotional communication. As a metaphor, 'spreadability' is linked to social media websites and platforms that have emerged in the transformation to Web 2.0. In the account of Jenkins et al., Web 2.0 involves 'a reorganization of the relations between producers and their audiences in a maturing Internet market, as well as a set of approaches adopted by companies seeking to harness mass creativity, collectivism, and peer production' (ibid.: 49). Spreadability denotes the pervasive forms of media circulation that define this culture. In promotional terms, it involves dispersing content widely through formal and informal networks as opposed to cultural and marketing models that aggregate audience attention through centralized media channels like broadcast television. This relies, fundamentally, on facilitating social connections and audience activity. Specifically it requires media creators to 'have to think about creating multiple access points to content and texts that are both "grabbable" and "quotable" – which are technically and aesthetically easy for audiences to share' (2013: 296). These imperatives are captured in T-Mobile's royal wedding spoof, a two-minute video released on YouTube in 2011 using fifteen royal lookalikes to stage a dance version of the wedding ceremony of Prince William and Kate Middleton. The video choreographed the royal family dancing down the aisle of Westminster Abbey to the East 17 pop song 'House of Love'. The video attracted 2.6 million views in the first two days, was posted on Prince Harry's Facebook page, and was widely reported on television and news media (Anon. 2011). As a form of branded entertainment, the video was humorous, easily grabbed, and blurred distinctions between marketers and audiences in the way that wedding guests were crowdsourced from T-Mobile's Facebook page. Moreover, the video maximized the likelihood of being shared by acting as fodder for conversations people were already having about

Figure 3.1 'One's life's for sharing': T-Mobile's royal wedding video (2011).

the royal wedding. By the terms of Jenkins, Ford and Green's argument, the T-Mobile spoof – which ended with the strapline 'One's Life's for Sharing' – was quintessentially spreadable.

Surveying the changing relationship between media and marketing in the twenty-first century, Jonathan Hardy observes that, by providing a greater range of vehicles for marketers to reach consumers, the digital environment has diminished the value and exclusivity of mass media channels. Considering newspapers, cinema and television, he writes: 'Content matters, since it attracts the consumers that advertisers seek to reach. However, marketers have much greater opportunity to reach consumers without subsidizing or accommodating media content providers' (2013: 147). While marketing bodies for commercial television have used econometric research to underscore television's ongoing significance to advertisers – noting, in particular, the ability of well-devised TV ads to drive online search activity (Thinkbox 2011) – the digital environment has nevertheless given rise to a new promotional ecology. The desire to 'pull' audiences to promotional material rather than 'push' media on consumers is witnessed in content-based campaigns for a wide variety of brands. In the same period as 'Life's for Sharing', for example, Fallon developed a series of quirky ads for Cadbury's that were designed to assume a viral life, the first of these (featuring a gorilla drumming emphatically to the Genesis song 'In the Air Tonight') released online in 2007 before its mainstream TV launch. Inscribed with their own entertainment value, such campaigns are viewed just as often on the web as they are on television and are frequently hosted on branded YouTube channels.

These marketing initiatives are not antithetical to the television ad. As Jeremy Orlebar suggests, 'apart from an initial wobble in the troubled economic times of 2008 when broadband and the Internet were confidently expected to kill off TV advertising, by 2012 the traditional moving image ad had adapted to the convergent environment and was confidently exploiting it' (2013: 195). While Jenkins et al. contrast 'stickiness' with 'spreadability' within marketing practice – the former based on 'aggregating attention in specific places' and the latter premised on 'dispersing content widely through formal and informal networks' (2013: 4–9) – they note that these 'logics' should ideally coexist. Indeed, an increasing number of television ads have been designed to work within different kinds of attention economies, leading critics like Orlebar and Iain MacRury (2009: 225) to identify new kinds of ad that depend less on product information than on 'their ability to create something that is likeable, captures attention, involves the consumer and engages in an educated dialogue' (Orlebar 2013: 195). Of course, commercial advertising has long striven for likeability and dialogue. Jennifer Gillan suggests that the 'friend and recommend' paradigm of US television and commercial advertising was firmly established in the 1950s, with 'content pro-motion hybrids' in this period defined by early 'peer-to-peer' forms of market-ing address (2015). Capturing attention and creating dialogue is nothing new in this sense. However, the logic of spreadable marketing has sought to involve the consumer more directly and visibly in the circulatory and meaning-making process of promotional communication. This has given rise to television ads and campaigns that are attuned to the sensibility of media sharing and conversation that pervade network communication. In designing television advertisements it is still necessary to create reasons to view in the sticky space of linear broadcasting. However, it is also important to use ideas or images that may seed a prospective digital 'afterlife' for ads and the campaigns to which they belong (Orlebar 2013).

As a marketing conceit 'Life's for Sharing' functioned as both a television and new media event. In particular, it played with the principle of developing audiovisual content for audiences to engage with, grab, excerpt and reuse. This captured a shift in T-Mobile's marketing approach in the mid-to-late 2000s. Steered by Saatchi & Saatchi, this shift was suggestive of broader transitions in the history and promotion of mobile media in this period. Of course, the advertising strategies used to sell mobile phones vary within and between markets. Promotional approaches are shaped in place and time by market-specific factors such as the technological and network capabilities of particular regions, habits of mobile use among populations (variously defined by age, vocation and socio-economic status), the brand identity of mobile operators and handset producers in global and local contexts, and the more general role of advertising as a cultural practice within specific territories and locales (Spurgeon 2008).[3] However, in major markets such as Europe, North America and China, mobile phones were increasingly imagined in the 2000s as a *screen* device. Heidi Rae Cooley (2004) observes this tendency in various US ads in the early 2000s, where human eyes peer from mobile LCD screens or where hands, and the act of holding a mobile, are associated with seeing. While camera phones would accentuate this sense of 'tactile vision', the establishment of third-generation networks in developed Western markets, and the subsequent launch of mobile television and other advanced data services, would see a growing number of ads presenting mobile phones as a medium for the delivery of audiovisual content. Jean Burgess posits the arrival of the iPhone in 2007 as 'the most emphatic assertion to date of the convergent future of the mobile phone', Apple ads promoting the 'endless generativity of the iPhone as a platform' (2013: 29, 40). Whether portrayed as a device for looking, listening, talking, texting, gaming, viewing or as an environment for apps, mobiles have been imagined to possess a transforming influence on projections of media self, space and, with it, screen behaviour.

This can be mapped onto transitions in the forms of address that mobile phone companies adopt at specific points in time. While network availability, price and handset choice became battlegrounds in the early market for mobile consumers, mobile services became relatively uniform in developed regions by the end of the 2000s, encouraging operators in especially competitive markets such as the UK to differentiate their brand identities. For example, when T-Mobile UK launched in 2002 (formerly known as Mercury One 2 One) it emphasized tariffs and new mobile features such as picture messaging. Following a maligned advertising campaign featuring the tennis stars Andre Agassi and Steffi Graf making joyful international calls to each other, Saatchi & Saatchi developed a pan-European advertising theme for T-Mobile in 2004 called 'Relax' that put price at the core of its brand message. This was replaced in 2008 by 'Life's for Sharing' which Saatchi's director of strategy, Richard Huntingdon, called a 'long-term brand proposition' encapsulating T-Mobile's desire to 'mobilise both personal and social networks' (Bussey 2008: 8). While not a wholesale shift, this change in emphasis from tactical product branding to affective corporate branding was influenced by the move towards engagement marketing models in the 2000s. For promotional intermediaries like Saatchi & Saatchi, this gave primacy to the development of brand communication (and content forms) that were suitably responsive to changes in the converged media environment.

This brings into focus Saatchi & Saatchi's own development as an agency in the 2000s and its relation with clients like T-Mobile. In October 2002, Deutsche Telekom decided to centralize its £27 million creative and media account for T-Mobile UK, moving it from BBH and Starcom Motive to Saatchi & Saatchi and the media agency Universal McCann. For Saatchi, this coincided with a period of creative and divisional reorganization, having lost its position, in terms of billings, as a top-ten London agency. Similar to other advertising and media agencies in the early 2000s, Saatchi & Saatchi sought to reinvent itself by declaring a 'media-neutral' approach to promotional planning. This was consistent with ideas of integrated marketing that emphasized the use of multiple communication channels for brand campaigns. Instead of being 'driven by preconceived ideas about a hierarchical communications mix with mass media advertising at the top' (Hackley and Hackley 2013: 79), Saatchi & Saatchi claimed that its planning was based on pragmatic creativity rather than mass media advertising by default. Its client relation with T-Mobile UK was set against this backdrop. Redefining its scope as an agency, Saatchi & Saatchi bought in specialist expertise in digital and mobile disciplines during the 2000s, and created new units such as a branded entertainment division (Gum), youth division (Friends of Johnny) and R&d lab (Industry@Saatchi). In different ways, Saatchi & Saatchi pursued content marketing strategies as a way to reconstruct its own creative status as an agency. This would be mediated in its work for T-Mobile.

Gum is indicative here. Launched in 2005, Gum's mission was 'to help clients achieve significant cut-through with leading-edge, young, urban consumers in the context of ever-increasing media fragmentation, the emergence of digital and wireless technologies and cynicism towards traditional marketing' (Bussey 2005: 20). Developing partnerships with specialists in different creative industries (including production companies, event organizers and music producers), it recruited two music industry professionals as equity partners to improve the unit's knowledge of popular culture. This foreshadowed the way that agencies would become increasingly outward facing in their creative approach, opening discussion with digital specialists, clients and consumers in developing ideas that could be promotionally leveraged. This openness was, in part, an attempt to reach the 18–30 target market whose experience of media was becoming increasingly shaped by Web 2.0 and the rise of mobile and social networks. In 2005, Saatchi & Saatchi's chief executive, Lee Daley, said that to target this market effectively 'we need to find out what these groups want without pushing into their lives. This group is massively cynical towards advertising and marketing and is fully versed in different media. We look at influences that fuel their culture, including the communication platforms' (cited in Bussey 2005: 20). As a venture, Gum was a response to uncertainties about traditional mass media advertising and mirrored attempts by other agencies to develop integrated marketing practices. While the unit closed in 2007 following a restructure by a new chief executive, Gum's focus on young consumers and early work for clients like T-Mobile seeded content strategies that would bear on the agency's development of spreadable media campaigns.

The redefinition of Saatchi & Saatchi as an agency was evident in the creation of new (albeit short-lived) divisions but also in corporate theorizing. This was captured in the idea of 'Lovemarks'. This term was coined by the company's worldwide chief executive Kevin Roberts (2006) and was taken up as an organizing concept for the agency as a whole. Lovemarks established a promotional philosophy about the emotions people bring to products they like. More interesting than the concept itself, which postulates the importance of weaving 'mystery', 'sensuality' and 'intimacy' into a brand, is the significance that 'Lovemarks' assumed in positioning Saatchi & Saatchi's market identity and promotional expertise. In the company's self-described move 'from an ad agency to an ideas company, to become the Lovemarks company' (Roberts 2007), Roberts' term became a corporate interpretive theory for how brands could 'inspire loyalty beyond reason' (Saatchi & Saatchi 2013).

In promotional terms, communication technologies became a site for creative ideas that focused on affect – that inspired feelings, called consumers to action and moved people to engage with technologies in a certain way. Jean Burgess suggests that 'the marketing of the iPhone consistently represents the device as a kind of magical object with which we are physically intimate, and which responds to our interior thoughts and desires with the mere touch of a finger' (2013: 39). By this account, Apple weaves mystery, sensuality and intimacy into the brand address of a key product. Mobile networks also developed promotional strategies that emphasized feelings and interactions, but in ways that often made less of the communication device itself than the role of the brand in facilitating media and popular cultural experiences. If 'Life's for Sharing' embodied Saatchi & Saatchi's approach to mobile promotion, leavened by the concept of Lovemarks, other agencies also developed affective strategies in their work for telecommunication companies. Saatchi & Saatchi's sister agency Fallon, for example, aligned the UK mobile network Orange with film culture in the 2000s, positioning Orange as a brand custodian of British cinema-going. In 2009, this involved sponsorship of the BAFTAs, a short-film competition, and a signature initiative called 'Orange Wednesday' that allowed Orange phone customers to buy two cinema tickets for the price of one across the UK on Wednesdays. Together with a long-running series of cinema ads that used

Hollywood actors to parody studio pitch meetings – so-called 'golden spots' that became part of the ritual of movie-going in the UK in the 2000s and that functioned as entertainments in their own right[4] – Orange launched a cinema-focused website, iPhone app and Facebook film club that translated popular cinephilia for a digital age. Steering away from explicit sales propositions, or ads that showed mobile phones, Orange appealed to youth and older-age demographics by associating its brand with the experience (and love) of popular film. By contrast, T-Mobile developed reality-inspired content for a target audience of young mobile users, in this case emphasizing themes of sociality and media sharing. In each example, Fallon and Saatchi & Saatchi developed content strategies with a calculated entertainment value and that also, portentously, associated mobile phones with screen media.

In 2004, Kevin Roberts suggested that telephone companies were likely to become critical players in media and marketing because they were putting screens into the hands of teenagers. He said: 'I know it's a communications device … but you are also enabling them [teenagers] to powerfully interact not only with their friends but with advertisers and products. It could easily be the new television set' (cited in Snoddy 2004: 5). While the significance of television would hardly diminish, mobile and social media would become a strategic promotional vehicle, of particular relevance to brands with a stake in net-worked communication. In the case of 'Life's for Sharing', this would involve agencies like Saatchi & Saatchi working with a range of creative partners. While advertising agencies provide ideas, direction, and oversight of integrated campaigns, especially those where television, mobile and social platforms work in tandem, producing and servicing content for these campaigns often relies on external companies with particular kinds of expertise. This extends from production companies that specialize in complex logistical shoots to digital publishers that facilitate 'always on' social media output.

Illustrating the blend of traditional and new media skills that cross-media campaigns require, Saatchi & Saatchi used a production company called Partizan to film the Liverpool Street flashmob that launched 'Life's for Sharing'. Partizan also produced ancillary media for this ad, including online trailers, 'making-of' documentaries and bonus material. Meanwhile, Saatchi & Saatchi used a digital publisher called Sabotage Times to generate social media content between the principal events and touch points of the 'Life's for Sharing' campaign. In one example, this included quirky, funny and shareable content (mostly articles and videos) from audience-contributors about the oddities of everyday British life that were circulated through Facebook, Twitter and Tumblr. In fulfilling its client brief 'to encourage people to create and share magical moments using T-Mobile', Saatchi & Saatchi developed a promotional strategy that established T-Mobile as a generator of media content. Creatively, this was the realization of agency planning and the work of the companies that Saatchi & Saatchi would sub-contract. However, 'Life's for Sharing' was also designed with a mind to the co-productive role of audiences. The next section uses the T-Mobile campaign to unpack this dimension of promotional screen practice, a feature that has accelerated with the proliferation of mobile and social networks. Critically, Saatchi & Saatchi's flashmob ads illustrate the development of promotional screen content by a major ad agency. However, they are also revealing of the way that audiences, and the activity of consumers, have been incorporated into the aesthetic and affective mode of promotional communication. Beyond the significance this holds for marketing practice, the flashmob ads connect with ideas of 'being digital' that would become a feature of media and policy discourse in the UK in the early twenty-first century (Carter 2009: 7).

Crowds, audiences and earned media: flashmobs and promotional co-production

The T-Mobile campaign is just one example of the culturally variable ways in which mobile phones have been imagined in marketing terms. However, 'Life's for Sharing' is notable for the way that it mediates promotional thinking and policy discussion surrounding mobile communication in a moment that Gerard Goggin associates with the rise of 'mobile Internet' (2013: 21–3). In launching the campaign, the Liverpool Street flashmob spoke directly to the advent of mobile social media. Moreover, it was situated against the backdrop of the regulatory thrust of UK government policy on digital life in the late 2000s. In January 2009, the same month as the flashmob, a major government report was published called *Digital Britain*. This would be followed by a lengthier final report in June that laid out plans for developing digital infrastructure and participation in the UK. Seeking 'to secure the UK's position as one of the world's leading digital knowledge economies' (Carter 2009: 7), the *Digital Britain* report proposed policy measures for developing the communications infrastructure of the UK and for enabling the wider social, cultural and economic potentialities of 'being digital'. For the mobile industry, this included recommendations for maximizing mobile and wireless networks, part of the Government's drive to achieve universal coverage for 3G mobile broadband through the allocation of spectrum licences and schemes of network sharing. Following the government auction of the 3G spectrum in the UK in 2000, mobile broadband coverage in the UK had reached 90 percent by the end of 2008, directly comparable with the US (92.3 percent), Italy (92 percent) and Norway (90 percent), although less than South Korea (99 percent), Australia (99 percent), Sweden (100 percent) and Japan (100 percent) (OECD 2010). However, it remained the case that only 17 percent of mobile users in the UK were on 3G when the report appeared. With the Government eager to maintain the position of the UK 'on the leading edge of the new mobile revolution' (Carter 2009: 74), the T-Mobile ads contributed to a wider set of cultural and promotional discourses surrounding 3G mobile communication. In a representational sense it resonated with the call of *Digital Britain* 'to put people at the centre of all our digital thinking' (ibid.: 27).[5]

In key ways, the 'Life's for Sharing' campaign was an example of the way that telecommunication companies projected shifts in the meaning of the mobile phone in the mid-to-late 2000s (May and Hearn 2005, Burgess 2013). Ever since the launch of the first commercial 3G services in Japan (2001), South Korea (2002), Europe (2003) and the US (2003), the diffusion of web-enabled phones has required marketing discourse to reconceptualize the type of social relationships and spaces that mobile phones mediate. Adriana de Souza e Silva (2006) argues that in allowing users to be constantly connected to the internet, mobile phones enable virtual communities to migrate to physical spaces. While the development of texting in the mid-1990s enabled people to exchange information with the purpose of coordinating face-to-face gatherings – social, political or otherwise – the increasingly locative nature of mobile media expanded the possibilities of virtual and corporeal communication. This was amplified by the emergence of cultural technologies like the iPhone which reconceived mobile technology as a portal, its haptic usability and integration with (geo-locative) apps enabling 'new kinds of verbal, visual, tactile, affective and sensory communication' (Goggin 2013: 21).

The first iterations of 'Life's for Sharing' played on these social, sensory and spatial meanings. In promoting free unlimited text and internet access, for instance, the television and new media advertising for 'Josh's Band' encouraged people to translate their *virtual* interest in Josh's musical quest – fostered through a dedicated Twitter feed, MySpace page and YouTube channel – into *physical* jamming sessions in London, Manchester, Birmingham and Edinburgh. In the marketing sequence of the 'Life's for Sharing' campaign, 'Josh's Band' built on two public events designed to elevate T-Mobile's brand status. The first of these saw the aforementioned flashmob in Liverpool Street Station. The second, four months later, involved a mass karaoke event in Trafalgar Square where 13,000 people gathered to sing the Beatles' 'Hey Jude' and Pink's 'So What' (where she also appeared) after T-Mobile corralled people by text and a YouTube video carrying the message: 'Remember the dance? Want to be part of the next event? Be at Trafalgar Square. This Thursday. April 30th 6 pm–7 pm'. In its first twelve months, the 'Life's for Sharing' campaign unfurled as a series of synchronized performances, all involving the public and with progressively deliberate integrations of mobile technology into mediated acts, and events, of social production.

According to T-Mobile's chief marketing officer Srini Gopalan, 'the flashmob ads were part of a strategy to build an emotional connection with consumers by using real people to give the campaign an element of a *Big Brother*-style reality television programme' (Costa 2010). The reference to *Big Brother* (Channel 4, 2000–2010) is consistent with mobile phone marketing strategy in the UK and elsewhere. Indeed, reality formats that rely on phone and text voting have frequently been sponsored by mobile phone companies in ways that foster audience interactivity. For example, a campaign for Carphone Warehouse/TalkTalk in 2009 built around *The X Factor* (ITV, 2004–) invited viewers to record their own online singing performances via a webcam, the resulting videos forming the basis for a series of television ads. In a different advertising market, Jing Wang (2008: 29) notes the connection in China between reality formats and mobile media, the Chinese pop-reality phenomenon *Super Girl* (Hunan TV,

2004–2011) developing audience interactivity by using sponsored content tie-ins with TV and mobile media. However, T-Mobile moved beyond these user-generated interstitials towards media content with its own 'crowdsourced' entertainment value. This strategy tapped the opportunities for 'mass creativity, collectivism and peer production' (Jenkins et al. 2013: 49) that have developed around networked communication technologies. If, as is widely theorized, 'new media environments extend the possibilities for conversational interaction and participation, and generate new possibilities for consumer productivity' (Spurgeon 2008: 7, Jenkins 2006), marketing has sought to capitalize on these dynamics. For corporate brands and the agencies who sell them expertise, this entails 'the diversification and integration of the range of techniques for facilitating advertiser-consumer interaction' (Spurgeon 2008: 104).

The 'Life's for Sharing' campaign is a clear example of the ways in which marketers have sought to build brand communities by connecting mass media advertising to the conversational possibilities of digital media. According to Lysa Hardy, head of brand communication at T-Mobile: 'the industry sees its future in mobile data so we should use it more to bring campaigns to life' (Farber 2009). Srini Gopalan concurred:

> If we're a brand that is about participation and sharing, then we need to drive real mass market mobile Internet. The Android platform is starting to make mass market mobile Internet more accessible, and out of that will come social networking and the related brand values.
>
> (Costa 2010)

These statements demonstrate the impetus in the late 2000s to connect 3G technology with new marketing approaches that emphasized consumer interaction and social participation.

Andrew McStay suggests: 'where traditionally brands have fought via straightforward representational means to make an impression and be number one, T-Mobile has sought to leverage sociality and community as a standing-reserve' (2013: 48–9). For Saatchi & Saatchi, this involved a creative strategy that offered a particular scenario of social and mobile interaction, captured symbolically in the initial flashmob. While mobile communication is often experienced as disruptive within public space – from the common frustration of phones going off at inappropriate times and places to the pedestrian hazards of people simultaneously walking and checking their screens – the Liverpool Street flashmob offered something thrilling, and even potentially moving, to watch. T-Mobile's 'Dance' attracted 3.5 million hits on YouTube within three weeks of its launch. During this time, the 'Life's for Sharing' channel became the most highly subscribed channel on YouTube in the UK. Creating 'an event that people would want to take part in and then share with each other' (Saatchi & Saatchi 2009), Saatchi & Saatchi used the performance of the crowd as a means of giving the campaign emotive currency. In accounting for this, it is instructive to consider the flashmob as a peculiarly contemporary cultural form.

As a practice, flashmobs were shaped in the late 1990s and early 2000s by the popularity of texting which could facilitate rapid, decentralized, one-to-many communication. Flashmobs became emblematic of mobile connectivity in this period, leading to a number of stunts in cities such as New York, London and Berlin that assumed the status of performance art. These would see groups quickly assemble to perform a random public act and then disband, leaving onlookers bemused. In a useful summary of its political and artistic inclinations, Judith A. Nicholson writes that 'flashmobbing straddled the boundaries between spectacle, activism, experiment and prank' (2005). Situated in a political climate where crowds and public places had become associated with terrorist intent, and where mobile and internet traffic was increasingly subject to state and commercial surveillance, Nicholson draws out the ideological ramifications of people being able very quickly to transform public space, whether to protest or, as a popular flashmob credo proclaimed, 'in the pursuit of nothing'. In cool-hunting for ideas, the T-Mobile dance echoed a planned flashmob in New York's Grand Central Station in 2003 (which itself was based on a piece of work called *Trainstation* (1998) by the performance and dance group 'Seven Sisters Group'). Whereas this particular 'mob ballet' had been cancelled due to concerns about the potentially twitchy response of armed law enforcement officials, the T-Mobile flashmob was suggestive of the way that corporate marketers and television executives had by 2009 transformed the practice into something popular and mainstream.[6]

Our interest here is less the manner in which advertising appropriated the form of the flashmob, or co-opted its potential for quasi-Situationist critique, than the particular means by which flashmobbing was turned into entertainment and put to imaginative work. Although the T-Mobile dance was an extensively rehearsed and pre-planned stunt, facilitated by the offices of Film London, it relied on unauthorized expressions within public space. Its affective power was a function of dance choreography but also of civic communication – of using laughter and amazement to jolt people out of their daily routines. If, as Judith Nicholson suggests, 'flashmobbing may be interpreted as a commentary or reflection on contemporary spaces and routines' (2005), the T-Mobile dance, much like the 'Welcome Home' flashmob at the arrival gate of Heathrow's Terminal 5, reimagined the space and sociality of the guarded urban crowd. As a physical and media spectacle, the Liverpool Street flashmob involved disguised dancers of varying ages, ethnicities and professions (from suited businessmen, station workers and coffee baristas to backpackers, commuters and tourists passing through). Switching between panning shots of the synchronized dance routine and close-ups of bystanders watching, taking pictures on their phones, laughing into their mobiles, and actually joining in, the ad seized upon moments of sociality in a space more often characterized by the passing of strangers. In one notable moment, a young male bystander with a tall Afro watches the dance on the sidelines, breaks into a half-smile, winks at the member of the public standing next to him, and submits himself to the spectacle, gyrating to the song 'My Boy Lollipop'. In other close-ups, we see

Figure 3.2 T-Mobile's Liverpool Street flashmob (2009).

pensioners dancing with shopping bags in hand, and spectators on the station balcony moving to the rhythm of the music. The director of the flashmob, Michael Gracey, explained in rehearsal to the pre-selected dancers that the 'real magic exists in you being able to convince members of the public to join in and do what you're doing' (T-Mobile 2009). This participatory principle was part of the aesthetic spectacle of the ad and was reflected in ancillary videos released on YouTube where interviews with members of the public described the event as 'delightful', 'contagious' and 'a moment of love'.

In promotional terms, 'Dance' was designed to capture attention within the television schedule and appeal in ways that encouraged audiences to seek out and watch the performance again. Rather than a long-form ad (lasting just over two minutes), the flashmob was conceived as short-form content, and was accordingly released with the paratextual apparatus of film and television promotion. As well as ancillary media such as making-of documentaries showing the auditioning and filming process, and bonus materials featuring off-screen interviews, T-Mobile fostered fan re-enactment by posting 'how to' videos breaking down the moves of the dance routine. This involved short choreographed actions that moved with fluid gear-shifts between songs by Lulu ('Shout'), Yazz ('The Only Way is Up'), The Pussycat Dolls ('Don't Cha'), Strauss ('Beautiful Blue Danube'), Kool and the Gang ('Get Down on It'), Rainbow ('Since You've Been Gone'), Millie ('My Boy Lollipop') and The Contours ('Do You Love Me?'). T-Mobile also posted two videos showing an England footballer and female British TV presenter parodying versions in their locker/dressing room. These instructional videos formed the basis of several amateur re-enactments of the flashmob in British shopping malls, demonstrating the strategic potential of dance to engage the productivity of ordinary consumers. As various critics observe, amateur home dance videos and the popularization of dance crazes have become a particular site of audience activity and co-creation on platforms like YouTube (Peters and Seier 2009, Jenkins, Ford and Green 2013: 182–8). This is demonstrated by video memes such as 'Crank Dat' (2007) and 'Harlem Shake' (2013) which spread globally as users created online versions, interpretations and adaptations of specific dance styles. While not a meme as such, flashmobbing offered an expressive and imitable form of choreography to copy, mash-up and emulate. In deciding on a trend to prioritize, Saatchi & Saatchi's 'Dance' was geared to participatory circulation and the launch of an aspiring online campaign.

According to Jenkins, Ford and Green, brands 'have seen spreadable media as a means of expanding the resonance of company messages and developing more meaningful relationships with current or potential consumers' (2013: 296). 'Dance' was exemplary of this corporate aim. Within Jenkins et al.'s argument, the 'logic of spreadability' responds to the potential for audiences to share content for their own purposes; it designates 'a movement toward a more participatory model of culture, one which sees the public not as simply consumers of preconstructed messages but as people who are shaping, sharing, reframing, and remixing media content in ways which might not have been previously imagined' (ibid.: 2). To facilitate the likelihood of content being spread, they suggest that media creators need to account for the 'producerly' elements of texts that 'leave open processes of analysis, meaning-making and activity for audiences to fill in' (ibid.: 219). While humour and the use of parody lend themselves to these producerly attributes, and were defining of the previously mentioned royal wedding spoof, the Liverpool Street flashmob can be seen as an example of 'unfinished content'. Jenkins et al. write:

> Content which is unfinished, or not immediately intelligible, drives the individual and collective intelligence of its audiences. Such texts or events often ask people to contribute something or encourage them to look twice because they can't believe what they are seeing; they need to verify its authenticity or figure out how it was done.
>
> (2013: 209)

In its staging and choreography, the flashmob encouraged audiences to look twice. The surprise and spontaneity of the dance was simultaneously mystifying and mesmeric. It invited questions about what the dance was, what it meant, and how it was achieved. These questions were addressed by the making-of documentary and bonus materials – ancillary texts that were designed to pull audiences into the campaign by providing insider knowledge of the production process. However, the 'how to' videos invited possibilities for further activity. This was consistent with the tone for the wider 'Life's for Sharing' campaign. While the final scenes of the Liverpool Street flashmob offered a model for sharing, dwelling on members of the public using their mobile phones to show and tell of their experiences, the 'how to' videos amplified the role of audiences *as* participants.

Consistent with postulations by the likes of Kevin Roberts about the 'age of the participation economy' (Roberts 2009), concepts like crowdsourcing, co-creation and user-generated content became prominent themes within marketing discussion in the 2000s and early 2010s. Indeed, *Advertising Age* included 'consumer control' and 'crowdsourcing' (as well as 'earned media', 'Madison & Vine' and 'Lovemarks') within a feature list of 'ideas of the decade' (Creamer and Parekh 2009). In promotional terms, the transformations brought about by Web 2.0 have led advertising and media agencies to devise communications strategies that motivate audiences to circulate content and become publicists in their own right. Describing changes to media planning since the late 1990s, Matt Andrews, Chief Strategy Officer at the media agency Mindshare UK, commented:

> It used to be that you just simply interrupted content with advertising, whichever medium that was, and now that's not the case anymore; you're trying to create reasons for people to want to engage – value within the connection, onward journeys to other things, creating social influence through those connections.
>
> (Andrews 2012)

This shift in communication strategy is captured in the trade distinction between *bought, owned* and *earned* media. While 'bought' media denotes the traditional model of buying advertising and media space between television programmes, 'owned' media describes the opportunity for brands to own and distribute original media content through broadcast channels, websites, online video channels and social media platforms. 'Earned' media becomes the point where viewers distribute that content for nothing because they are engaged by it; it is the moment where boundaries between producers, marketers and audiences potentially blur.

As a term, 'earned media' implies something worked for and acquired by promotional intermediaries. This can involve editorial coverage achieved through public relations activity but it also relates to the earned labour of audiences. In a marketing sense, audience labour involves the participation of consumers in the promotional process, either as unpaid ad creators or as publicity distributors through the circulation of videos, blogs, commentaries, tweets and the like. More broadly, it describes the production of online social relations, and the use of social media to generate valuable personalized information. This involves 'transforming data collected through people's useful, satisfying or entertaining interactions on these sites into products that can be sold' (Cohen 2013: 182). Saatchi & Saatchi's concept for the 'Life's for Sharing' campaign was premised on the co-creative labour of audiences. From the crowdsourced participation of fans/consumers at live events to their production and sharing of content through mobile and social media networks, T-Mobile created a community of productive viewers that could be used and surveyed for commercial purposes.

This taps into wider debates about the 'contradictions of user-generated labour' (Andrejevic 2009). Indeed, the T-Mobile campaign highlights critical questions about the significance and meaning of 'prosumer' activity, a critical neologism describing consumers who become producers or co-promoters. Within the field of mobile promotion, harnessing the free labour of audiences undoubtedly serves the interests of companies like T-Mobile. However, this does not mean to say that such relations are wholly exploitative. In their discussion of contemporary media literacy – what they call 'media literacy 2.0' – Michael Hoechsmann and Stuart R. Poyntz suggest that 'youth today experience media as actors in an immersive environment, not just as external spectators of entertainment and information' (2012: 152). In focusing on young mobile users, Saatchi & Saatchi used dance and musical performance as a particular value-basis for T-Mobile to facilitate social interaction among consumers. Adam Arvidsson calls this the 'ethical economy of customer co-production' (2008). He writes that in a fragmented social environment where durable ties are scarce, 'promoters thrive by giving affective strength, for a short time at least, to what are essentially weak ties between participants in a scene. These ties entail commitment, trust and solidarity – that is, they are experienced as ethically significant' (2008: 333). Exemplifying Saatchi & Saatchi's 'Lovemark' philosophy, the 'Life's for Sharing' campaign was premised on the giving of affective strength. By the terms of Arvidsson's argument, value for participants is not primarily of the product but of the process (and in T-Mobile's case the *performance*) that allows them 'to have their efforts socially recognized as creative, inventive or beautiful in a sustained way' (ibid.: 333). The value for marketers, in turn, is the way that user activity deepens the circulatory life of a promotional text and lends itself to data mining and free market research.

Achieving this balance of value is not always straightforward for advertising agencies and their clients. While audiences may derive affective rewards from their interaction with brands, and may willingly participate in commercially driven campaigns if they provide cultural or social benefits, content-based campaigns can backfire if they are not seen as credible. This was something that Saatchi & Saatchi had to manage in the case of 'Josh's Band'. Unlike the song and dance flashmobs, which were widely embraced, the grassroots credentials of 'Josh's Band' were received far more sceptically within online discussion. Creating a band through mobile and social networking – purportedly developed as a challenge to a random member of the public when asked by a T-Mobile film crew what he would do with free texts and internet for life – the impromptu gigs and music-making activities raised suspicions of contrivance. The project attracted claims and counter-claims about the authenticity of Josh and his band, and the transparency of the project as a whole. One British TV critic excoriated 'Josh's Band' as 'so clumsily contrived it wouldn't fool a hen' (Brooker 2009). The accompanying description of Josh as a 'simpering middle-class mop' touched the surface of numerous online barbs levelled at the campaign and its apparent claim to be a grassroots musical phenomenon. This relates to what Jenkins et al. call audience suspicion of 'astroturfing' within marketing practice, a term for the production of 'fake grassroots' (2013: 77–8). While 'Josh's Band' didn't disguise its status as a marketing initiative, it did ask audiences to believe that the band and accompanying song were spontaneous and unmanufactured. The hint that paid session musicians were involved, and that the song was written by a professional tunesmith, weakened the bounds of credibility and trust in Josh's band. If transparency refers to the 'degree to which brands and audience members alike are forthcoming about their ties to one another' (ibid.: 76), 'Josh's Band' raised questions for marketing managers at T-Mobile and Saatchi & Saatchi about the terms upon which corporate brands develop user-driven campaigns.

Although brands have increasingly sought to position themselves as facilitators in the lives of consumers, the 'new strategic imperatives of ubiquity, mobility and interactivity' have often been a source of improvisation rather than sure-footed marketing design. In transforming T-Mobile into a locus of social and creative activity, Saatchi & Saatchi used branded entertainment to enact scenarios of mobile living. While some argued that 'Josh's Band' was lacking in authenticity, the 'Life's for Sharing' campaign would highlight wider efforts in the promotional industries to mobilize advertising as a content and cultural resource. This occurred in a period where the dream life of connectivity – of being 'effortlessly digital' to cite internal marketing language at Orange[7] – had become central to the imagination of mobile media.

'Effortlessly digital'?: the cultural work of promotional media

So far, we have focused on the industrial and textual dynamics of spreadable mobile marketing. This can deliver perspectives on the brands, promotional intermediaries and creative work involved. However, mobile promotion can also help us think about the cultural function of promotional texts. In this last section, we want to consider briefly the role that promotional materials play in constructing vernaculars around digital audiovisual technology. This brings into focus the social and ideological bearing of self-representations of mobile media within specific contexts and periods.

Analysing the way that contemporary popular media attempts to educate audiences about the uses of digital technology, Will Brooker (2010) suggests that mobile phone advertising can offer a 'kind of training' about the digital world. Focusing on texts pitched at 'middle market' audiences – those who are neither entirely native nor wholly removed from the world of digital media – he suggests that the mini-narratives of advertising help to

> … teach their viewers the gestures and language, the possibilities and advantages of technology, but also, crucially, they enforce the social importance and status of mastering the world-as-data; of transforming the environment, through technology, into digital form and being able successfully to manipulate it.

(2010: 558)

This relates to a broader contention that popular entertainment, including advertising, film, television and video games, has a tutorial function within twenty-first-century capitalism. Within his argument, Brooker suggests that such cultural forms help audiences to acquire the attitudes, understanding and mentality necessary to live in a world of digital media.

In a broad-ranging essay, Brooker's discussion of mobile phone advertising concentrates on promotional examples that are explicit in their show-and-tell approach to mobile technologies; he focuses on ads for Apple, Windows and Nokia that demonstrate what can be done with specific handheld devices.[8] However, the tutorial function of mobile promotion has different modes, and can be applied to the examples discussed in this chapter. For example, the Orange 'golden spots' that ran in British cinemas for much of the 2000s would always end with the admonishment: 'Don't let a mobile phone ruin your movie. Please switch it off'. These tongue-in-cheek ads offered tutorials in mobile etiquette for movie audiences, and aligned with Orange's brand position as the guardian of mobile-owning film communities. Meanwhile, the 'Life's for Sharing' campaign offered training in a different kind of social behaviour; set in a range of open public spaces (stations, airports, city squares, shopping malls), T-Mobile ads provided examples of everyday content sharing. By the terms of Brooker's argument, 'mastering the world-as-data' meant in this case developing habits in the circulation of digital texts, and of building up and belonging to physical/network communities (which offered their own world-*of*-data to marketers). While the tutorial function of 'Life's for Sharing' also provided lessons for marketers in how to encourage audience participation in brand initiatives, the flashmob ads chimed with a wider set of cultural discourses about digital living that took hold in the UK. This included government promotional campaigns (cum-tutorials) designed to prepare people for a shift from analogue to digital in the late 2000s and early 2010s, and was notable in public information ads and posters foreshadowing the national switchover to digital television in 2012. According to *Digital Britain*, 'Digital technology is no longer simply desirable. It is rapidly becoming an essential facility to citizens and consumers in a modern society' (Carter 2009: 28). With phones reconceived in the late 2000s as personal computers able to send and receive digital text, image and audio files, mobile communication was increasingly figured as a source of connectivity, creativity and communal participation. This was reflected in both the tenor and execution of the T-Mobile campaign.

While promotional materials can have a pedagogic function, they are also a site of ideological investment. They are in this way potentially revealing of the way that new media technologies have been framed, debated and taken up in specific periods. In his perceptive study of the launch of radio, television and digital media in the United States during the twentieth century, William Boddy suggests that promotional materials help uncover the 'fantasies of consumption that can speak eloquently of the larger cultural ambivalence regarding new communications technologies' (2004: 1). In considering the cultural work of promotional media, we might ask finally what ambivalences about mobile technology (if any) are revealed in promotional initiatives such as the T-Mobile campaign. While content strategies such as 'Life's for Sharing' point to equivocations about mass media advertising among marketing practitioners, the campaign also uncovers ambivalences of a social and political kind. For example, T-Mobile gave tacit acknowledgment of the generational, gender and ethnic divisions of 3G mobile ownership in a series of promotional poster images that accompanied the multiplatform screen campaign. In one image that appeared in March 2010, a smiling black woman in her late forties is accompanied by the message 'who says a smartphone with apps can't be available to everyone?' In a different image, a younger black woman is shown chatting at a water cooler with the message 'who says smartphones aren't for everyone in your business?' These images addressed the implicit assumption that smartphones were for a certain kind of consumer in the late 2000s, mainly hypersocial twenty-somethings or white professional men.[9] Within the wider T-Mobile campaign, these images revealed underlying cultural ambivalence about the extent of 'sharing' taking place within and between market segments, and of the uneven diffusion of smartphones among social groups.

In drawing attention to assumptions about smartphone ownership, the 'Life's for Sharing' campaign posed questions about the extent of cultural participation in the era of mobile internet. However, the campaign would also, unwittingly, throw into relief ambivalences that were more political and corporate in nature. Indeed, while T-Mobile was conducting its song and dance in 2009, 'Life's for Sharing' assumed an unexpected legal and regulatory meaning. Notably, it was discovered that T-Mobile staff had unlawfully sold private data from thousands of customers to third-party brokers. This trade in personal records raised issues of data protection and posed an altogether different set of questions about life sharing: namely whose life is being shared, by whom, for whom, and with what consequences for digital privacy rights? It is here that content ventures such as 'Josh's Band' would dovetail with developments in data gathering. As various critics have shown, online marketing is posited on the trade of data (McStay 2010, Cohen 2013, Turow 2013). Within the digital environment, audiences are often only able to watch, play or join in a discussion if they give companies access to such as their Facebook account, sign in to a Cookies policy, or give other kinds of data about themselves. 'Josh's Band' was an example of the way that content was leveraged *in relation to data*. To borrow from Mark Andrejevic, it offered people 'a modicum of control over the product of their creative activity in exchange for the work they do in building up online community and sociality upon privately controlled network infrastructures' (2009: 419). Although the unlawful trade in personal records was not directly tied to the 'Life's for Sharing' campaign, T-Mobile's development of mobile and social network marketing was part of what Joseph Turow calls the 'data-gathering, media-planning and ad-serving ecosystem' (2013: 110). While 'Josh's Band' raised questions about marketing transparency in this sense it was also inextricably linked to the commoditization of the digital audience and to associated concerns about the way that large companies and digital businesses use, exchange and sell data.

The size of telecommunication companies became a site of further ambivalence in the course of the 'Life's for Sharing' campaign, giving rise to regulatory friction about media ownership and market competition. Just as 'Josh's Band' was gathering steam, T-Mobile UK and Orange UK announced plans to merge. This created the largest mobile phone operator in the UK, with 29.5 million customers and a combined market share of 37 percent, significantly ahead of its nearest rivals, Vodafone (27 percent) and O2 (25 percent). More significantly, it meant that the merged company had 84 percent of the strategic 1800 MHz spectrum band, key to enabling fourth generation (4G) wireless technologies. For rival mobile operators, this flew in the face of a government settlement designed to ensure the spectrum was fairly shared between competitors. Although T-Mobile and Orange agreed to give up bandwidth to see the merger approved, the British media regulator Ofcom would subsequently give the company permission to establish a new 4G network ahead of its competitors. Launched in 2012 as a joint venture between France Telecom and Deutsche Telekom (called EE or 'Everything Everywhere'), this saw one of the largest promotional campaigns of its kind in the UK, with a reported marketing budget of £100 million.[10] While the agenda of *Digital Britain* was to facilitate conditions for broadband access to all homes by 2012, it seemed that network sharing was not for life in regulatory terms, creating disquiet about the concessions the British government was prepared to give to a single corporation for the UK to stay apace with the rollout of 4G services in other developed countries.

These different flashpoints provide an appropriate coda to this chapter's consideration of mobile promotion. William Boddy suggests that the 'unique legal and political relationship of electronic media industries to the state in the USA and elsewhere has sensitized the major corporate actors to the strategic importance of being able to define the electronic media's ontologies, audience demands and social rationale' (2004: 4). Within developed markets such as Britain, the vernacular of mobile communication in the late 2000s and early 2010s was built around ideas and images of cultural and network connectivity, the prospects of which were elaborated in content forms that strategically – although not unambiguously – promoted the corporate-political agenda of harnessing digital technologies for new ways of living. The T-Mobile flashmobs were performance spectacles in this context. Set against a backdrop of corporate re-alignment and public policy discussion surrounding the digital economy, and tied to developments in mobile and social media marketing, the 'Life's for Sharing' campaign provided a site where the rationale of mobile media was played out. Mobilized as screen entertainment, the campaign illustrates how, within the UK and beyond, being 'effortlessly digital' has required, and will continue to require, significant promotional and imaginative work.

Conclusion

This chapter has focused on the way that advertising agencies like Saatchi & Saatchi have sought through forms of content marketing to create images and interactions that demonstrate the social and cultural possibilities of mobile media. In a series of respects, the dissemination of mobile technology in the 2000s had a major bearing on both the marketing and media industries. Most immediately in the former case, mobile phone advertising became a growth field. This would range from the sending of promotional messages to idle screens, to the introduction of apps, games and ad-supported mobile services. More broadly, mobile and smartphone technology would become central to online advertising, mobile devices presenting new possibilities for communicating with targeted consumers in real time and within specific locations (the subsequent chapters will also consider the ways in which mobile social media offered new opportunities for the promotion of audiovisual content while also threatening established business models, particularly in the TV industry). Meanwhile, as these technological, economic and aesthetic developments were taking shape, network operators and handset providers in the major markets of Europe, North America and the Asia Pacific took a lead in conveying the relation of mobile and smartphones to the converged media environment, shaping the promotional imagination of mobile communication and projecting a sense of the 'dream life' of electronic media in the digital era (Boddy 2004).

We have argued that 'Life's for Sharing' is revealing of industrial, textual and cultural transitions in the move towards mobile social media in the first decades of the twenty-first century. To this end, we have used the campaign as a lens to analyse the way that promotional screen practices have developed within, and responded to, the convergent media environment. T-Mobile is clearly not the only telecommunications brand to associate itself with mobile social media. However, its attempt to fashion a long-term brand proposition in this area, and its work with a major advertising agency also concerned with remodelling its own promotional identity, makes it a suggestive case study for this book. Our period of focus between 2005 and 2014 coincides with a particular conjuncture in the history of mobile media that witnessed the embedding of mobile and social networks in everyday life. The creation and circulation of 'Life's for Sharing' corresponds with the development of this networked culture. Moving seamlessly between new and traditional media outlets, the campaign is an example of marketing and media confluence; it illustrates the playful and participatory way that advertisements collapse the boundaries of promotion and content and have been consciously designed to spread.

In serving the needs of global telecommunication companies, the imaginative work of mobile promotion has been mainly developed by advertising agencies. These are often themselves part of transnational advertising conglomerates like WPP, Publicis, Omnicom and Interpublic. While global brands may seek promotional expertise beyond the agencies they roster, client work for major corporations is generally handled by large advertising and media agencies. As part of the Publicis Group in the late 2000s, Saatchi & Saatchi and Fallon took different approaches to mobile promotion, the former associating T-Mobile with social media and the latter associating Orange with film and cinema-going. However, the merger of T-Mobile and Orange, and the subsequent launch of EE, would suggest the growing promotional importance of digital content strategies. Before the $35 billion mega-merger of Publicis and Omnicom in July

2013 – which, by some accounts, was driven by the increasingly fierce battle to control data and consolidate digital businesses (Sweney 2013)[11] – Publicis aligned Saatchi & Saatchi and Fallon into a mini group structure in 2007 to invigorate the presence of both agencies in the UK and US market. It was Saatchi & Saatchi, however, that was given the prized EE account. According to Spencer McHugh, EE's director of brand, 'we felt that the work Saatchis had been doing with T-Mobile was more culturally relevant to the UK market' (cited in Tylee 2012: 14). By 2011, 27 percent of adults and 47 percent of teenagers owned 3G smartphones in the UK (Ofcom 2011), a significant jump from the 17 percent of total recorded users of 3G in 2008. Furthermore, the UK had the third highest proportion of mobile users accessing the internet with a smartphone. This stood at 36 percent, behind China (64 percent) and Spain (43 percent) (Ofcom 2012). If the smartphone represents new modalities of communication in the world of mobile internet – phones becoming platforms serving multiple screen and telephonic functions – one result, according to Gerard Goggin, has been 'the intensive reassembling of the social' (2013: 23). Saatchi & Saatchi's focus on social media illustrates how a major advertising agency has accounted for the 'new strategic imperatives of ubiquity, mobility and interactivity' on behalf of the mobile industry (Boddy 2011: 72). As we shall see in the following chapter, these imperatives extend beyond the realm of commercial advertising and mobile communication, and bear on other cross-cutting promotional and media sectors as well.

Notes

1 At this point, T-Mobile was the world's third-largest multinational mobile network after Vodafone (UK) and Telefonica (Spain), with international subsidiaries in Germany, the UK, the US, Austria and the Czech Republic, and a brand presence stretching across Europe and North America.

2 Apple launched its app store in 2008, a year after it launched the iPhone. As Gerard Goggin notes, 'this establishment of a platform and marketplace for software brought mobile computing alive, establishing it henceforth as a feature of mobile devices – in which Apple was in the vanguard but which other smartphones also quickly copied, contended with and sought to better' (2013: 20). Google, Nokia, Blackberry, Microsoft and Samsung all launched their own app stores in the immediate years following.

3 In case specific terms, the UK has one of the largest mobile markets in Europe, both in revenue and in the number of subscribers (76 million in 2009). When 'Life's for Sharing' was launched, the UK was served by five major providers that would all offer 3G services: Orange, Vodafone, O2, T-Mobile and 3. This highly competitive market required companies in the UK to differentiate not only their network packages but also their brand identities in very deliberate terms.

4 Beginning in 2003, these spots involved a film pitch by a Hollywood actor to the 'Orange Film Commission Board', chaired by the comedy writer Steve Furst. In each case, the executives of the board would crudely attempt to leverage mobile-related ideas such as texting or the colour orange into the movie concept. This was met with incredulity and resignation by the talent giving the pitch. The spots featured stars including Snoop Dogg, Macauley Culkin, Michael Madsen, Val Kilmer, Patrick Swayze, Mena Suvari, Steven Seagal, Sean Astin, Carrie Fisher, Angelica Huston, Roy Scheider, Verne Troyer, Darth Vader (in character), and Spike Lee.

5 The transition to 3G became a source of wide-ranging policy discussion in the 2000s. The launch of the first commercial 3G services in Japan, South Korea, Europe and the US in the early 2000s was underpinned by policy protocols about the standards required for wireless communication, as well as competition policy rules governing the activities of mobile operators and the cost of licence fees within particular regional markets (Tilson and Lyytinen 2006, Bjorkdahl and Brolin 2003). While the development of 3G mobile communication intersects with the *Digital Britain* report at the end of the 2000s, it is important to note that the technological and political trajectory of 3G has a longer history, dating back to the launch of the first web-enabled phone in 1999 and, in the European context, to wider attempts by the EU to establish the necessary standards and regulatory systems for the creation of convenient, reliable telecoms networks and services for a pan-European market.

6 Flashmobs became something of a television fad in 2009 and 2010. The mob dance style featured in episodes of US programmes ranging from *Glee* (FOX, 2009–) to *Modern Family* (ABC, 2009–) in 2009, and formed the basis of UK channel idents and TV promos in dance-based reality shows such as *Got to Dance* (Sky, 2009–) and *Strictly Come Dancing* (BBC, 2004–) in 2010.

7 Spencer McHugh, brand director of Orange, who would later direct brand promotion for the company EE, the merged Orange UK and T-Mobile UK, explained in 2010: 'We have a term we use internally about being "effortlessly digital", which is something we've been trying to do for the last couple of years, where the digital landscape, or digital media, affects everything we do. We want to continue to develop and grow that' (Farey-Jones 2010).

8 According to Jean Burgess, a new phase in Apple branding in the late 2000s would emphasize the 'effortless' rather than 'extraordinary' creativity of Apple users, marketing around Apple products such as the iLife software suite and devices such as the iPhone and iPad emphasizing the 'social and cultural generativity' of Apple technologies (2013: 37, 40).

9 As in other mobile markets, the T-Mobile campaign in the UK was especially geared to youth culture. In their broad survey of mobile communication in global markets, Manuel Castells et al. observe that the European mobile market has long been oriented towards young people (2007: 127-69). In the 1990s and early 2000s, Northern and Western Europe, together with Japan, saw younger generations readily embrace mobile technology, leading to particularly fast rates of diffusion in these regions among those in the 15–25 and 25–34 years age brackets. Accordingly marketing efforts tended to focus on these groups. This compared with the United States where the largest group of mobile users in the same period were young professionals in the thirty-plus age range, leading the mobile industry to focus on the corporate market.

10 EE was introduced as a technology-based brand aimed at a segment of the market wanting 4G. The EE launch made extensive use of digital platforms and placed at its centre the Hollywood star Kevin Bacon. This played on the parlour game 'six degrees of Kevin Bacon' (which posits that any individual in Hollywood is only six links or acquaintances apart from the Hollywood character actor) to illustrate the principle of connectivity.

11 This merger collapsed in May 2014 as negotiations between the two advertising giants turned into a power struggle, with increasing talk of Omnicon (revenues of $15.9 billion) taking over Publicis (revenues of $9.5 billion) (Sweney 2014).

Bibliography

Acland, C. R. (2009) 'Curtains, Carts and the Mobile Screen', *Screen*, 50 (1): 148–66.

Andrejevic, M. (2009) 'Exploiting YouTube: Contradictions of User-Generated Labor', in P. Snickars and P. Vonderau (eds) *The YouTube Reader*, Stockholm: National Library of Sweden.

Andrews, M. (2012) *Interview with authors*, 1 November.

Anon. (2011) 'T-Mobile Wedding', *Campaign*, 22 April: 5.

Arvidsson, A. (2008) 'The Ethical Economy of Customer Coproduction', *Journal of Macromarketing*, 28 (4): 326–38.

Bjorkdahl, J. and Brolin, E. (2003) 'Competition Policy and Scenarios for European 3G Markets', *Communications and Strategies*, 51 (3): 21–34.

Boddy, W. (2011) '"Is it TV Yet?" The Dislocated Screens of Television in a Mobile Digital Culture', in J. Bennett and N. Strange (eds) *Television as Digital Media*, Durham: Duke University Press.

——(2004) *New Media and Popular Imagination*, Oxford: Oxford University Press.

Brooker, C. (2009) 'Screen Burn', *Guide (Guardian)*, 5 November: 52.

Brooker, W. (2010) '"Now You're Thinking With Portals": Media Training for a Digital World', *International Journal of Cultural Studies*, 13 (6): 553–73.

Burgess, J. (2013) 'The iPhone Moment: the Apple Brand and the Creative Consumer: From "Hackability and Usability" to Cultural Generativity', in L. Hjorth, J. Burgess and I. Richardson (eds) *Studying Mobile Media*, London and New York: Routledge.

Bussey, N. (2008) 'Will Conviction Sell Mobiles or is it about Price?' *Campaign*, 18 July: 8.

——(2005) 'Live Issue – Gum Hopes to Make Content Chimera a Reality', *Campaign*, 16 September: 20.

Caldwell, J. T. (2008) *Production Culture: Industrial Self-Reflexivity and Critical Practice in Film and Television*, Durham: Duke University Press.

Carter, S. (2009) *Digital Britain*, London: HM Government, Department of Business Innovation & Skills and Department for Culture, Media & Sport.

Castells, M., Fernández-Ardèvol, M., Linchuan Qiu, J. and Sey, A. (2007) *Mobile Communication and Society*, Cambridge, MA: MIT Press.

Cohen, N. S. (2013) 'Commodifying Free Labor Online: Social Media, Audiences, and Advertising', in M. P. McAllister and E. West (eds) *The Routledge Companion to Advertising and Promotional Culture*, London and New York: Routledge.

Costa, M. (2010) 'Bride Vows to Carry on Regardless', *Marketing Week*, 21 January. Online. Available: http://www.marketingweek.co.uk/bride-vows-to-carry-on-regard less/3008868.article (accessed 10 March 2010).

Creamer, M. and Parekh, R. (2009) 'Ideas of the Decade', *Advertising Age*, 14 December: 8.

de Souza e Silva, A. (2006) 'From Cyber to Hybrid: Mobile Technologies as Interfaces of Hybrid Spaces', *Space and Culture*, 9 (3): 261–78.

Facebook (2012) 'Investors Relations'. Online. Available: http://investor.fb.com/release detail.cfm?ReleaseID=736911 (accessed 16 June 2013).

Farber, A. (2009) 'YouTube Campaign Success Leads T-Mobile to Up Digital Spend', *New Media Age*, 5 February: 5.

Farey-Jones, D. (2010) 'Turning Geek into Brand Chic', *Marketing*, 27 January: 24.

Gillan, J. (2015) *Television Brandcasting:The Return of the Content Promotion Hybrid*, London and New York: Routledge.

Goggin, G. (2013) 'The iPhone and Communication', in L. Hjorth, J. Burgess and I. Richardson (eds) *Studying Mobile Media*, London and New York: Routledge.

——(2011) *Global Mobile Media*, London and New York: Routledge.

Hackley, C. and Hackley, A. R. (2013) 'From Integration to Convergence: The Management of Marketing Communications in Promotional Culture', in H. Powell (ed.) *Promotional Culture and Convergence*, London and New York: Routledge.

Hardy, J. (2013) 'The Changing Relationship Between Media and Marketing', in H. Powell (ed.) *Promotional Culture and Convergence*, London and New York: Routledge.

Hespos, T. (2003) 'Entertainment Advertising Moves the Needle', *iMediaConnection*. Online. Available: http://www.imediaconnection.com/content/1995.imc (accessed 6 April 2004).

Hjorth, L., Burgess, J. and Richardson, I. (2013) (eds) *Studying Mobile Media*, London and New York: Routledge.

Hoechsmann, M. and Poyntz, S. R. (2012) *Media Literacies*, Oxford: Wiley-Blackwell.

Hosea, M. (2008) 'Orange: A Ringing Endorsement of the Silver Screen', *Brand Strategy*, 8 September: 48.

IAB (2012) 'Internet Advertising Revenue Report 2012'. Online. Available: http://www.iab.net/media/file/IAB_Internet_Advertising_Revenue_Report_FY_2012_rev.pdf (accessed 10 June 2013).

IAB Europe (2013) 'European Online Advertising Market Surpasses €24.3b in Value'. Online. Available: http://www.iabeurope.eu/news/european-online-advertising-market-surpasses-243bn-value (accessed 9 September 2013).

Jenkins, H. (2006) *Convergence Culture: Where Old and New Media Collide*, New York: New York University Press.

Jenkins, H., Ford, S. and Green, J. (2013) *Spreadable Media: Creating Value and Meaning in a Networked Culture*, New York: New York University Press.

Ling, R. and Donner, J. (2009) *Mobile Communication*. Cambridge: Polity Press.

MacRury, I. (2009) *Advertising*, London and New York: Routledge.

McDonald, P. (2009) 'Digital Discords in the Online Media Economy: Advertising Versus Content Versus Copyright', in P. Snickars and P. Vonderau (eds) *The YouTube Reader*, Stockholm: National Library of Sweden.

McStay, A. (2013) *Creativity and Advertising*, London and New York: Routledge.

——(2010) *Digital Advertising*, Basingstoke: Palgrave Macmillan.

May, H. and Hearn, G. (2005) 'The Mobile Phone as Media', *International Journal of Cultural Studies*, 8 (2): 195–211.

Nicholson, J. (2005) 'Mobility, New Social Intensities and the Coordinates of Digital Networks', *Fibre culture*, 6. Online. Available: http://journal.fibreculture.org/issue6/ (accessed 17 February 2010).

OECD (2010) 'Indicators of broadband coverage', Online. Available: http://www.oecd.org/sti/telecom (accessed 15 January 2010).

Ofcom (2012) 'Smartphones are the Most-Connected Handheld Devices'. Online. Available: http://stakeholders.ofcom.org.uk/market-data-research/market-data/communications-market-reports/cmr12/international/icmr-5.10 (accessed 27 July 2012).

——(2011) 'A Nation Addicted to Smartphones'. Online. Available: http://consumers.ofcom.org.uk/2011/08/a-nation-addicted-to-smartphones/ (accessed 26 June 2013).

Orlebar, J. (2013) 'The TV Ad and Its Afterlife', in H. Powell (ed.) *Promotional Culture and Convergence*, London and New York: Routledge.

Peters, K. and Seier, A. (2009) 'Home Dance: Mediacy and Aesthetics of Self on YouTube', in P. Snickars and P. Vonderau (eds) *The YouTube Reader*, Stockholm: National Library of Sweden.

Powell, H. (2013) 'The Promotional Industries', in H. Powell (ed.) *Promotional Culture and Convergence*, London and New York: Routledge.

Rae Cooley, H. (2004) 'It's All About the Fit: The Hand, the Mobile Screenic Device and Tactile Vision', *Journal of Visual Culture*, 3 (2): 133–55.

Rheingold, H. (2002) *Smart Mobs: The Next Social Revolution*, Cambridge: Perseus.

Roberts, K. (2009) 'The Participation Economy', *New Zealand Herald*, 22 October.

——(2007) 'Kevin Roberts on the Making of Lovemarks', *Advertising Age*, 1 January: 2.

——(2006) *Lovemarks: The Future Beyond Brands*, New York: Powerhouse Books.

Saatchi & Saatchi (2013) *Corporate homepage*. Online. Available: http://www.saatchi.com/ (accessed 23 June 2013).

——(2009) 'Saatchi & Saatchi Create Dance Mania at Liverpool St Station', press release, 26 January. Online. Available: http://www.saatchi.co.uk/news/archive (accessed 10 March 2010).

Snoddy, R. (2004) 'It's an Ad, Ad, Ad, Ad World: The Interview with Kevin Roberts', *The Independent*, 13 December: 4–7.

Spurgeon, C. (2008) *Advertising and New Media*, London and New York: Routledge.

Sweney, M. (2014) 'Merger of Omnicon and Publicis Fails', *Guardian*, 10 May: 22.

——(2013) 'Digital Age is Driving Force Behind Merger', *Guardian*, 30 July: 23.

Thinkbox (2011) 'Payback 3: Ad Success in Tough Times', Online. Available: http://www.thinkbox.tv/server/show/nav.1818 (accessed 17 July 2013).

Tilson, D. and Lyytinen, K. (2006) 'The 3G Transition: Changes in the US Wireless Industry', *Telecommunication Policy*, 30 (10–11): 560–86.

T-Mobile (2009) 'Making of T-Mobile Dance'. Online. Available: http://www.youtube.com/watch?v=uVFNM8f9WnI (accessed 9 August 2013).

Turow, J. (2013) 'Media Buying: The New Power of Advertising', in M. P. McAllister and E. West (eds) *The Routledge Companion to Advertising and Promotional Culture*, London and New York: Routledge.

Tylee, J. (2012) 'The Advocates – Mobile "Game-Changer" Makes Grand Entrance', *Campaign*, 2 November: 14.

Walker, R. (2003) 'We're all connected?' *New York Times Magazine*, 24 August: SM11.

Wang, J. (2008) *Brand New China: Advertising, Media and Commercial Culture*, Cambridge, MA: Harvard University Press.

4 Television
Transmedia Promotion and Second Screens

> Welcome to the 65th Primetime Emmy Awards. Tonight we celebrate the best of
> television. For our younger audience that's the thing you watch on your phones.
> (Neil Patrick Harris, 2013 Primetime Emmy Awards,
> opening monologue)

Neil Patrick Harris's opening gag at the prestigious Primetime Emmy Awards
held the very definition of television up for question. In doing so, it revealed the
industry's anxieties about the rapid changes to the contemporary media landscape in the early 2010s. Yet Harris did go on to offer reassurance, noting that

> over thirty million people around the world will see this broadcast. And
> why not? These are remarkable times for television. The content has never
> before been more varied. The viewing has never been easier. You can now
> watch TV on your TV, on your laptop, on your mobile device ...

Television's content and audience may now be dispersed across multiple platforms and devices, but television (so the rhetoric goes) still has the power to
capture a global audience of thirty million viewers. Indeed, the implication here
is that the changes to the media landscape might, in fact, be facilitating the
continued global reach of television as a mass medium.[1] In key respects, Harris's
monologue encapsulated the central dilemma of the television industry in the
twenty-first century: how might the rapid transformations to television in the
digital era be used to maintain its established position as the mass medium par
excellence?

Chapter 3 explored the impact of new media technologies and audience behaviours on promotional screen culture through the specific lens of mobile communication, examining the ways in which digital mobile devices have encouraged
strategies of content sharing and consumer co-production within advertising
practice. In this chapter we examine the ways in which promotional screen
content produced by and for the television industry responds to and attempts to
manage the uncertainty caused by digitalization. While the nature and rate of
digital change varies across the globe, the transformation of television by

digitalization can be characterized by the 'new strategic imperatives of ubiquity, mobility, and interactivity' (Boddy 2011: 76) established in Chapter 1 as a connective thread running through this book. The increase in the number of television channels, combined with the rise of the internet as a site for accessing audiovisual content (whether on a connected television set or a desktop computer, laptop, mobile or tablet), has made television content more *ubiquitous*, fragmenting audiences across a wider range of channels, services and platforms. The increased *mobility* with which television content can travel has, in turn, facilitated greater circulation of television programmes by broadcasters and viewers across these multiple platforms. Meanwhile, the adoption of technologies such as digital video recorders and TiVo has enabled viewers more easily to time-shift, live pause and view television on demand, increasing the potential for *interactivity* and giving audiences more control over how, when and where they watch television.

These changes threaten the control that broadcasters have traditionally had over the circulation of their programming and make visible the increasing number of ways in which viewers engage with television beyond just watching programmes at the time of broadcast. In doing so, these changes affect the relationship between the television industry and its audience. Historically, this relationship has been dominated by what Philip Napoli terms the 'exposure model' (2011) in which ratings measure audience exposure to programming and advertising content. Digitalization undermines the exposure model in three ways. First, the fragmentation of the audience makes it harder to measure reliably who is watching television. Second, services such as TiVo make it easier for viewers to skip television adverts. Third (as we saw in Chapter 3), the internet and mobile devices offer increasingly attractive alternatives for advertising spend. The unsettling of established business models brought about through digitalization has led to industry experiments in programming and promotion hybrids that attempt to encourage, measure and monetize audience interactivity (Napoli 2011: 96).[2] These content-promotion hybrids (Gillan 2015), often created by promotional screen intermediaries, invite us to think more deeply about what we mean by 'promotional content' and to consider the place of the promotional screen industries in contemporary television production.

The impact of digitalization on our understanding of the television industry, the television audience and television production has been the subject of a number of studies (see, for example, Lotz 2007, Andrejevic 2008, Doyle 2010, Murphy 2011, Gillan 2011, Bennett and Strange 2011, Creeber 2013). However, less attention has been paid within this literature to the promotional screen industries. Building on the work of Jennifer Gillan (2015), this chapter argues that promotional screen intermediaries play an important role in navigating broadcasters through the changes to television as a medium in the first decades of the twenty-first century. Specifically, we ask how television's promotional screen texts and their producers are negotiating the sometimes competing and conflicting demands between long-standing business models based on exposure and the emerging possibilities offered by digitalization. In doing so, we examine the ways in which forms of promotional screen content advocate fantasies of digital living that operate to reinforce the established place of television as mass medium at the same time as positioning television as a site of audience interaction and participation.

Television's promotional screen intermediaries and the case of Red Bee Media

The production of television's promotional screen content principally takes place in-house within the marketing departments of broadcasters, networks and studios. Given the large number of different programmes typically transmitted by television channels, creating this promotional content entails high volume, high turnover work, produced to tight deadlines. For example, Tim Hughes (On-Air Marketing Director, Discovery Networks, 2012) explained that Discovery UK typically produces thirty campaigns a month to promote its programmes and brands across eleven channels. The majority of this output is created by an in-house team (made up of around forty producers, editors, creatives, designers and marketing managers) that works alongside the scheduling, programming, research and commercial teams within Discovery.[3] Retaining an in-house team not only suits the production demands of such high volume content, but also offers the benefit of a workforce that has a strong understanding of the broadcaster's brands. However, while taking work out of house can be more expensive, external companies are used for campaigns that require specific technological, creative or strategic expertise, including brand agencies, advertising and media agencies, and specialist broadcast, digital design and creative agencies.

One such agency is Red Bee Media, a company whose work culture we examined in detail in Chapter 2. At the time of writing, Red Bee is the largest broadcast and digital communications agency in the UK, with a creative division responsible between 2005 and 2015 for the majority of the promotional work of the BBC and UKTV, as well as a host of television networks in Europe, America and East Asia.[4] Although Red Bee is a commercial company (acquired by Ericsson in 2014), in its current incarnation its creative division can be understood as sitting somewhere between an in-house marketing team and an external creative agency. Red Bee was formed in 2005 from a commercial subsidiary of the BBC with a creative division that was established out of the Corporation's design and presentation teams (Johnson and Grainge 2015). From its formation in 2005 until December 2015, Red Bee held the contract to produce the majority of the BBC's promotional content, effectively acting as an external supplier of work that would previously have been produced by the Corporation's in-house marketing team. However, Red Bee also operates as a commercial agency, not only in its relationship with the BBC but, in addition, producing promotional content for a range of other broadcast clients in the UK and overseas. This makes Red Bee a fairly atypical company within the promotional screen industries over this period. As Andy Bryant (Director of Creative, Red Bee Media, 2012) claimed,

> the work that we do in Creative tends to be done by most broadcasters in-house. There are very few companies like us out there and most of them tend to be smaller lifestyle businesses. So we are by far the biggest game in town. But that's largely because most broadcasters choose to do what we do in-house, because they feel it's core to their creative soul.[5]

While Red Bee is in some sense unusual as one of television's promotional screen intermediaries, the company provides a useful case study for this chapter in that its work is characteristic of both segments of this sector – in-house marketing teams and specialist external agencies.

As an external agency, Red Bee has to pitch for work and explicitly sell itself to potential clients. The ways in which Red Bee positions its commercial expertise is revealing of the current challenges facing television's promotional screen industry. Amidst industrial uncertainty about how to respond to the changing media landscape, Red Bee has promoted itself as a *navigator*, able to guide clients 'through the maze of new market opportunities' presented by changes in media consumption (Red Bee Media 2012).[6] In a manner akin to the ways in which market research companies produce white papers and reports that act as self-advertisements (Clarke 2013: 125), in 2011–12 Red Bee under-took a yearlong programme of research, think tanks, white papers and industry events called 'Tomorrow Calling' that attempted to build a picture of the media landscape in 2020. An exemplary piece of industrial self-theorizing, 'Tomorrow Calling' functioned as a 'semi-embedded' (Caldwell 2009: 203) textual activity that engendered a form of symbolic communication between media profes-sionals on topics such as the future of media consumer behaviour, new business models and the evolution of platforms, networks and devices. Along with reg-ular blogs and work case studies, such forms of industrial self-theorizing posi-tioned Red Bee as 'thought leaders', able to predict and to prepare clients for an uncertain future.

Red Bee Media's website in 2014 characterized the media landscape as one of dynamic change in which (in typical promotional hyperbole) 'connecting view-ers to content is the ultimate endgame' (Red Bee Media 2014). Red Bee here is selling itself as a navigator in two senses: not just promising to navigate its clients through a tumultuous media landscape, but also offering the expertise to navigate the audience in order to 'build bridges between content and viewers'. The emphasis on navigation in Red Bee's industrial self-theorizing responds to the increased mobility, ubiquity and interactivity of television, and finds particular articulation in two current trends within the television industry: transmedia and second screens. Akin to the development of integrated advertising, transmedia promotion attempts to manage and exploit the increased ubiquity and mobility of screen media and has become commonplace in contemporary television marketing. This chapter will begin by focusing on an example of transmedia promotion produced by Red Bee for the BBC natural history programme *Planet Earth Live* (2012). If *Planet Earth Live* typifies the kind of promotional work usually produced by broadcasters in-house, the chapter will then go on to examine a more experimental form of promotional content – the second screen companion app – through the case study of the Walkers' Kill Count app created by Red Bee for digital channel FX. Both examples demonstrate the ways in which promotional screen intermediaries are navigating broadcasters through the new strategic priorities of ubiquity, mobility and interactivity with the production of promotional forms that attempt to manage the relationship between viewer and content. In doing so, these case examples also demonstrate the ways in which the contemporary media landscape is challenging established working practices within the television industry, specifically the boundaries between marketing and programme production.

Red Bee offers a specific, UK-based case study for this chapter. However, transmedia and second screening can be understood as concerns that extend beyond the realms of the UK television industry (Jenkins 2006, Holt and Sanson 2014). While there are differences in the nature and production of promotional television content between countries (see Johnson 2012 and 2013), focusing on transmedia and second screens enables this chapter to use key instances of Red Bee's work as stepping off points for examining the ways in which promotional content has come to function in the broader television ecology. Although changes in the media landscape are being negotiated by established broadcasters (such as the BBC and FOX) and new entrants to the television industry (such as Netflix), it is the established broadcasters whose business models and practices are most overtly under threat. In this context, the case example of Red Bee Media enables this chapter to examine the role of television's promotional screen intermediaries in navigating traditional broadcast companies through the changes wrought by digitalization.

Transmedia promotion: *Planet Earth Live*

Accounts of transmedia television describe the ways in which programmes are extended across multiple media platforms. Part of a broader set of cultural practices in which the boundaries between marketing and programming are blurring (see Chapter 1), core to the conceptualization of transmedia television is the argument that transmedia texts have both narrative and promotional functions (Evans 2011: 38). Indeed, in production terms transmedia texts sit somewhere in between programming and marketing. Some transmedia properties are closely managed by the programme's creator or showrunner and commissioned through the same team responsible for the television episodes themselves.[7] However, other transmedia texts are created through marketing teams and budgets (or specific online or commercial licensing teams), often with little input from the creative personnel responsible for the original broadcast episodes (Clarke 2013). Over and above this, any transmedia extensions created by the production team will sit alongside promotional texts produced by marketing, often together with a wide range of other ancillary content such as licensed products and merchandise.

Perhaps inevitably, studies of transmedia television have tended to focus on those programmes that display extensive transmediality, such as *Lost* (ABC, 2004–2010), *Heroes* (NBC, 2006–2010) or *Doctor Who* (BBC, 2005–).[8] Although characteristic of contemporary television production, such programmes are not typical of transmedia television.[9] Whilst most television programmes contain transmedia elements, these are more commonly limited to a website and assorted online materials. As Sheila Murphy argues of the transmediality of US series *The Middleman* (ABC Family, 2008),

> the marketing and launch of this new programme is typical of the contemporary television industry: the show had a Web site with interactive features, posted regular Webcasts and podcasts by the show's creator and actors, and translated its aesthetic – the sights and sounds and style – of the television program onto its Internet Web site.
>
> (2011: 67)

By focusing on the exceptional rather than the typical in accounts of transmedia television, we lose sight of these now quite routine ways in which the industry extends its programmes onto new media platforms.

Rather than selecting a case that reveals extensive 'transmedia storytelling' (Jenkins 2006), this section will examine BBC natural history programme *Planet Earth Live*, an example that demonstrates the ways in which transmedia promotion has emerged as a commonplace industrial strategy that aims to manage the seemingly more complex relationships between audience and content. *Planet Earth Live* was an eight-part series broadcast on BBC One and simulcast in 140 countries over three weeks in May 2012. The programme followed the real-time stories of families of wild animals from six countries around the globe, with live commentary and discussion from presenter Richard Hammond, who was based in Kenya. *Planet Earth Live* offers a useful case study of the ways in which transmediality has become an integral, expected and everyday part of television's promotional strategies. Furthermore, while viewers were encouraged to engage with the programme across a range of platforms (the television broadcast, the programme's website, a programme-specific Facebook page and Twitter), *Planet Earth Live* is also exemplary of the ways in which the industry's strategic use of transmedia intersects with attempts to reassert television as a medium that brings the family together to watch live. Moving discussion beyond the focus on transmedia storytelling (Jenkins 2006), this section demonstrates how transmedia promotion attempts to discipline an unruly audience by offering models of digital television viewing that embrace the ubiquity, mobility and interactivity of the contemporary media landscape, while attempting, crucially, to drive live viewing. In doing so it offers a detailed examination of Red Bee's work for *Planet Earth Live* in order to reveal the processes and production dynamics involved in the creation of television's promotional screen content.

The process of creating promotional content at Red Bee begins with a creative brief. Drawn up by the account director and strategic planner (see Chapter 2), the creative brief condenses the business objectives, marketing strategy, programme information and audience data for the campaign into a single compelling message designed to inspire the imagination of the creative team. For the BBC, *Planet Earth Live* was a programming experiment that drew on the Corporation's significant global reputation in high-end natural history programming, epitomized in its *Planet Earth* brand, a flagship BBC natural history programme co-produced with Discovery in 2006 and broadcast to over one hundred countries. At the same time, however, the BBC attempted to draw in new audiences by adopting a novel magazine-style 'live' format that it had used for science documentaries (*Bang Goes the Theory*, 2009–) and domestic wildlife programming (*Springwatch*, *Autumnwatch*, 2005–). In the words of Red Bee's creative brief, *Planet Earth Live* aimed to reinforce the BBC's place 'as the home of the biggest, most innovative factual programming in the world', while also encouraging new audiences to engage with the documentary genre, in particular, those aged between 25 and 45 with young families, who usually find factual television hard work. With characteristic promotional élan, the programme was described in the creative brief as a piece of BBC One 'event' programming offering 'a whole new way of experiencing wildlife on the BBC' by combining the liveness and address of a 'global news bulletin' with the glossy footage and expertise of the traditional BBC natural history documentary. Using Richard Hammond (a presenter more associated with quiz shows, motoring and children's television) for a natural history programme was intended to draw new audiences to this genre. However, it also posed a risk to the natural history brand, which is of significant value both to the BBC's public service reputation and commercially as one of its major overseas exports (see Wheatley 2004). Similarly, attempting to create a natural history series live, in a genre whose programmes typically take years to produce, threw up real production challenges for both the BBC and Red Bee.

Part of Red Bee's role as promotional screen intermediary was to navigate the BBC through the potential pitfalls of this new form of programming. Specifically, the BBC asked Red Bee to come up with a 'big idea' to launch the series on television and online and to encourage audience participation between episodes, while also emphasizing the brand links to BBC One, *Planet Earth* and BBC natural history more broadly. The promotional campaign aimed to set the tone for the programme overall, operating as an 'entryway paratext' (Gray 2010: 79). This term describes promotional forms that help determine and control entrance to a text and that create clusters of meaning, expectation and engagement around that text. The promotional content created by Red Bee, then, functioned to create anticipation for the programme and to construct the frames within which the series was interpreted.

The pre-launch campaign focused specifically on driving viewing of the programme as broadcast on BBC One. The campaign began ten days before the programme launched, with a number of 'countdown' bumpers. These were five

Figure 4.1 Planet Earth Live bumper (2012).

to ten seconds long and were broadcast in the junctions of the BBC's linear schedule. Each bumper depicted the BBC One logo in a variety of wild settings – in the hull of a boat at the moment when a whale leaps out of the sea, in a forest being pushed and prodded by a black bear – with a graphic counting down the days until launch of *Planet Earth Live*. Conceived by Red Bee but shot by the production team on location in the build-up to the series, the bumpers functioned to create anticipation, not only through the device of the countdown to the first live broadcast, but also through providing short narratives full of intrigue and emotion (What is the animal going to do? How exciting was that encounter!). They also aimed to reassure the audience that *Planet Earth Live* would be intrinsically 'BBC One' in its tone and feel, the channel logo becoming a character in the bumpers whose close encounters with wildlife acted as a cipher for the potential excitement on offer within the series.

The relationship between the programme and the BBC One brand was reiterated through the creation of a bespoke ident for *Planet Earth Live* that was broadcast in the junctions between programmes in the lead up to and during transmission of the series. According to Emma James (Account Director, BBC One, Red Bee Media, 2012), bespoke idents are reserved for large event programmes, including all natural history programming.[10] Event programmes like *Planet Earth Live* reinforce BBC One's channel positioning ('unite and inspire') and its personality and tone of voice ('big, inclusive and generous') by aiming to bring together different generations and draw new audiences to natural history. The ident positioned *Planet Earth Live* as a core component of BBC One's brand identity.

Meanwhile, the forty-second launch trailer (broadcast on 29 April 2012, one week before transmission of the first episode on 6 May) consolidated the construction of the series as a piece of natural history event programming.

Figure 4.2 Planet Earth Live ident (2012).

It opened by replicating the image of the earth from space used in the trailer and titles for *Planet Earth*, followed by narration from Hammond that described the series as 'the most ambitious live wildlife experience ever attempted by the BBC'. However, the reference to traditional BBC natural history was tempered through intercut footage of wildlife families and a focus on the intimate, emotional and unexpected, as Hammond's voice-over emphasized that 'the month of May is make or break time for young animals. Share the drama with us as *Planet Earth* goes live'. Before the broadcast of the first episode, then, these entryway paratexts revealed the BBC's preferred interpretation for the series as one that encapsulated the drama and scale of BBC natural history but with a tone and address that was more intimate, unpredictable and family-friendly. They also explicitly emphasized the broadcast of the first episode, the intention being to drive viewing of the programme when initially transmitted on BBC One.

The pre-launch promos demonstrate the ways in which promotional screen content attempts to manage audience behaviour through the creation of anticipation for the initial broadcast transmission and the construction of a specific interpretive framework for the programme. Once the series began broadcasting, however, the promotional screen content shifted to focus on navigating the audience between television viewing and other forms of mediated engagement with the programme through the creation of two types of 'appointment-to-view' (ATV) trailers to be broadcast in between episodes.[11] The 'water cooler' ATVs highlighted those moments from previous episodes that had got everyone talking, encouraging viewers to participate online and tune in to find out what happens in the next episode. The 'cliff-hanger' ATVs drew on elements of jeopardy from the last episode (Will the meerkat survive that snake bite?), encouraging viewers to return for the next instalment. As Emma James described, 'both will point to the programme, obviously, but it is sort of "didn't you love this moment? Carry on the conversation online" and "What is going to happen next? Watch us tomorrow"' (2012). This points to the dual intention of the promotional campaign: to drive linear, scheduled television viewing of the episodes and to encourage online interaction and engagement. By posing open-ended questions to the audience (What must it be like to be that close to wildlife? What is going to happen to the bear cub?), the trailers aimed to create anticipation about forthcoming episodes, while, equally, encouraging conversations about the series that could be continued online.[12]

As with the multiplatform reality television programmes analysed by Espen Ytreberg (2009), *Planet Earth Live* provides an example of the ways in which participation across new media platforms is being strategically engineered in order to enhance (rather than distract from) live television viewing. The various invitations to participate online around *Planet Earth Live* – such as inviting viewers to use social media to discuss what will happen to the meerkats – aimed to drive the viewer to watch the next episode of the programme and remain up to date with their viewing in order to be able to join in online. Such strategies encourage participation by linking television's liveness with the internet's sense of immediacy (Ytreberg 2009: 478).

The use of transmedia as a means of driving live viewing has been identified as a key strategy by the television industry in the wake of the rise of time-shifted viewing and video-on-demand. As Adam Gee (Multiplatform Commissioner of Factual, Channel 4) argued of interactive television, 'It throws the emphasis back on live TV, which is good for advertising. There is a sweet spot between TV and interactive where you can get mass participation and rewarding new experiences' (cited in Farber 2013).[13] Hye Jin Lee and Mark Andrejevic have argued that 'from a marketing standpoint, the promise of interactivity is about closing the circle of monitored consumption: linking TV content to ad exposure and consumption behavior' (2014: 44). The BBC is not driven by these commercial dynamics, generating the bulk of its funding from a licence fee rather than the sale of advertising. Yet for marketers, interactivity offers other benefits in terms of monitored consumption. Andy Bryant argues that social media is essential when promoting event television: 'It's a way to engage key influencers, it can act as a barometer to content that's most worth watching and it can help to encourage people to watch the linear TV transmission' (2012). Indeed, the promos for *Planet Earth Live* can be understood as a series of triggers that are intended to encourage particular forms of audience behaviour at certain moments in time. For example, by counting down to transmission, the pre-launch bumpers constructed eventfulness around the programme itself. However, by minimizing the information provided about the programme (simply giving programme title, channel, number of days until launch and a suggestion that its focus is on wildlife), these bumpers also invited the audience to actively find out more about the programme by searching online. Rather than thinking of promotional content as texts designed to promote or sell a particular programme, it is more useful to think of them as texts designed to manage audience behaviour through attempts to trigger certain actions within the viewer.

Such triggers are a central part of contemporary television promotion, from the placement of URLs and hashtags on promos and idents, to the use of open-ended questions, elusive editing or specific calls to action within trailers or online. New companies are forming that actually sell expertise in promoting and facilitating television interactivity online to broadcasters. For example, since 2009, communications agency Five by Five has scripted posts and content for Facebook and Twitter as part of the BBC's marketing for primetime entertainment series *Strictly Come Dancing* (2004–) with the intention of encouraging conversations about the series across social media. For UKTV's magic show *Dynamo: Magician Impossible* (Watch, 2011–), Five by Five used monitoring tools to tailor its social media content in response to topics trending online. Managing and monitoring social media interaction is an increasingly important part of the work of promotional intermediaries. For the BBC's high profile natural history series *Africa* (2013), Red Bee developed a content plan that mapped out 80 percent of the messages that they were going to post across social media (specifically Facebook, Twitter and Pinterest), leaving 20 percent to be spontaneous and responsive to audience participation. Monitoring social media allowed the campaign to respond to buzz, particularly from those with online influence. It also informed the trailers for forthcoming episodes, which were edited to include those moments that were generating most discussion online. This points to the ways in which promotional screen intermediaries are shaping how the television industry uses new media to engage in two-way interactions with its audience.

If the promotional campaign for *Planet Earth Live* attempted to create a seamless transmedia experience in which the viewer was encouraged to move easily between online participation and live viewing, an examination of the production process for Red Bee's promotional work for *Planet Earth Live* reveals the complex negotiations that sit behind transmedia content. The promotional screen work for *Planet Earth Live* involved the negotiation of boundaries in relation to what was produced, by whom and how it was released. The assets that Red Bee could create for the campaign were shaped by two major factors: the production processes for the programme itself and the professional boundaries between marketing and programme production at the BBC. Unlike a traditional advertising campaign where the product is known in advance and in which there is a long lead-in before launch, television's promotional screen intermediaries are often working with a product that is still in production and whose end result is not yet known.[14] This is particularly pronounced for a live programme, such as *Planet Earth Live*, where the bulk of the programme footage will not be available until broadcast. Red Bee initially saw this as an opportunity to shoot original material for the campaign (as is typical for the promotion of event television such as *Planet Earth Live*) and to replicate its previous experiments with live trailers. However, any live trailers would have needed to be created in close collaboration with the production team in Bristol who were responsible for capturing and processing the footage from the production locations around the globe. Commenting on the logistics of delivering a programme such as *Planet Earth Live*, with daily footage coming in from six different locations around the globe, Emma James reflected, 'I mean they are working out how to deliver a programme let alone our trailer ... with such a new format things do change' (2012). As the programme production developed, it became apparent that the series would need to rely largely on recorded material captured in the days between live broadcasts because of the practical difficulties of wildlife filming. At the same time the BBC took the decision to focus its promotional budget for the series on maintaining interest and excitement during the three weeks of broadcast, rather than on pre-launch promotion.[15] This shifted the emphasis away from the 'liveness' of the programme in the campaign, but also meant that Red Bee was dependent on *Planet Earth Live*'s production team (and archival material) for much of the footage that was used in the campaign, with relatively little of the promotional budget spent on shooting original material.

These kinds of changes and negotiations could be said to reinforce the idea that promotional work is of lesser creative value than other forms of cultural production. However, such an argument fails to acknowledge the creative challenges of having to be adaptive within the limitations of changing production circumstances. In effect, promotional intermediaries such as Red Bee have to be particularly agile in their working practices, able to respond at short notice to the shifting demands of their clients. Indeed, as promotional campaigns attempt to harness and respond to social media buzz (as in the case of *Africa*), such agility becomes an increasingly central component of the production process for promotional content. This extends from the actual creative design of promos and idents to the strategic decision-making about how a campaign is delivered. Red Bee's creative presentations for *Planet Earth Live* contained a plan for the way in which the campaign should be delivered, with dates and themes for the 'pre-launch', 'launch' and 'post-launch' elements of the campaign. However, such decisions have to be negotiated with the broadcaster's media planning team that is responsible for deciding where promos and other interstitials play out. Emma James described this as a 'fluid' process (2012), Red Bee providing expertise around the best strategy for releasing promotional material in order to achieve the objectives of the campaign as laid out by the broadcaster, and media planning within the BBC bringing insight into the content and schedules of the broadcaster, particularly the best programmes around which to place promotional material in order to attract the series' target audience.[16]

Red Bee's promotional work is also shaped by the established professional boundaries between marketing and programme production, boundaries that are coming under significant pressure in the digital era. The account directors at Red Bee primarily work and liaise with the marketing teams for their major clients, although certain projects will involve sign-off from channel controllers or even the Director General.[17] The marketing teams within broadcasters are typically separate from programme production and commissioning, responsible for devising promotional campaigns for programmes that are in production (as well as corporate and channel branding). As such, within the traditional structures of the television industry there are professional boundaries in terms of content creation between marketing (whose staff largely come from advertising backgrounds) and programme production and commissioning. One account director that we interviewed at Red Bee in 2012 described the complexity of this situation:

> There's a very grey area about are you creating content or are you creating marketing. I think that there's a funding issue, in the sense that marketing aren't allowed to spend their budget on content. There's a relationship issue in the BBC that if someone is creating content they don't want anyone else creating content. ... I guess our role is how do you use social spaces to engage people and market stuff and I think that's where the lines get blurred.

In the case of *Planet Earth Live*, Red Bee was charged with creating a promotional strategy and trailers that encouraged audience participation online. However, the actual web content and engagement was managed by the BBC's programme team through sites like Facebook, Twitter and the programme's website. As Emma James described,

> when we first presented we had lots of digital ideas – what they might do with Facebook, what they might do online. But there is a very fine line from marketing. You can't be seen to be generating new content. That is the programme's job. ... we might feed in ideas and they can give them to the programme to make it a richer experience.

(2012)

However, the distinction between marketing and content is a difficult one to police, with James going on to discuss examples where Red Bee had created apps for the BBC when they were seen to be a continuation of the on-air campaign or for the BBC's smaller digital channels where there would be less scrutiny about how the production budget was spent. The difficulties that transmedia raises for established production practices are not specific to the BBC. Red Bee staff that worked with the company's other major client (UKTV) described the challenges of creating transmedia promotional content arising from the tendency for the broadcaster's marketing, commissioning and web teams to operate in isolation. The production of transmedia promotion places these organizational distinctions under pressure by blurring the disciplinary boundaries of marketing, programme-making and online.

Indeed, the role of marketing within the television industry has changed dramatically since the 1990s when broadcasters largely focused on on-air promotions and print. Marketing departments now have to generate campaigns across both traditional (print, broadcast television and radio) and new digital media for programmes and services, as well as overseeing product placement and integration deals (Marich 2008: 26). The broadening scope of the work of television promotion involves the negotiation of a series of professional boundaries between programme production, marketing, online and media planning. Although transmedia programmes might attempt to seamlessly navigate viewers across media platforms, in production terms transmedia texts unsettle established working practices that have historically been based on the separation, rather than the interrelation, of programme and promotion.

Social TV and second screens: *The Walking Dead* (AMC 2010–)

The production processes for television's promotional screen content are further complicated through the emergence of new forms of mediated interaction around television viewing. The forms of audience participation encouraged through the transmedia extensions of *Planet Earth Live* are not new to the digital era. What has changed is that social interactions around media content are increasingly mediated and thus more visible, particularly to the media industries themselves. The television industry's interest in audience participation has been intensified by the rise of second screening, sometimes referred to as 'dual screening' or 'social TV'. Social TV, a term that Gerard Goggin claims was coined in 2007, was nominated as the most important emerging technological trend by *MIT Technology Review* in 2010 (Goggin 2012: 89–90). It tends to be used to describe the ways in which audiences are using new media to converse with other viewers about television content (Creeber 2013: 106). While social TV can refer to audience interaction beyond the specific moment of viewing, industry research reveals that a significant proportion of audiences are 'media multitasking', using other media technologies while watching television (Parr 2011, Nielsen 2012, Ofcom 2013). The rise of 'always on' devices, such as smartphones and tablets, is fuelling media multitasking. While 53 percent of all UK adults are regular media multitaskers, this rises to 81 percent for tablet owners (Ofcom 2013: 4).[18] Indeed, Lee and Andrejevic argue that '*second screen* is a credible candidate for 2012 buzzword of the year in the television industry' (2014: 41).

The rise of second screening and media multitasking challenges the television industry to address the significance of audience engagement for their business models. As Claire Tavernier (Managing Director, StoryTechLife) explains,

> The engaged viewer is watching, tweeting, chatting. The non-engaged viewer is watching and doing email. Do we care? It's a big question. … And on the face of it, a viewer is a viewer. If the non-engaged viewer is as likely to switch on the show as an engaged one, and if they both watch the ads (or don't watch them, but in equal measure), these two people have the same value to advertisers, and therefore to network executives.
>
> (2013)

Media multitasking, then, demands that the industry attempts to understand the differences between what Tavernier describes as the 'engaged vs the non-engaged viewer' (ibid.). This has resulted in a number of debates about the value of media multitaskers to the industry. Mirroring Henry Jenkins, Sam Ford and Joshua Green's (2013) arguments about spreadable media (see Chapter 3), Tavernier goes on to suggest that the engaged viewer should be understood as an 'acquisition tool' that helps to promote television content and increase audiences.[19] It is unsurprising in this context that media multitasking has instigated a flurry of interest, particularly from promotional screen intermediaries, about how to capitalize and control what Kris Hardiman (Head of Product Management, Red Bee Media) referred to as the 'new frontier of television' (2012).

The rhetoric of a 'new frontier' speaks to a fundamental change in the relationship between television and technology. Analogue technologies, such as the television set, effectively functioned to convert and transmit television programmes from one form into another. By contrast, digital technologies transfer television programmes into numbers, 'abstract symbols rather than analogous objects' (Lister et al. 2009: 18). These numbers can then be mathematically altered through algorithms contained within software (ibid.). New media technologies, such as the home computer, contain both hardware (for example, the chips that allow large amounts of data to be compressed and stored) and software (the programmes that allow that data to be used in different ways). If, in the analogue era, it was hardware producers (television set manufacturers) and content producers (broadcasters and television studios) that controlled how television could be used, the digital era introduces the additional level of the software producer into the relationship between television and technology. While P. David Marshall (2004: 92) argues that it is software that differentiates computers from television, we want to argue that software design is now a central component of the television industry.

The role of software is particularly significant in relation to the internet. Essentially the internet is an 'end-to-end' network in which the infrastructure carries data, but in which what happens to that data depends on its use (Meikle and Young 2012: 17). Software can shape what happens to the content that circulates as data through the internet, without involvement from the producers of that content or the technology for receiving that content. As the speeds of broadband and data processing have increased, new platforms and applications have emerged based on software that facilitates the circulation of and interaction with audiovisual content. As such, the television industry's decreased control over the circulation of its content, outlined at the opening of this chapter, is shaped in part by software that enables television programmes to be shared (whether through peer-to-peer, video-on-demand or video-sharing services). Similarly, the mediatization of the audience's engagement with television is also shaped by software applications that enable social networking sites such as Facebook to operate. Therefore, the digital era brings an additional player into the heart of the television industry, digital intermediaries that Tarleton Gillespie describes as 'now the primary keepers of the cultural discussion as it moves to the internet' (2010: 348).

In the digital era it is not just broadcasters that are attempting to march on the new frontier of television. Technology developers, content owners, platform owners and advertisers are all jostling to take advantage of the potential opportunities of social television and second screening. These different players often have competing interests, leading to considerable uncertainty about how the industry should respond to media multitasking. At the heart of this debate are three interrelated questions: What forms of media interactivity do the audience want to engage in while watching television? How might this media interactivity be monetized? Who should control or facilitate this interactivity? The industry discourse in 2012–2013 surrounding the television companion app Zeebox (re-branded as Beamly in April 2014) was indicative of the terms of this debate. Zeebox was one of a number of second screen apps (generally available on smartphones, tablets and, sometimes, the web) developed by digital promotional screen intermediaries outside of the television industry to facilitate audience interaction around television viewing.[20] Zeebox originally marketed itself on its website as 'your TV sidekick' that will help you 'discover, connect, share and interact – all live as you watch' by using audio-synching to link its content with whatever the user was watching (Zeebox 2013). It facilitated content discovery through social buzz metrics and recommendations and mediated social interactions through offering opportunities for participation within programmes and with stars.

As an aggregator, Zeebox's business model depended on partnering with broadcasters, advertisers and other developers. For broadcasters and producers, it offered a web-based content management system that enabled non-technical editors to add metadata, images, tags and widgets (such as polls, trivia, quizzes and competitions) to appear on the app when their content aired. Audience engagement could even be linked back to broadcast television, with (for example) quiz results from the app displaying on-air. Advertisers could bypass the broadcaster and sponsor programmes directly on Zeebox, with the opportunity to develop branded interactions around the programme being sponsored. They could also place advertising on Zeebox synched to broadcast adverts that included click-to-buy tags to allow direct purchase. Meanwhile, Zeebox offered developers a range of widgets and APIs (application programming interfaces, which enable the construction of software applications) to link the app to other websites and applications. Zeebox also offered minute-by-minute social and platform engagement analytics for broadcasters, advertisers and content owners about the audience activity around their brands and products.[21]

Third party applications, such as Zeebox, offer both an opportunity and a challenge to broadcasters. The benefit of such cross-channel apps is that they offer a single platform for social TV experiences. As Gareth Capon (Product Development Director, Sky) argued,

> It's a challenge to ask customers to use lots of different apps or devices, to move through them and remember what they are. We need to simplify things and offer a singular, crossplatform experience that they know is always available. That's why we support investment in Zeebox, a platform for second-screen experiences, and put some of its capabilities into our own applications.
>
> (cited in Farber 2013a)

Sky is not the only broadcaster to partner with Zeebox.[22] In September 2012 the company struck a deal with Comcast Cable, NBC Universal, and HBO and its Cinemax service to enhance hundreds of their programmes on Zeebox. As HBO co-president Eric Kessler argued of the deal, 'Zeebox offers a unique, comprehensive platform that drives discovery, engagement and conversation around our most beloved programs and stars' (cited in Szalai 2012). For broadcasters, then, Zeebox facilitated the creation of second screen content that encouraged audiences to watch and participate with their programmes within one centralized platform.

Although an app such as Zeebox might simplify engagement for the audience, it takes some of the control and ownership away from the broadcaster, while also acting as competition for advertising revenue. As Tom Cape (Chief Executive, Capablue (a company that offers expertise in cloud technology to broadcasters)) argued, 'they are making money out of your programme by selling adverts on the second screen. Zeebox is selling ads around BBC content on the second screen. It's really important to take a stake in the market – if you don't, other people will' (cited in Farber 2013a). Clare Phillips (former Head of Strategic Planning, Red Bee Media, 2006–2012) concurred, arguing,

> I don't want to go through Facebook or Zeebox for people to comment on my programmes, or to get additional content, because I don't own that relationship with the viewer and I can't monetize it and I don't get the data. And so it doesn't make sense for a broadcaster to go through Zeebox.
> (2012)

What is at stake in second screening from an industry perspective, therefore, is ownership of the relationship with the audience. The mediatization of audience interaction with television not only makes that interaction visible, it also makes it open to surveillance, effectively turning audience interaction into data that can be monitored and monetized. Digital developers with expertise in software applications and platforms are seeking to usurp the broadcasters' traditional ownership of this relationship.

In this context, content owners (studios, broadcasters and producers) and platform owners have sought to develop their own apps. Platforms and broadcasters have created multiplatform user interface experiences designed to navigate viewers around their content. For example, the BBC, Channel 4, Sky, TiVo and Virgin have all launched apps (alongside the video-on-demand services made available online and through set-top boxes) that facilitate content discovery and (to differing degrees) audience interaction. Most broadcaster and platforms apps are versions of online video-on-demand players, such as the BBC iPlayer and 4OnDemand.[23] However, broadcasters and content owners have also created programme-specific apps that encourage media multitasking around series such as *Antiques Roadshow* (BBC, 1979–), *The X-Factor* (ITV, 2004–) and *Million Pound Drop* (Channel 4, 2010–). Tom Cape argues that audiences 'will start at programme level because it's easier to bite off', claiming that it is only once you

have a portfolio of programme apps that you can aggregate this into channel-wide or cross-channel apps (cited in Farber 2013a). As such, there is a lack of consensus about whether the development of second screen apps should be focused at programme, channel or cross-channel level. Underlying this is uncertainty about how best to capture, control, facilitate and monetize audience interaction with television. This uncertainty intersects with competing industry interests. As Luke Gaydon (Vice President, Brightcove (an online video platform)) argues, what is at stake in the development of social TV apps is not the limits of the technology but the competing interests of the parties involved (ibid.).

While social TV apps are complicating the relationship between the broadcaster and the viewer and increasing the competing interests faced by the television industry, they are also expanding what television is and what television promotion can be. As with *Planet Earth Live*, social TV apps force us to think more deeply about what we mean by 'promotional content'. As a companion app, Zeebox augmented the television viewing experience. Yet in doing so it played an important promotional role. As a form of promotion, Zeebox encouraged, facilitated and shaped television viewing, much as the promotional strategy for *Planet Earth Live* attempted to manage viewer behaviour. Social TV apps, therefore, form a fundamental part of the new ways in which broadcasters are attempting to attract, engage and manage the seemingly more unruly audiences of the digital era. It should come as no surprise, then, that many of the broadcasters' efforts in the area of social TV and second screening are created through marketing budgets and by promotional screen intermediaries.

Indeed, social TV is a central concern for the promotional screen industries, evidenced by the array of industry events in the US and Europe dedicated to examining the consequences of social media.[24] Identifying social TV as an emerging trend, Red Bee created a specific presentation on the potential benefits of second screening that they took to broadcasters, content owners and producers in order to sell their expertise in this nascent area.[25] It was through one such presentation that FX (Fox International Channels' UK entertainment channel, re-branded as FOX in 2013) approached Red Bee to help them to create a second screen experience around their highest-rated show, zombie series *The Walking Dead*. It is indicative of the industry uncertainty surrounding second screening that Red Bee's work for FX on a second screen app for *The Walking Dead* came through a pitch *to*, rather than as something solicited *from*, the client.

For Red Bee Media, the technological innovation within second screening made it a particularly strategic area of future business development. Although the majority of the work undertaken by the Creative department of Red Bee is the kind of promotional material produced for *Planet Earth Live*, Creative is only one part of a larger company that also includes Media Delivery and Access Services (see Chapter 2). The development of second screen apps is one area where the work of the Creative department intersects with the more technology-oriented aspects of Red Bee's business. It is, therefore, a potential site where Red Bee's unique combination of technological and creative expertise could be sold to clients. As a former senior strategic planner at Red Bee claimed in an interview with us in 2012, 'Social TV is massively important, hugely important. It is one of the areas where you know Red Bee really makes sense because we have the guys who can technically build the second screen ... we have also got designers who can make it appropriate for the brand and we've got planners who understand what type of additional content works'. One of the reasons why digital intermediaries have moved into the area of second screening is because it involves specific technological expertise in its development. Red Bee have a digital interactive team that sits within a larger design section in the Creative department and that works across all multiplatform experiences, from transmedia promotions to interface designs. This team combines staff with specific technological expertise in user experience with designers who have skills in interface design. For projects such as *The Walking Dead* app, both the technologist and designer would work together with creatives, a strategic planner and the account director on creating an initial concept to sell to the client. Once approved, the technology team would create user journeys and a wire frame for the app that would then be passed to the design and creative team to overlay the front-end design. This development process points to the close interrelation between design and technology in the production of new media applications and platforms. As Kris Hardiman argues, the development of Red Bee's business in the area of second screening cannot be purely technology-based and is 'wrapped up with the user interface and the creative design and the look and feel of the thing' (2012).

Key to the development of multiplatform projects is an understanding of the affordances of different platforms. As Casey O'Donnell argues, platforms matter; they bring their own hardware specificities, programming languages, software development kits and data formats (2011: 277). They also bring specific requirements in terms of design. For example, Paul Fennell (Head of User Interface Design, Red Bee Media, 2012) described to us the ways in which tablets are revolutionizing interactive design. Whereas design for the web could use grid patterns translated from those used to design for television or print, the significance of gesture control on tablets makes it more important to understand how the user moves through the content and to design around the transitions *between* content. As such, Fennell argues that designers need to understand both the technological processes behind the more gestural user interface within tablets as well as the experience of actually using them.

A key issue in the development of second screens apps, therefore, is an understanding of the audience. This extends from the ways in which audiences interact with specific technologies, to the ways in which audiences might move from one platform or technology to another. Gerard Goggin (2012: 91) describes social television as the unrealized dream of convergence, one that requires considerable work on the part of the viewer in having to navigate across multiple platforms and devices. Indeed, Sheila Murphy argues that the potential interactivity offered by new media technologies is characterized by compromise:

> Whereas early theorists of new media were quick to recognize that inter-
> activity is shot through with great potentiality, one can now see that nego-
> tiating and using new media is often about switching modes and making
> trade-offs: will I sacrifice interaction to engage in a closed but satisfying
> narrative experience? Will I watch one, two or three programs 'at once',
> deftly switching between them?
>
> (2011: 121)

Second screen apps attempt to navigate the viewer (and the industry) through
these compromises, offering an interface that encourages certain behaviours at
particular moments in order to manage the potentially competing desires to
engage in an immersive viewing experience while also interacting and sharing
that experience online with others. This was a particular issue in developing an
app around a serialized drama such as *The Walking Dead* that demanded
attentive viewing. In their creative presentation to FX, Red Bee claimed that
there was significant appetite amongst viewers to engage in media multitasking
around broadcast drama by drawing on audience research that suggested that
television dramas with the highest numbers of tweets were also those that
rated the highest. The challenge for Red Bee was to create a second screen
experience that enhanced (rather than detracted from) engagement with the
unfolding story and characters.

As with *Planet Earth Live*, the temporality of the experience was central
here. Red Bee designed a second screen experience that made most demands
for participation from its audience immediately before and after broadcast,
with limited interaction expected during the viewing of the programme itself.
The Walkers' Kill Count app created by Red Bee allowed viewers to predict
the number of zombie kills before each episode, including which weapon
would be used and which character would be responsible. Using innovative
audio-synching technology that linked the app to the broadcast, the app could
then count the kills as they happened, measure the viewer's predictions
against the actual kills and allow viewers to post their scores on Facebook or
Twitter. The app integrated with Twitter and Facebook so that viewers could
play along with friends and comment through the app while watching the
episode. In addition, the app attempted to augment the viewing experience
by including a 'thrill meter' and heartbeat sound synched to the impending
zombie attacks in each episode. The app also included trailers for forthcoming
episodes, push notifications that alerted viewers to the broadcast of the next
episode and a range of stats that could be engaged with after broadcast. As
with *Planet Earth Live*, the Walkers' Kill Count app attempted to drive live
viewing. Although the audio watermarking would allow the app to synchro-
nize with time-shifted viewing, the app alerted viewers when the episode
was to be broadcast and invited social interaction through the sharing of
tweets and Facebook updates that encouraged viewers to watch at the time
of broadcast.[26] The Walkers' Kill Count app, therefore, attempted to negotiate
the viewer through a range of interactions with television content, from

Figure 4.3 The Walkers' Kill Count companion app (2012).

predicting before broadcast, to viewing during broadcast, and socializing after broadcast.

The construction of this user journey was based on audience research which was used by Red Bee to justify to FX the different forms of interaction being invited by the app before, during and after broadcast. Red Bee examined patterns of mediated interaction around the first series of *The Walking Dead* in order to identify the established forms of media multitasking around the series. Analysis of the volume of tweets related to the broadcast of season one revealed that tweeting peaked just before the broadcast of each episode, reduced in volume during the episode before increasing again just before the end of the episode. Red Bee turned this data into strategic insight that identified three potential roles that a second screen app could have around the broadcast of the episode. In the words of its creative presentation to FX, just before broadcast the app could 'fuel the excitement', during the episode it could 'deepen the engagement', while towards the end of the episode it could 'extend the revelry'. Red Bee also researched the nature of the tweets and other forms of online interaction already circulating around the series. They noted significant audience interest in the zombie kills themselves, with fans counting the number of kills, describing pleasure in the ways in which they were filmed, and posting videos that edited together all of the zombie deaths from the series. These two insights formed the basis of Red Bee's proposed second screen app for FX. As such, the app was responding to a particular set of identifiable audience behaviours, while at the same time attempting to control and exploit those behaviours. In this sense, the Walkers' Kill Count app accorded with Ethan Tussey's observation that companion apps can be understood as a form of digital enclosure in which 'emergent audience practices are identified and repackaged in ways that affirm the traditions of the entertainment industry rather than transforming them' (2014: 204).

In doing so, the Walkers' Kill Count app privileged certain forms of social behaviour around the series over others, resulting in an app that favoured a particularly masculinized reading of the series. In emphasizing the visceral thrill and gore of the zombie attacks over the series' more melodramatic examination of the attempts by the survivors to construct a community and retain their humanity amidst post-apocalyptic horror, the app conformed to Jenkins et al.'s argument that transmedia extensions tend to reward masculine interests over feminine ones (2013: 151). While this may be a consequence of FX's brief to attract heavy internet users, it also stems from the industry requirements that content strategies are justified by audience data. In a nascent area engaged in by a limited proportion of the television audience, this can lead to the privileging of the most visible audience interactions in the shaping of second screen apps.

The problems of audience measurement in such a nascent area extend to the evaluation of the success of these new forms of promotional content. According to Red Bee's strategic planner on the project, because the Walkers' Kill Count app was defined by FX as a marketing endeavour, the primary measures of success for the project were determined by marketing objectives, namely to increase ratings for, and buzz about, the series. The combination of Broadcasters' Audience Research Board (BARB) ratings with proxy measures of engagement (such as uplift in social buzz) and in-event app metrics (such as downloads, dwell time, views of trailers within the app) points to the ways in which engagement is becoming increasingly valued by the industry. However, while second screen apps are positioned as marketing and produced through marketing budgets, emphasis is placed on encouraging (and measuring) certain forms of audience interaction over others, namely viewing, endorsing, sharing and recommending the broadcast programme and its related promotional texts. Over and above this, new forms of audience measurement, such as in-app metrics, lack the longitudinal and comparative data of ratings that Red Bee or FX could use to measure the success of the Walkers' Kill Count app against. Although Red Bee could measure the number of viewers that downloaded the app, there was little industry consensus on what this figure needed to be to constitute a good result. As such, evaluations of success depend not only on what kinds of audience interactivity are measured, but also on negotiations within the industry about what is understood to constitute the boundary between success and failure. Promotional screen intermediaries are, therefore, not only functioning as navigators for broadcasters in the development of social media applications, but also play a central role in the ongoing negotiations about how to measure and evaluate their success.

Conclusion

This chapter has focused on two case examples to examine the ways in which promotional screen intermediaries are acting as navigators for the television industry in the face of changes to the media landscape that offer both oppor-tunities and threats to established business models. It has explored the ways in which promotional screen content does more than simply sell programmes. Screen promotion functions to manage the relationship between viewer and content, doing so by constructing an interpretive framework for television programmes (and channels/broadcasters), by favouring certain forms of parti-cipation, and by encouraging specific audience interactions with and between content. In these ways, promotional screen forms contribute to the popular imagining of television as a medium in the digital era, normalizing mediated interaction as an intrinsic part of television viewing while simultaneously reas-serting television's position as a mass medium of broadcasting by attempting to drive live viewing. This function can be understood as an industrial reaction against forms of audience behaviour (such as binge viewing and watching on-demand) that disrupt the traditional relationship between viewer and content.

In attempting to manage audience behaviour, these promotional texts act as facilitators that help the audience to negotiate the new technological possibi-lities for mediated interaction around television. If, as Andrejevic (2008) argues, interaction requires skills, promotional screen forms attempt to reduce the level of skill required to participate by navigating the viewer through different modes of engagement with television content. This is not to suggest, however, that the audience has no freedom here. The control that can be exerted over audience behaviour through a second screen app or transmedia promotion is limited. While the Walkers' Kill Count app may attempt to encourage certain forms of mediated interaction around *The Walking Dead*, it cannot fully control how audiences engage with the series. Similarly, although some audiences responded to the calls to action within *Planet Earth Live* and its promotional paratexts, others used the internet to complain that the series' liveness and non-expert presenters undermined the BBC's reputation for quality natural history pro-grammes. As Jennifer Gillan argues, promotional screen content 'is always conflicted and often contested because as much as it tries to precreate meaning, it cannot predetermine it' (2015).

Indeed, industry engagement in the 'new frontier' of social television stems from recognition that the audience's interactions around television are unruly and beyond the industry's control. In a blog on transmedia and interactivity, Tim Whirledge (former Strategic Planner on the Walkers' Kill Count app at Red Bee Media) argued that the two drivers of multiplatform development in the television industry are the increased penetration of portable media devices such as the tablet, and improved understanding of audiences in the digital world (2013). Lee and Andrejevic suggest that we should be wary of the tele-vision industry's tendency to describe itself as attempting to 'keep up' with audience behaviour by positioning developments such as second screen apps as a 'consumer-led revolution' rather than a strategy for monitoring and manipu-lating consumers (2014: 53). Yet, despite improvements in research techniques, the industry's understanding of and relationship with its audience remains a contested area of activity. As Philip Napoli writes,

> The audience marketplace is a complex and contentious institutional environment, with many divergent, competing stakeholder interests that are frequently brought to bear in an effort to influence technologies in terms of both how audiences consume media and how these consumption behaviors are represented – sometimes in an effort to prevent, or at least impede, certain technological transitions from taking place.
>
> (Napoli 2011: 117)

Rather than seeing developments in second screen applications and transmedia promotion as simply attempts by the industry to control audience behaviour, we could characterize these areas as sites of industrial negotiation.

The relationship between viewer and content can, therefore, be understood as contested ground upon which new industrial battles are being forged. These battles involve a growing range of players, from large media conglomerates and established broadcasters, to new online providers such as Google, Apple and Netflix, to start-ups and digital entrepreneurs such as Zeebox. Often overlooked, but central, are promotional screen intermediaries, from the in-house marketing teams producing routine transmedia campaigns, to external agencies experimenting with second screen apps. As television transforms into a digital medium, the form of promotional screen content changes, and with it the skills required by those intermediaries charged with marketing television's programmes, channels and broadcasters.

Television's promotional screen intermediaries actively work to 'educate' their clients about the changes to the media landscape through forms of industrial self-theorizing that position themselves as 'thought leaders'. Yet this is a two-way process. As with the transmedia producers studied by Clarke (2013), the work of television's promotional screen intermediaries is subject to approval and evaluated through marketing objectives (such as increasing ratings and buzz). The attempt to educate the client is, therefore, tempered by the need for client sign-off on any work produced. In their working practices, television's promotional screen intermediaries have to be particularly agile, responding not only to new developments in media technology and audience behaviour, but also to shifting client demands and uncertainties. This is a particular challenge for the television industry, whose business models have been most affected by the increased ubiquity, mobility and interactivity of the digital media landscape (Holt and Sanson 2014: 4–5). The following chapter will move our focus from television to examine the promotional challenges faced by the Hollywood film industry in response to digitalization. As movie studios also attempt to navigate a changing relationship with their audiences, we explore the shifting status of trailers and the creative agencies responsible for their production within a globalized marketplace.

Notes

1 Research into the global television market suggests that there has been a sustained reduction in the collective audience share of the top channels. At the same time,

however, global television revenues continue to rise and, despite the increase in online television, scheduled linear viewing remains popular (Ofcom 2013a: 8).

2 The new opportunities and possibilities presented through digitalization have added to the pressures being placed on the traditional exposure model. For commercial broadcasters, research that suggests a link between engagement with content and engagement with embedded advertising has spurred attempts to enhance audience participation (Napoli 2011: 96). For public service broadcasters, increasing audience interactivity can help to demonstrate the value and significance of their television services across a range of criteria, such as facilitating citizenship.

3 While the exact structure of marketing departments varies from company to company, typically broadcasters retain in-house marketing teams staffed by marketing directors and creatives capable of producing a significant proportion of their promotional content.

4 UKTV is a broadcaster with ten British digital channel brands, co-owned by BBC Worldwide (the BBC's commercial arm) and Scripps Network Interactive. In July 2014 it was announced that the BBC would not be renewing its contract with Red Bee and that from December 2015 its core creative and operational promotional work would be brought in-house (Swift 2014).

5 It is notable that the BBC decided to take the core clip-based promotional work undertaken by Red Bee back in-house once its initial ten-year contract with the company came up for renewal in 2015. This supports Bryant's argument that broadcasters feel that such promotional content is a core part of their production operations.

6 Indeed, its very name, Red *Bee*, drew associations with what its own marketing described as one of 'nature's expert navigators' (cited in Grainge 2010: 51).

7 Denise Mann argues that transmedia television places increased pressures on show-runners whose attention is diverted from running the writing room to managing a complex and on-going slate of post-production and promotional content (2009: 100).

8 See for example, Creeber (2013: 105–6), Evans (2011) and Clarke (2013).

9 This is particularly the case in the UK where a wider range of television programmes are produced than in the US, with only a selection of UK programmes displaying such pronounced transmediality.

10 The production of an ident for this specific programme is the one element that differentiates it from most other more routine transmedia television promotional campaigns.

11 ATVs are short films promoting forthcoming episodes that conclude with an end board giving the date and time of the next episode.

12 This was enhanced through specific calls to action within the programme itself, such as asking members of the public to suggest names for some of the animals, as well as regular posts on Facebook and Twitter reminding viewers of upcoming episodes, asking for viewer questions to be posed to experts during the broadcast programmes or sharing additional video content. The interrelationship between programme content (both broadcast and online) and promotional content was emphasized by the placement of the bumpers and the launch promo alongside clips from the programme and exclusive content on the series' website, effectively positioning the promotional material as BBC content. This is indicative of the ways in which the texts produced by the promotional screen industries largely remain unattributed to their creators, with their authorship generally being co-opted by the client (whether a broadcaster such as the BBC or a brand such as Nike).

13 Indeed, although the digital era is often characterized by a shift from mass to niche audiences, the increased fragmentation of the audience actually makes the mass audience even more valuable. As Peter Bazalgette (Chairman, Mirriad) argues, 'in an era of diffuse diverse audiences, mass audiences have more value' (2012: 10). This is particularly important for commercial broadcasters whose ad revenues are threatened by the move of viewers away from live viewing.

14 This is particularly pronounced for a new series. Emma James suggested that it is possible to be more experimental and innovative with a returning series where both the audience and the creatives are already familiar with the programme's format (2012).

15 This is in part a consequence of reduced marketing and multiplatform budgets at the BBC. The BBC licence fee was frozen for six years in 2010 and the Corporation was additionally required to fund the BBC World Service and the Welsh language service S4C, equating to a 16 percent reduction in its ongoing licence fee funding (BBC 2012: F4).

16 In the case of the *Planet Earth Live* launch trailer, this was in a primetime Sunday evening slot between the rural and farming programme *Countryfile* (BBC, 1988–) and the singing competition *The Voice* (BBC, 2012–).

17 The channel controller for BBC One, Danny Cohen, was involved in the decision-making processes for the promotion of *Planet Earth Live*.

18 Tablet ownership in the UK rose 24 percent in the first quarter of 2013 (Ofcom 2013: 5). Holt and Sanson offer similar statistics from the US, noting a Nielsen study that suggests that 40 percent of tablet owners in the US are using their devices while watching television (2014: 9).

19 The value of engaged audiences was a subject of debate at the Westminster Media Forum's 'TV Bites Back', held on 31 January 2012, where the assertion that engaged viewers are more passionate about the content they are viewing was repeated.

20 Other examples include Peel, tvtag and Viggle.

21 These features remain an integral part of the rebranded Beamly. The main change has been to position the app more explicitly as a social network that functions as a site for news and gossip around television, introducing a number of 'TV Rooms' hosted by celebrities and fans where users can engage in discussion and speculation.

22 BSkyB bought a 10 percent stake in Zeebox in 2012.

23 However, in 2013 Channel 4 launched 4Now, an app specifically designed to aggregate audience interactions around its four primary digital channels.

24 For example, the Media and Entertainment Services Alliance, which supports service providers in the media and entertainment industries, has established a Second Screen Society which holds conferences in the US and Europe 'to meet the needs of the rapidly evolving ecosystem for companion screen viewing of broadcast television and home entertainment' (Second Screen Society 2014). In the UK, the Westminster Media Forum's 'TV Bites Back' event (see footnote 19) brought together broadcasters, advertisers and a range of communications and digital agencies to debate the impact of dual-screen viewing, while the UK's annual Promax conference in April 2012 included a session dedicated to second screening.

25 This presentation was based on insights developed in three white papers (produced in conjunction with digital media consultancy Decipher) for Red Bee's 'Tomorrow Calling' research programme in 2012.

26 The second season of *The Walking Dead* aired in the UK five days after the US, allowing viewers to engage in online discussion across the Atlantic.

Bibliography

Andrejevic, M. (2008) 'Watching Television Without Pity: The Productivity of Online Fans', *Television and New Media*, 9 (1): 24–46.

Bazalgette, P. (2012) 'The Power of the Television Event – for Producers and Audiences', paper presented at *TV Bites Back: Dual-Screen Viewing, Social Media and the Power of the Schedule*, Westminster Media Forum. London: 31 January. London: Westminster Media Forum.

BBC (2012) 'Full Financial Statements 2011/12', *Annual Report and Accounts 2011–12*, July. Online. Available: http://downloads.bbc.co.uk/annualreport/pdf/bbc_ar_online_2011_12.pdf (accessed 11 August 2014).

Bennett, J. and Strange, N. (eds.) (2011) *Television as Digital Media*, Durham: Duke University Press.

Boddy, W. (2011) '"Is it TV Yet?" The Dislocated Screens of Television in a Mobile Digital Culture', in J. Bennett and N. Strange (eds) *Television as Digital Media*, Durham: Duke University Press.

Bryant, A. (2012) *Interview with authors*, 2 July.

Caldwell, J. T. (2009) 'Cultures of Production: Studying Industry's Deep Texts, Reflective Rituals and Managed Self-Disclosures', in J. Holt and A. Perren (eds) *Media Industries: History, Theory, and Method*, Oxford: Wiley-Blackwell.

Clarke, M. J. (2013) *Transmedia Television: New Trends in Network Serial Production*, London and New York: Bloomsbury.

Creeber, G. (2013) *Small Screen Aesthetics*, London: British Film Institute.

Doyle, G. (2010) 'From Television to Multi-Platform: Less from More or More for Less?', *Convergence*, 16 (4): 431–49.

Evans, E. J. (2011) *Transmedia Television: Audiences, New Media and Daily Life*, London and New York: Routledge.

Farber, A. (2013) 'The new rules of engagement', *Broadcast*, 14 March.

——(2013a) 'How to use the second screen', *Broadcast*, 21 March.

Fennell, P. (2012) *Interview with authors*, 2 July.

Gillan, J. (2015) *Television Brandcasting: The Return of the Content Promotion Hybrid*, London and New York: Routledge.

——(2011) *Television and New Media: Must-Click TV*, London and New York: Routledge.

Gillespie, T. (2010) 'The Politics of Platforms', *New Media and Society*, 12 (3): 347–64.

Goggin, G. (2012) *New Technologies and the Media*, Basingstoke: Palgrave Macmillan.

Grainge, P. (2010) 'Elvis Sings For the BBC: Broadcast Branding and Digital Media Design', *Media, Culture and Society*, 32 (1): 45–61.

Gray, J. (2010) *Show Sold Separately: Promos, Spoilers, and Other Media Paratexts*, New York: New York University Press.

Hardiman, K. (2012) *Interview with authors*, 11 June.

Holt, J. and Sanson, K. (2014) 'Introduction: Mapping Connections', in J. Holt and K. Sanson (eds) *Connected Viewing: Selling, Streaming, and Sharing Media in the Digital Era*, London and New York: Routledge.

Hughes, T. (2012) *Interview with authors*, 25 October.

James, E. (2012) *Interview with authors*, 1 May.

Jenkins, H. (2006) *Convergence Culture: Where Old and New Media Collide*, New York: New York University Press.

Jenkins, H., Ford, S. and Green, J. (2013) *Spreadable Media: Creating Value and Meaning in a Networked Culture*, New York: New York University Press.

Johnson, C. (2013) 'The Continuity of "Continuity": Flow and the Changing Experience of Watching Broadcast Television', *Key Words: Journal of the Raymond Williams Society*, 11, pp. 23–39.

——(2012) *Branding Television*, London and New York: Routledge.

Johnson, C. and Grainge, P. (2015) 'From Broadcast Design to "On-Brand TV": Repositioning Expertise in the Promotional Screen Industries', in V. Mayer, M. Banks and B. Conor (eds) *Production Studies, Volume II*, London and New York: Routledge.

Johnson, D. (2013) *Media Franchising: Creative License and Collaboration in the Cultural Industries*, New York: New York University Press.

Lee, H. J. and Andrejevic, M. (2014) 'Second-Screen Theory: From the Democratic Surround to the Digital Enclosure', in J. Holt and K. Sanson (eds) *Connected Viewing: Selling, Streaming, and Sharing Media in the Digital Era*, London and New York: Routledge.

Lister, M., Dovey, J., Giddings, S., Grant, I. and Kelly, K. (2009) *New Media: A Critical Introduction*, 2nd edition, London and New York: Routledge.

Lotz, A. (2007) *The Television Will Be Revolutionized*, New York: New York University Press.

Mann, D. (2009) 'It's Not TV, It's Brand Management TV: The Collective Author(s) of the *Lost* Franchise', in V. Mayer, M. J. Banks and J. T. Caldwell (eds) *Production Studies: Cultural Studies of Media Industries*, London and New York: Routledge.

Marich, R. (2008) 'Lisa Gregorian: Defining Marketing's Boundaries', *Broadcasting and Cable*, 9 June: 26.

Marshall, P. D. (2004) *New Media Cultures*, London: Hodder Arnold.

Meikle, G. and Young, S. (2012) *Media Convergence: Networked Digital Media in Everyday Life*, Basingstoke: Palgrave Macmillan.

Murphy, S. C. (2011) *How Television Invented New Media*, New Brunswick: Rutgers University Press.

Napoli, P. M. (2011) *Audience Evolution: New Technologies and the Transformation of Media Audiences*, New York: Columbia University Press.

Nielsen (2012) *The Cross-Platform Report: a New Connected Community*, 13 November. Online. Available: http://www.nielsen.com/us/en/newswire/2012/the-cross-platform-report-a-new-connected-community.html (accessed 12 December 2013).

O'Donnell, C. (2011) 'Games Are Not Convergence: The Lost Promise of Digital Production and Convergence', *Convergence*, 17 (3): 271–86.

Ofcom (2013) *Communications Market Report 2013*, 1 August. Online. Available: http://stakeholders.ofcom.org.uk/binaries/research/cmr/cmr13/2013_UK_CMR.pdf (accessed 11 August 2014).

——(2013a) *International Communications Market Report 2013*, 12 December. Online. Available: http://stakeholders.ofcom.org.uk/binaries/research/cmr/cmr13/icmr/ICMR_2013_final.pdf (accessed 11 August 2014).

Parr, B. (2011) *The Rise of Digital Multitasking*, 1 February. Online. Available: http://mashable.com/2011/02/01/deloitte-survey/ (accessed 12 December 2013).

Phillips, C. (2012) *Interview with authors*, 12 May.

Red Bee Media (2014) 'About Us'. Online. Available: http://www.redbeemedia.com/about-us/overview (accessed 29 August 2014).

——(2012) 'Tomorrow Calling'. Online. Available: http://www.redbeemedia.com/insights/tomorrow-calling (accessed 11 August 2014).

Second Screen Society (2014) 'About Us', 6 January. Online. Available: http://www.2ndscreensociety.com/ces2014/about/ (accessed 11 August 2014).

Swift, J. (2014) 'BBC to End Exclusive Red Bee Media Production Deal', *Campaign*, 21 July. Online. Available: http://www.campaignlive.co.uk/news/1304512/ (accessed 11 August 2014).

Szalai, G. (2012) 'Comcast, NBCUniversal Take Stake in U.K. TV Companion App Maker Zeebox', *Hollywood Reporter*, 27 September. Online. Available: http://www.hollywoodreporter.com/news/comcast-nbcuniversal-uk-app-zeebox-374827 (accessed 12 December 2013).

Tavernier, C. (2013) 'If Everyone is Tweeting About the Show, Why Aren't More People Watching It?', Red Bee Media, 3 December. Online. Available: http://www.redbee media.com/blog/claire-tavernier-if-everyone-tweeting-about-show-why-aren-t-more-pe ople-watching-it (accessed 12 December 2013).

Tussey, E. (2014) 'Connected Viewing on the Second Screen: The Limitations of the Living Room', in J. Holt and K. Sanson (eds) *Connected Viewing: Selling, Streaming, and Sharing Media in the Digital Era*, London and New York: Routledge.

Wheatley, H. (2004) 'The Limits of Television? Natural History Programming and the Transformation of Public Service Broadcasting', *European Journal of Cultural Studies*, 7 (3): 325–39.

Whirledge, T. (2013) 'Is Transmedia Finally Growing Up?', Red Bee Media, 6 August. Online. Available: http://www.redbeemedia.com/blog/transmedia-tv-finally-growing (accessed 12 December 2013).

Ytreberg, E. (2009) 'Extended Liveness and Eventfulness in Multi-Platform Reality Formats', *New Media and Society*, 11 (4): 467–85.

Zeebox (2013) 'Welcome'. Online. Available: http://zeebox.com/uk/welcome (accessed 1 December 2013).

5 Movies

Trailers and the Infrastructure of Blockbuster Marketing

It's amazing – though taken for granted – that the century-old marketing tool that is the film trailer has emerged as the most potent marketing tool for movies in cyberspace.

(Robert Marich 2013: 125)

More people see the trailers than actually see the movies because they go out everywhere.

(Suneil Beri, Managing Director, Create London, 2012)

What we create is one of the most highly consumed digital things on the internet.
(David Stern, Managing Partner, Create Advertising, 2012)

A robot encounters a hoover that accidentally sucks up his cockroach friend leading to a tussle that covers the room with dust and debris. The cockroach survives. In the middle of the night, scary monster Sulley sneaks into his spherical chum Mike's bedroom with a pot of glue as a prank for their fraternity party. Mike awakes to discover he is covered in reflective squares and storms out of his room as Sulley turns on the lights transforming him into a giant mirror ball. These scenes are not extracts from larger feature films. Neither are they independent short animated movies. Rather they are teaser trailers produced to promote Pixar's *Wall-E* (2008) and *Monsters University* (2013) respectively. They form part of what Christopher Holliday (2013) has argued is a new type of teaser trailer pioneered by Pixar that actively blurs the line between promotion and content. Rather than 'previewing' a forthcoming movie, these trailers are '*comprised of* footage, not edited or cut *from it*' (ibid.). Here the trailer is recast as a short film designed to be enjoyed in its own right.

This form of teaser trailer is not confined to Pixar's animated movies. As discussed in Chapter 2, the promotion of *Prometheus* in 2012 involved the creation of a range of original video shorts, such as a Ted talk by fictional character Peter Weyland, and a Weyland Industries film promoting its new cybernetic humanoid, David 8. More recently, the first two teaser trailers for *The Hunger Games: Mockingjay Part 1* (2014) were presented as television addresses from the fictional leader of the Capitol, President Snow. As with the conventional trailer, these original shorts function as entryway paratexts that set up an initial framework for viewing the film (Gray 2010: 72). Each short reveals something of the 'genre, stories and stars' that Lisa Kernan argues 'constitute the three principal rhetorical appeals' of trailers (2004: 41). Yet, at the same time, they avoid the explicit promotional address of many conventional trailers, speaking to the viewer more as 'audience' than 'consumer'. In this sense they function as *in medias re*s paratexts, narrative segments that come from within the diegesis of the film even if they may not feature within the final movie itself.

The blurring of promotion and content, evident in the aforementioned teaser trailers, extends to the industrial structures shaping the production of many such materials. Within Disney/Pixar, any original promotional content containing the characters from the movie (as opposed to being re-cut from the movie's footage) will be produced by the film's creative staff. As such, in production terms, these teaser trailers are part of the film-making process for the movie, rather than a separate marketing effort. Yet we should be wary of over-determining the separation of marketing and film-making here. While the film-makers create these shorts, Disney/Pixar's marketing team (responsible for devising the broader marketing strategy for each movie) makes the decisions about what form they should take. Beyond the example of Disney/Pixar, such promotional texts can be produced in-house (the *Prometheus* Ted talk was directed by Ridley Scott's son Luke Scott (Ostrow 2012)) or by external creative agencies, such as Ignition, which created the 'David 8' short as part of its larger promotional work for *Prometheus*.

Indeed, while these teasers demonstrate a particularly clear example of the blurring of promotion and content, digitalization has turned the trailer more generally into valuable short-form content that is sought out by both viewers and platform owners. Trailers have become an in-demand form of digital content with film distributors able to negotiate exclusive premieres with online platforms in exchange for the promotion of their trailer (Marich 2013: 125). A special feature in *Wired* magazine on 'The Art of the Trailer' claimed that 'the movie preview has become a genre unto itself – and a viral sensation', stating that in 2013 movie fans watched more than a billion movie trailers on YouTube (Kehe and Palmer 2013). As Keith M. Johnston argues, the internet has actually increased the profile of the movie trailer within marketing departments, highlighting the attraction of all forms of movie trailers to audiences as 'unique short films in their own right' (2009: 143). Trailers are often sought out, circulated, dissected and appropriated by fans, all processes facilitated by digitalization (Tryon 2010). To borrow the language of Henry Jenkins, Sam Ford and Joshua Green, trailers have particular potential for 'spreadability' (2013). As inherently open and unfinished texts, they provide glimpses into a larger filmic world and offer resources for shared discussion, gossip and speculation about films that might be (or have been) watched.

The continued value of the trailer can be understood in relation to the economics of the Hollywood film industry in the early twenty-first century. As with the advertising and television industries examined in Chapters 3 and 4, the Hollywood film industry has been affected by the development of new digital technologies. Movies themselves are more mobile and ubiquitous, increasingly circulated by new distribution intermediaries (both legal and illegal) that challenge the control that studios have traditionally had over how, when and where their films are viewed (Tryon 2013). Indeed, since the early 2000s the distribution of movies in theatres has acted as a loss leader for Hollywood (Schatz 2008: 37). The Hollywood film industry generates the bulk of its profits not from domestic (US and Canada) box office, but from ancillary markets and international theatrical revenues (Drake 2008: 64). In terms of ancillary markets, revenues have been threatened by the decline of DVD sales since 2008 and Hollywood conglomerates have responded by moving into the video-on-demand (VOD) market through deals with major companies such as Google, as well as acquisitions of internet companies (Schatz 2008: 38). Chuck Tryon argues that experiments with premium VOD in the early 2010s were exploited by the industry as a new form of domestic movie consumption to make up for declining DVD sales (2013: 37).[1] Although 'persistent online availability ultimately diminishes the urgency of seeing a movie on the big screen' (ibid.: 10), Hollywood theatrical revenues have nevertheless increased. This is largely due to international theatrical box office revenues, which rose by 32 percent between 2008 and 2012 (MPAA 2012: 2) and accounted for around two-thirds of overall gross box office for the top ten movie releases in 2013 (Box Office Mojo 2013).

Within Hollywood's shifting economy, theatrical exhibition remains central, with box office success positioned by the industry as *the* indicator of a movie's marquee value, meaning its potential revenue in overseas and ancillary markets (Marich 2013, Drake 2008). As such, the premiere of a movie in the cinema can be understood as akin to a product launch for a larger brand. The more successful a movie in its opening weekend, the more likely (so the Hollywood rhetoric goes) it is to generate revenues across the other markets where movies typically make their profits. It is, then, unsurprising that domestic marketing typically accounts for around a third of the combined production and domestic release costs for the major Hollywood studios (Drake 2008: 63, Gerbrandt 2010). Indeed, Larry Gerbrandt argues that 'for every dollar spent on producing a major film, the studios have been spending 51 cents – 58 cents to release and market it in the U.S. and Canada' (2010). Theatrical exhibition, therefore, has become a show for a product that reaps its profits in other windows. As international box office supersedes domestic box office, this is a show of global reach and proportions. As John Caldwell argues, the movie itself becomes a 'viral marketing stream', one stratum in a complicated global multimedia industrial marketing and consumption strategy (2005: 95, 2008: 307).

Within this viral marketing stream, where theatrical box office is positioned as the key indicator of a movie's broader economic value, trailers have particular status. Robert Marich argues that 'Hollywood film marketers view them as the most persuasive in convincing moviegoers to buy cinema tickets' because they share the audiovisual nature of movies and can be easily distributed and circulated online (2013: 10). As Finola Kerrigan notes, 'in the age of YouTube, where people are developing the practice of consuming short media clips on a range of media devices, the film trailer may be seen as the ideal promotional tool for film' (2010: 142).

In the emergent field of 'trailer studies' within film and television studies, the trailer has mostly been analysed textually, leaving the role of the trailer industry largely unexamined (see, for example, Kernan 2004, Johnston 2009, Tryon 2010).[2] This chapter addresses this lacuna by focusing on the industrial and production cultures that sit behind trailer-making. It does this in two ways. It begins with the case example of the LA- and London-based trailer house Create Advertising, exploring the processes that underpin the production of trailers as a key form of promotional screen content. However, trailers do not function as promotional texts for movies in isolation; unlike the companies examined in Chapters 3 and 4, trailer houses do not actually steer or strategize promotional campaigns or manage how trailers are used and circulated. In order to examine the role of the trailer within the contemporary digital economy of Hollywood, then, this chapter broadens its scope to look at the role of the in-house marketing departments that coordinate theatrical marketing campaigns for movies. Using the Lionsgate franchise *The Hunger Games* (2012–) as a case study, it examines the ways in which marketing departments within studios and distributors manage trailers as assets that make up part of a larger promotional campaign.

In many ways, *The Hunger Games*, as one of the most successful franchises of the early 2010s, is exemplary of the promotional strategies used by contemporary Hollywood. Yet *The Hunger Games* is also in some sense atypical, produced not by one of the majors, but by the independent studio Lionsgate. In this respect the franchise is indicative of the ways in which new players are competing with and adopting many of the industrial practices of the Hollywood majors.[3] However, it is important to recognize that the blockbuster franchise is not representative of all movie promotion, and this chapter will contextualize its analysis of blockbuster marketing in relation to the often quite different promotional strategies for mid-budget Hollywood and low-budget independent movies.

In taking Create Advertising and *The Hunger Games* as case examples, this chapter builds on the broader concern of this book to open up perspectives on the different production and work cultures of the promotional screen industries that operate outside of Los Angeles. As international box office has become more important to Hollywood, the question of localization in the marketing of movies looms large. This chapter uses its case examples to examine the relationships between Hollywood studios, localized distributors and the agencies (such as trailer houses) that studios use to create promotional content within global flows. In doing so, we argue that Hollywood's promotional screen intermediaries are increasingly producing promotional screen content that attempts to position cinema-going as part of a broader network of digital social behaviours that are shaped and enacted online.

Trailers, trailer houses and the case of Create Advertising

In this section we use the example of the trailer house Create Advertising as a lens through which to examine working practices and cultures in the production of promotional screen content within Hollywood. Create Advertising was founded in 2004 by Managing Partner David Stern, with an initial staff of ten. By 2014 the company had expanded to a staff base of around eighty. Based in LA, the company focuses on creating audiovisual promotions for the film industry, including theatrical trailers and television spots. Although distributors control the marketing for most movies, they typically produce very little promotional content in-house. The majority of promotional content is produced through collaboration with media and creative agencies.[4] Media agencies are responsible for buying the advertising space for movies and devising a media plan based on analysis of the target market and the media advertising landscape. Creative agencies produce the actual promotional content used by Hollywood, and have historically specialized in either print-based marketing (such as posters and newspaper ads) or, as in the case of trailer houses like Create, audiovisual promotion (such as trailers and television spots).

By the early 2010s there were around fifty trailer houses in Los Angeles specializing in the production of audiovisual promotional content for movies. The size of companies ranges from boutiques and start-ups with a handful of employees to large integrated agencies such as Trailer Park that employ around 200 staff and combine expertise in trailers and print, interactive and digital marketing for movies. The importance of the trailer to Hollywood film-making is reflected in the changing status of the trailer editor. Rather than seeing trailer work as a stepping stone to a job in feature film editing, David Stern claimed that applicants to Create now tend to have a much greater understanding of the role of trailer houses and often harbour specific ambitions to pursue careers as trailer editors (2012). Trailer editor Frank Frumento concurred, claiming that around half of the editors he knew in LA in 2013 were specifically pursuing a career as a trailer editor (2013). This speaks to the growing cultural status of trailers as forms that have an aesthetic and circulatory value of their own.

The changing status of trailers, combined with the technological changes wrought by digitalization, has affected the working practices of trailer houses. In production terms, the shift to non-linear digital editing has had a significant impact on the trailer industry. Once a film-based art in which trailers were cut on flat beds, digital editing makes it easier to produce a wider number of trailers and has increased the importance of sound and motion graphics in trailer-making. The ability to cut more versions enables greater targeting of trailers to specific audiences and an increase in the number of trailers produced. As David Stern describes of the ways in which studios commission television spots and trailers:

> I would say on an average film a studio probably cuts upward of 200 thirty-second TV spots. And they're probably doing it with three to five companies in an attempt to finish somewhere between ten and twenty spots. So they're

cutting 200 to get twenty. And the reason they cut 200 is that 200 helps them learn what are the twenty that work the best. And that even happens on trailers.

(2012)

Digital enables studios to adopt a 'try it and see' attitude towards their promotional content, with one trailer editor even arguing of the studios, 'they often use us to figure out how they want their movie to be marketed' (Frumento 2013).[5]

At the same time, the circulation of trailers as digital assets online makes them open to greater scrutiny by viewers, akin to the forensic fandom that Will Brooker argues has emerged around the online viewing of television series (2009).[6] One consequence is that marketing executives are more concerned with the details of their trailers. As Frumento argues, 'you get the marketing executives in LA saying "we need to go through and make sure that every single shot is the perfectly best shot", because you know that you're going to have some blog with a hundred thousand readers that is going to go through it and post freeze frames' (2013). With trailers forming a central part of a film's promotional campaign and representing the largest spend in term of media buying, studios are keen to ensure that the trailer works in aesthetic and marketing terms. Trailers have to go through a number of levels of approval and it is not unusual for twenty-five to thirty versions of a single trailer to be produced before the client is satisfied (Frumento 2013).

Although studios exercise significant control over their trailers in terms of scrutinizing the work created by agencies, trailer editors provide an important creative input into a film's promotional campaign. Indeed, while some distributors will provide written creative briefs for their trailers, it is not uncommon for the brief to be open and sketchy. This provides the trailer editor the space to experiment, in part because the distributor may have approached that creative agency because it trusts the type of work that it produces. It is common for studios to commission work from a number of different creative agencies that develop reputations (often through the skills of star editors) for cutting specific kinds of trailers (Marich 2013: 30, Beri 2012). Editors might specialize, for example, in trailers for comedy or for action movies. This industrial practice sometimes results in 'star editors' with strong reputations or relationships with studios being poached by rival companies or these editors setting up individual boutique agencies.

Indeed, digitalization has lowered the costs of establishing a new trailer house. As an indication, David Stern suggested that Apple's Final Cut software reduced the cost of setting up an editing bay from $150,000 to $20,000 (2012). Yet barriers to entry remain. As Stern observed, 'the barrier to entry is not technological. The barrier to entry is relationships' (ibid.). Across our interviews with those working in marketing and promotion in the film industry, the centrality of relationships recurred as a theme. The need for promotional content to conform to strict contractual requirements (such as those negotiated with core talent) and the highly pressured timescales within which promotional content is produced can lead distributors to commission work from creative agencies with which they have an established relationship. As marketing manager Katie Sexton argued of the relationship between film distribution marketing departments and their creative agencies,

> Our agencies know what to expect from us and we know what to expect from them, they know what deliverables we need, what the layout of our key messaging should look like, they know where we need to put our logos and billing and lots of things that can be tedious to explain to an agency unfamiliar with film advertising. We work with agencies that have been doing film advertising design work for decades and so we tend to use them for digital advertising as well, even though there might well be other younger companies out there that have more insight into certain technical elements or have other expertise, because we know and trust their specific design skills.
>
> (2013)

Maintaining these relationships is a core part of the job for those working within both film distribution marketing departments and the creative agencies from which distributors commission work (Kerrigan 2010, Marich 2013).

The importance of relationships is reflected in the structure and practices of trailer houses, where work is typically organized around two key permanent roles: the account handler/producer and the editor. The account handler/producer manages the relationship with the studio's marketing department, from the initial brief through revisions to the final cut of the trailer. The account handler works closely with the editor who has overall responsibility for the creation of the trailer itself. These roles help us to understand the process of trailer making. This begins with the account handler receiving the client brief, followed by the delivery of the movie to the trailer house. Typically this is not the final cut of the movie, and it may even be dailies, depending on when the trailer is required. In part, this stems from the relative timescales, with trailers often being cut before shooting is complete. However, it can also reflect client concerns regarding piracy, with some studios leaving deliberate gaps in the versions of the movies that they deliver to trailer houses (Beri 2012). Security is also ensured for the client by locating all the materials for a trailer within a control room with permissions set to restrict access to content. Once the material and the brief have been delivered to the agency, the editor undertakes the creative work of cutting the trailer. The editor will begin by breaking the movie down, a laborious process that involves transcribing the dialogue and dissecting the movie into different elements, such as all the moments with a particular character, all of the jokes, all of the dramatic turns, and so on.

While the editor is positioned as the creative leader in trailer production, the process of creating a trailer is a collaborative one that depends on a range of usually freelance creative staff. Working closely with the editor and producer, a copywriter will draft a script for the trailer that will shape a point of view or angle on the movie. Music supervisors will be employed to identify the soundtrack to be used on the trailer. Typically this is not the score used for the movie itself. The need for trailers to generate interest in a short space of time means that the demands of trailer soundtracks can be quite different from the demands of the film score and there are companies that specialize in creating music specifically for trailers.[7] The editor will work with the copy and the music to create a rough cut onto which graphics will be laid (created by in-house designers) and a voice-over added. The trailer is then subject to multiple revisions requested by the client and negotiated through the account handler/producer. Within LA this can often include a 'trailer derby' in which all of the agencies that have cut trailers for a specific movie are brought together to view each other's work (Marich 2013: 30). Trailer houses are paid even if the studio does not use their work. However, in such a highly competitive industry, trailer houses are keen to produce work that is commissioned in order to maintain their relationship with the studio.

Although the trailer remains a core component of movie promotion in the twenty-first century, the trailer industry does face a number of challenges. Studios have seen their marketing costs soar, particularly in the face of the growing importance of international markets. *The Hollywood Reporter* claimed that marketing costs rose by 33 percent between 2007 and 2014 to around $200 million per picture (McClintock 2014). As these rising marketing costs place pressure on the studios' margins, spend on creative comes under pressure as there is far less space to negotiate in relation to media buying, which accounts for the majority of most marketing budgets.[8] Some trailer houses have responded by producing a wider range of content for movie promotion or by merging with other companies in order to offer integrated creative promotional work across a range of media and platforms. For Create these commercial pressures have led towards diversification in two areas: expanding its client base by producing trailers for the video game and entertainment technology industries, and developing its expertise within the area of multicultural and international movie marketing. Having considered features of the process of trailer-making, we want to look briefly at these forms of diversification as revealing of the shifting status of the trailer in the contemporary media ecology. In doing so, we examine the ways in which the trailer has become a significant form of promotional screen content beyond the film industry, and explore how trailer production is enmeshed within the international production cultures that characterize global Hollywood.

Video games and entertainment technology

The US computer and video game industry has been expanding over the past decade with annual growth exceeding 10 percent between 2005 and 2009 (Siwek 2010: 1). Indeed, video games have surpassed the total box office receipts for feature films since 1988 (Caldwell 2008: 277). There are a number of similarities between the film and video game industries. Both require significant up-front investment but have minimal reproduction costs and both produce 'experience goods' that can only be experienced by the consumer after purchase. In addition, there has been significant improvement in the technology of video games, allowing the industry to produce products with cinematic visuals and complex narratives (Brookey 2010). Finally, the video game industry has become an 'A-title driven business' (Stern 2012), in which producers are spending more money on big titles rather than on generic games. As in the film industry this has led to the rise of video game franchises, as well as games developed out of other media, such as movies and comic books.

Much like the film industry, marketing is a core component of the video game industry, with Peter Zackariasson and Timothy L. Wilson claiming that the largest game publishers (Activision, Electronic Arts and Ubisoft) typically spend 50 percent of revenues on promoting business in one aspect or another (2012: 65). André Marchand and Thorsten Hennig-Thurau argue that 'prerelease advertising has a critical role, and game producers devote a substantial portion of their advertising budget to the time prior to a new game's release' (2013: 150). As with movies, marketing is the primary way in which gamers can experience a video game before it has been released. In addition, technical quality has been identified as playing an important role for consumers of games (ibid.: 148) and a high quality trailer can help to construct the impression of technological quality, as well as communicating the experience of playing the game in emotional and immersive terms. Trailers can also help to promote a video game before the producers have actual gameplay footage to reveal to consumers. David Stern argues that 'four or five years ago the video game industry started to accept the model of the movie business and they said ... "let's advertise like the movie business does" and smartly they came to companies like ours that were doing the movie advertising' (2012). Video game producers have, therefore, turned to trailer houses within Hollywood for their long experience of promoting movies.

However, video game trailers present specific production demands for trailer houses. Producing a trailer for a video game requires staff skilled in motion graphics and with the technological ability to interface with the game's design team. In addition, trailer houses need the technology to capture footage from within a game and/or to create specific content for the trailer related to the world of the game. This can alter the role of the trailer editor, requiring greater collaboration with digital animators, but also enabling the editor to request footage to be created to fulfil the requirements of the trailer. The move into video game trailers, therefore, requires specific technological and creative skill-sets, and trailer houses face competition from digital design and animation specialists for this work.

In addition, despite their similarities, movies and video games are quite different experiences and trailer editor Frank Frumento (2013) argued that this can lead to divergent requirements from clients. He claimed that while clients from film studios often require trailers that clearly communicate the experience and basic plot of the movie, video game trailers tend to be closer to a 'teaser' format, in which the trailer is required to communicate a sense of the game's world and gameplay in ways that can be more narratively open and suggestive. The 'Improvise' trailer produced by Axis Animation for the video game *Alien: Isolation* (2014) is a case in point.[9] As with the teasers described at the opening of this chapter, this three-minute trailer played like a short film, depicting the protagonist, Amanda Ripley, attempting to escape from an alien xenomorph. Rather than displaying the mechanics of gameplay, the trailer placed the viewer within the fictional world of the game through a narrative focus on the protagonist's fear in the face of danger (enhanced by computer-generated animation that emphasized the character's facial performance). 'Improvise' was one of a number of trailers and behind-the-scenes videos released for the game, with other trailers more concerned with gameplay ('Survive') or establishing the narrative premise of the game ('Pre-order Trailer'). This points to the way in which the video game industry, much like the film industry, is looking towards the production of a range of differentiated short-form promotional paratexts to frame and create anticipation for their products.

Of course, the video game industry is made up not only of game publishers, but also of console manufacturers. The area of home entertainment technology has provided another new client base for Hollywood's trailer industry, particularly where the focus of the promotional campaign is on the content rather than the technology. For example, Create has produced a series of trailers for PlayStation 4 in which game footage is used as a key selling point for the new technology. In addition, the agency has devised promotions for other new technologies and media service providers such as BluRay and Netflix that similarly use films and television programmes to sell their platforms. As trailers become desired forms of content in their own right, particularly online, a wider range of entertainment-based businesses are looking towards the trailer industry for promotional content that, in Frank Frumento's words, can 'stand alone as a two-minute short film' (2013). Indeed, David Stern argues that the trailer industry should

> stop defining ourselves by our clients and start defining ourselves by our core capabilities … we make short-length marketing material that combines the capabilities of editorial, music, sound design and graphics … and we are uniquely positioned as a company to be able to provide that material to a new host of clients.
>
> (2012)

In many ways, Stern's statement is indicative of the broader movement being traced across this book in which promotional screen content is repositioned as short-form screen entertainment of value to a wide range of industries and audiences. At the same time, it is noticeable that the trailer industry has primarily diversified into clients from within the entertainment industries more broadly. Indeed, while Create has produced trailers for home entertainment technologies, in the main these have used footage cut or created from the die-getic world of games, television programmes and/or films – different from ads designed to explain the technology itself. This suggests that there continues to be significant specialization within the promotional screen industries that dis-tinguishes the trailer industry from, say, the advertising industry. Such specia-lization stems in part from the creative expertise on sale, with editorial skill being central to the work of trailer houses. However, this can be set alongside other cultural and business factors, the relationship-based workings of the video game and Hollywood movie industries facilitating the diversification of the trailer industry into video game marketing.

Multicultural and international marketing

In addition to diversifying its client base to new industries seeking cinematic audiovisual promotional content, Create has also sought to develop specialist expertise that reflects the changing nature of the Hollywood film industry by focusing on multicultural and international marketing. Multicultural marketing is tied to the development of targeted marketing but recognizes the increased ethnic diversity of the US population, with the Hispanic demographic by 2013 representing the largest minority ethnic group in the US (Tornoe 2013). According to the MPAA (2012: 12), while Hispanics make up 17 percent of the US population, in 2012 they represented 26 percent of 'frequent moviegoers' (those going to the cinema once a month). Identifying this shift, Create has begun to specialize in multicultural trailers, with a specific emphasis on cutting trailers targeted at the Hispanic market.[10]

Kerrigan notes that because the cost of placing media far outweighs the cost of making trailers and other forms of promotional content, there is a financial logic to creating culturally specific marketing communications (2010: 138). This applies not only to the development of multicultural and demographically tar-geted promotional content for the domestic market, but also to the ways in which promotional content is localized for international markets as movies are released across the globe. Indeed, the increasing importance of international box office makes localization central to the promotional process, and Create has set up a London office that focuses on the production of UK-specific and inter-national trailers as one way of expanding its business. As with the development of the London office of the Chinese digital media company Crystal CG, explored in the next chapter, the establishment of Create London in 2009 was driven in part by specific contracted work. In this case, Sony required Create to send a producer/editor team to London to cut the trailers for *Casino Royale* (2006) and *Quantum of Solace* (2008) in an attempt by production company Eon to main-tain as much control over the movie as possible (Beri 2012). This opened up the possibility of expanding Create's client base within London as a strategic film territory. The establishment of Create London can be understood, then, as part of a broader shift in the development of what Ben Goldsmith, Susan Ward and

Tom O'Regan term 'local Hollywood' in which a variety of places and people around the world are actively shaping Hollywood production (2010: 1–2).

While Goldsmith et al. focus on film production, the localization of promotional paratexts plays a significant role in the global circulation of movies and film culture. The demands of localization are cultural (including different tastes, demographics and calendars) and political (including different codes for advertising and quotas for foreign imports). David Stern gave the example of the ways in which cultural assumptions about movie audiences shaped the trailers cut for the promotion of *Real Steel* (2011) for theatrical release in the US/Canada and in Japan. The domestic trailer placed the action at the forefront to maximize appeal to a young male audience, while the Japanese trailer emphasized the emotional relationships between the characters.[11] Through such methods, promotional screen intermediaries participate in localization practices that tend to 'strategically reify localities, as well as local tastes, humour, and meanings – in hopes of successfully anticipating the desires of regional audiences and generating a profit' (Carlson and Corliss 2011: 68).

However, these localization practices are also shaped by the different production cultures of promotional intermediaries operating outside of Los Angeles. A brief examination of the trailer industry in London reveals the ways in which specific factors can shape the production cultures of local promotional screen intermediaries. The UK has the third highest international box office for Hollywood movies (after China and Japan) (MPAA 2012) and is also home to a number of international distributors.[12] While a significant amount of the international promotional screen content for Hollywood movies is produced by trailer houses based in LA, there are a number of creative agencies in London that produce promotional screen content for Hollywood and non-Hollywood distributors. The cultural and economic factors that shape the UK trailer industry stem in part from the UK film industry's reliance on Hollywood (see McDonald 2008), but also function to create an industry with a production culture distinct from that in LA.

Despite the increasing significance of international box office for Hollywood, international campaigns within specific territories for Hollywood movies tend to receive smaller marketing budgets than North American campaigns. This, combined with the lower marketing budgets for non-Hollywood movies, means that the UK trailer industry is far smaller than the US industry, with approximately eight trailer houses operating in the UK, compared to around fifty in the US (Beri 2012). The smaller scale and lower budgets of the UK industry intensify the relationship-based nature of promotional work, but also change the nature of the relationship between the trailer house and its client. While the Hollywood majors in LA employ marketing executives to oversee specific parts of a promotional campaign (such as print or audiovisual), within the UK, marketing executives will typically be responsible for all aspects of a local campaign. One consequence is that the clients commissioning work from trailer houses are less specialized and, according to one trailer editor, therefore more likely to trust the expertise of the creative agency.[13] The lack of client specialization, combined with smaller marketing budgets and shorter production schedules, means that clients tend to demand fewer revisions and there is far less tendency in the UK to create multiple versions of a trailer or television spot.[14] In some ways this increases the creative freedom of the editors, who can work with less interference from the client, particularly on smaller budget films. In other ways, however, the creative labour of UK trailer houses is more constrained. For example, the creative agency that cut the UK television spots for *The Hunger Games: Catching Fire* (2013) did not have access to the feature film and had to rely on the audiovisual promotional content that had already been released by Lionsgate US. A significant proportion of the work of UK trailer houses is what the industry terms 'adapts', US trailers adapted for the UK market, rather than original work. Frank Frumento claimed that around half of the trailers cut by Create London are international and half are original work specifically for the UK market (2013). However, Create London also produces work for the US market, particularly for movies that want to convey a more 'independent' or 'transatlantic' sensibility (Beri 2012). In addition, Suneil Beri argued that Create London has a larger 'administrative function' in the coordination of a campaign. While the scale of the industry in the US means that LA-based trailer houses focus solely on creative work, in the UK, Create London's work can include coordinating with the media agency for the client and dealing with music licensing (Beri 2012).

In many ways, the UK trailer industry is shaped by its relationship with Hollywood. Yet to see this local industry as simply an offshoot or adjunct to Hollywood is to overlook the specificities of the production culture of the trailer industry in the UK. As Goldsmith et al. argue of Hollywood's internationally dispersed production cultures, the Hollywood studios may retain control of the 'design function' of movie production, but this is an industry characterized by flexible specialization in which a wide range of components are contracted out to companies across the globe (2010: 17). While Hollywood distributors retain significant control of the 'design function' of the promotion of their movies, locally based distributors and creative agencies play an important role in the production of promotional paratexts created (as in the case of London) within an industrial context that differs in terms of scale, competition and budgets. This alternate context can limit the creative agency of trailer houses to producing campaigns based on existing promotional content produced in the US. However, it can also extend the role of the trailer house beyond the production of creative content and provide the trailer editor with greater creative freedom than his/her US counterpart, able to operate with less interference and scrutiny from the client. In being attentive to the specificities of the production cultures that shape the global circulation of Hollywood movies, we can paint a more complex picture of the negotiation of control that reveals the structuring role that local practices and relationships have on the creation of promotional paratexts.

These local practices and relationships in the promotional screen industries extend beyond the trailer house to include the negotiations of control between

Hollywood and local distributors. Indeed, although trailer houses play a central role in the production of promotional screen content, it is the marketing departments of distributors that control the promotional campaigns for movies. The next section will, therefore, examine the ways in which the trailer operates as just one part of a larger marketing campaign constructed through a network of relations between global and local players. Using the example of the marketing of *The Hunger Games* in the US and the UK as a stepping off point, it will examine the ways in which the promotion of the franchise appealed to its digitally literate target audience by positioning cinema-going as part of a broader network of digital behaviours. In doing so, it will argue that the promotional screen content for movies can be understood as contributing to the popular imagination of what cinema is, and might be, in the early twenty-first century.

Trailers and the infrastructure of blockbuster marketing: the case of *The Hunger Games*

> A film is a brand that has no public awareness. In a really short amount of time a film needs to become culturally prolific and people need to be talking about it.
>
> (Beri 2012)

> There might not be a more daunting challenge than opening a major motion picture: create an internationally recognized brand name that lasts a lifetime, and do it in a couple of weeks.
>
> (Gerbrandt 2010)

If marketing campaigns for Hollywood movies typically used to begin four weeks before theatrical release (Kerrigan 2010), it has now become commonplace for studios and distributors to begin promoting their biggest movies up to two years before their release, as movies emerge as components of larger brands that need 'to be explained, positioned, and promoted to consumers' (Marich 2013: 5). The repositioning of movies as brands not only affects when the marketing process begins, but also the nature of the promotional campaign. In this section we want to use the example of the promotional campaign for *The Hunger Games* franchise to examine the nature of blockbuster marketing within Hollywood in the digital era and the changing role of the trailer in this.

The Hunger Games is a franchise of four movies based on a trilogy of books of the same name set in the fictional nation of Panem.[15] At the heart of the franchise is a narrative of oppression and revolution. The ruling 'Capitol' of Panem exercises brutal authoritarian control over the rest of the nation, which is divided into twelve districts each determined by a different industry (mining, fishing, farming and so on) responsible for providing the wealth through which the Capitol maintains power. The subjugation of the districts is further maintained through the annual 'Hunger Games' in which one boy and one girl from each district are selected in a lottery to compete in a televised fight to the death as punishment for a past rebellion against the Capitol. The franchise follows the experiences of Katniss Everdeen, a young woman from District Twelve, who becomes an emblem for rebellion against the Capitol after surviving the Hunger Games. *The Hunger Games* franchise has been a significant success for Lionsgate. In 2013 Lionsgate was the only studio other than the Hollywood majors to break the $1 billion mark in domestic box office revenues (Lionsgate 2013), with the first two movies in the franchise reporting gross domestic box office over $400 million as of the end of 2013 (Box Office Mojo 2013a).[16]

Alongside its purchase in 2012 of Summit Entertainment (the independent studio responsible for the *Twilight* films), Lionsgate's production of *The Hunger Games* signalled the studio's move into the youth demographic, as well as an expansion of its emphasis on franchising. While franchising has typically been understood as a strategy employed by major media conglomerates in order to generate revenue from one movie across the full range of their subsidiaries (Schatz 2008), the move of Lionsgate (and Summit Entertainment) into franchising points to the benefit of this strategy to independent studios as well. Derek Johnson argues that media franchises function as a 'cultural resource' shared across a network of social and labour relations within the media industries (2013: 45). For an independent studio this cultural resource can be exploited through deals with partners keen to share in the financial benefits of a successful franchise. Over and above this, the blockbuster franchise typifies the shifting context of the movie itself as one of a number of content streams that not only generate revenue but that aim, more broadly, to create extended and loyal customer relationships. Franchising can also ameliorate marketing costs, which can be aggregated across a number of movies, and can also, if successful, construct each movie as an anticipated event in order to enhance box office and ancillary revenues. The blockbuster movie franchise can be understood, therefore, as a 'sustained event' (Grainge 2008: 130–50) that invites consumers to participate across the extended life of the franchise, and generates revenue over time.

The internet has become central to the creation of the contemporary blockbuster franchise as a sustained event, with websites and social media now a core component of movie marketing (Kerrigan 2010, Marich 2013). Historically the promotional campaign for Hollywood movies began with the premiere of the trailer in cinemas and on television, with distributors vying for the most coveted television spots such as in the US magazine programme *Entertainment Tonight* (Beri 2012). In the digital era, blockbuster movie campaigns begin online, with distributors using social media to position themselves into non-linear channels that viewers use to discover and discuss the popular cultural forms that interest them. As such, the promotional campaign for the first *Hunger Games* movie began not with the release of a trailer, but with the launch of a Facebook site in February 2011. This appeared before the film went into production and over a year before the first movie premiered in theatres on 23 March 2012. At this point casting decisions remained uncertain and the site began by circulating news and gossip about the casting and production of the show. In this early pre-production and production phase of the campaign, social media sites like Facebook and Twitter were used to disseminate the kinds of content typically produced for the electronic press kit (EPK) of a movie, such as interviews with the cast, behind-the-scenes content from the set, posters and stills. While prior to the internet the EPK was circulated to journalists who then chose how, when and where to use the promotional content provided, digital technologies provide distributors with the ability to sidestep these gatekeepers and speak directly to the consumer.[17]

The internet, therefore, makes it far easier for distributors to circulate promotional material without the need for cultural intermediaries such as journalists. However, content online has to work far harder to find an audience. As Katie Sexton argued of social media marketing for movies, 'when you set up social media accounts (Facebook, Twitter and so on) you can't really target large groups of people without spending – so you're starting from zero in most cases, and you need to be imaginative to get audiences into the conversation early' (2013). Adopting the logic of spreadability, Lionsgate aimed to 'get fans in' to the film world of *The Hunger Games* through the construction of promotional content that acted as a participative online fictional extension of the movie itself. Working with creative agency Ignition, Lionsgate created a multichannel narrative based around the world of Panem. This part of the campaign began in August 2011, with a hashtag displayed in the first teaser trailer for the movie that enabled fans to discover the Capitol and its online location, www.theca pitol.pn. Unlike the traditional movie website, the site communicated with the user not as a potential film-viewer, but as a citizen of Panem. Users were invited to log in through Facebook or Twitter in order to register as a 'citizen', providing Lionsgate with valuable demographic information about their core fanbase for the franchise. Users were then assigned to different districts of Panem, each of which had its own Facebook site, and were invited to elect their own mayor, with fans posting videos and text in an attempt to generate votes. Positioned as the website of the official government of Panem, www.thecapitol.pn and its related Facebook pages encouraged viewers to participate within the fictional world of the movie by playing citizens of the districts of Panem while also educating viewers about the world of the movie. Information about and promotion for the film was released in the guise of official Panem statements about the forthcoming Hunger Games, and the totalitarian nature of the Capitol was emphasized.[18] Participation was further encouraged through the Facebook game *The Hunger Games Adventures* (produced by social gaming company Funtactix with the involvement of the novels' author Suzanne Collins) that revealed aspects of the fictional world of the franchise not explored in the films or novels. Launched in March 2013, the game aimed to maintain interest in the franchise between the first and the second movies while also generating its own revenue through in-game purchases in an explicit example of the blurring of promotion and content.

While the Capitol website and *Hunger Games Adventures* focused on positioning viewers as oppressed workers within the districts, in January 2012

Figure 5.1 The Hunger Games as interactive experience: 'The Capitol Tour' (2012).

Lionsgate launched the fashion magazine Capitol Couture (www.capitolcouture.pn) that addressed viewers as citizens of the wealthy Capitol. The magazine included fake articles on the characters and events within the world of the film series, offering sneak peeks of footage from the film itself, as well as cross-promoting a product line from the American cosmetic brand CoverGirl inspired by the Capitol's outrageous fashion. Ignition also worked with Microsoft and inter-active production company The Nerdery to create 'The Capitol Tour', an interactive and immersive HTML experience that allowed viewers to access new areas of the Capitol such as the control room for the Hunger Games. In addition, the Capitol Tour provided information about the cast, characters and world of the series and links both to the other promotional platforms and to the official trailers and posters for the movie.

By creating websites and games that addressed viewers as participants within the fictional world of *The Hunger Games* movies, Lionsgate created an online infrastructure through which other forms of promotional content could be released directly to viewers who were already engaged with the franchise. All of the online initiatives discussed above were used to disseminate traditional pro-motional content such as trailers, posters and publicity, often positioned as significant events in their own right. For example, Lionsgate used the Capitol Couture website to create Capitol Portraits of eleven main characters to be featured in the second film, *The Hunger Games: Catching Fire*. The release of the portraits was an event in itself, with anticipation stirred through the pub-lishing of images of empty chairs with a hashtag, date, time and venue for release of the full image through exclusive deals with partners such as MTV, IGN, Empire, MSN and through the fake magazine's Instagram, Tumblr and

Figure 5.2 (a) Teaser Capitol Portrait poster for *The Hunger Games: Catching Fire* (2013);
(b) Official Capitol Portrait poster for *The Hunger Games: Catching Fire* (2013).
Courtesy of Lionsgate/The Kobal Collection.

Facebook feeds. The promotional infrastructure created online for the movies, therefore, became a site through which more traditional promotional materials could be positioned as valuable short-form content.

Lionsgate used this promotional infrastructure to encourage ongoing interaction with the franchise. Between the theatrical exhibition of the first two movies, these sites were used to promote the release of the first film on DVD and to share reviews and gossip about the franchise and its actors. As the franchise expanded with the production of the second movie, Lionsgate launched *The Hunger Games Explorer*, created in partnership with Internet Explorer and RED Interactive Agency. Tied in with the launch of the official trailer for the movie (which premiered at the MTV Movie Awards on 14 April 2013 before being released globally online), *The Hunger Games Explorer* website aggregated all promotional activity surrounding the movie, from posters and trailers, to links to *Hunger Games* online sites and games. In addition, the website encouraged participation and repositioned promotional materials not as marketing, but as desirable content that rewarded fan devotion. Fans received 'sparks' and 'badges' for participating online by liking posts (using the #HungerGamesExplorer in social media posts) and entering competitions. Each week a new 'featured fan' was chosen, often based on creative participation with the site (such as producing fan videos or images), and the site constructed a leaderboard of the top fans according to the number of sparks and badges they earned. As well as inviting fan participation the site also aggregated user-generated content (UGC), reposting official and fan content from other sites based on the user's location and language to create a tailored experience that constantly updated. In this, user-generated and official promotional content sat side by side.[19]

The immersive promotional infrastructure created by Lionsgate can be understood as an attempt to manage the unruly and unpredictable nature of social media (Marich 2013: 123). As Julie Levin Russo (2009) argues of the uses of UGC in film and television marketing more broadly, Lionsgate strove to contain fan productivity within its proprietary (promotional) spaces. It did this by constructing these spaces as a fictional expansion of the world of the franchise itself and by rewarding fans with promotional material that was repositioned as valued content. The promotional infrastructure of *The Hunger Games* also attempted to construct a temporal journey through the film's promotional content that functioned to prioritize the changing marketing aims of Lionsgate. Viewers could potentially access promotional content related to any moment from the campaign. However, Lionsgate constructed its promotional infrastructure to direct viewers to the most recent material in an attempt to ensure that its specific marketing objectives (such as creating anticipation for a forthcoming theatrical release or pushing a DVD launch) were emphasized at any given time. New issues of Capitol Couture, for example, were released at strategic moments in the campaign, allowing Lionsgate to build up anticipation and to archive older, and less relevant, material. The promotional infrastructure for *The Hunger Games* aggregated the wide range of official and fan-generated content around the franchise in ways that attempted to manage audience behaviour in order to support the marketing aims of the studio.

Lionsgate's use of the participative potential of the internet to manage audience behaviour and create consumer loyalty built on strategies established through previous tent-pole blockbusters, such as *The Lord of the Rings* and the *Harry Potter* series (Grainge 2008: 134–45). Through its promotional infrastructure for *The Hunger Games*, Lionsgate constructed a developing set of fictional encounters with the franchise where the films functioned as just one part of an extended transmedia world. In the process, the films were positioned as a component of a more extensive social digital experience in which the consumer was invited to actively participate. Far more than just functioning as paratextual frames that shaped the interpretation of the movies, the promotional surround for *The Hunger Games* established sets of social interactions around the fictional world of the franchise online. In doing so the promotional campaign aimed to manage audience engagement with the franchise. However, it also functioned to reimagine movies as an intrinsic part of the digital landscape and to position cinema-going within the everyday digital behaviours of viewers.

These online forms of promotion need to be understood as adding to, rather than replacing, traditional media. Although online marketing was a core component in the promotion of *The Hunger Games*, the franchise relied on traditional forms of media and movie marketing (cinema and television trailers and posters), particularly in the run-up to the theatrical release of each movie. For example, there was a significant increase in the media spend on television, outdoor advertising, radio and digital promotions after ticket sales opened for *The Hunger Games: Catching Fire* on 1 October 2013 in the lead up to its cinema release on 22 November 2013.[20] In fact, although spend on online film marketing has increased (Marich 2013: 119), for most mainstream movies television marketing remains a primary expenditure (Kerrigan 2010: 147). Marich claims that film marketing is the fifth-largest category in paid for advertising in the US and that 73 percent of US theatrical advertising spend was on television in 2010 (2013: 78). While television advertising can deliver reach, it also benefits from being what Marich terms a 'fast-load' media (2013: 87–8). Fast-load media, such as network television, can reach millions of potential movie-goers in an instant, in comparison to outdoor billboards (or most online campaigns) which can reach large numbers but at a slower rate. Unlike the internet, where it is harder to ensure that a mass audience receives promotional content when it is released, a spot in a highly rated television programme can potentially attract millions of viewers just before the release of a movie, constructing a sense of eventfulness designed to encourage cinema-going. Of course, as with other forms of television advertising, the increase in time-shifting has affected the commercial spot's ability to deliver mass audiences (see Chapter 4). This is particularly important for the marketing of movies, where television advertising has been understood by the film industry as the central means of reaching mass audiences in the build-up to theatrical release. Marich argues that the temporal demands of the marketing of movies, whose success is deemed to depend on their box office revenue in the opening weekend, has made advertising spots within non-scripted programmes particularly popular because they create a greater urgency to watch in real time (2013: 98).

The marketing for *The Hunger Games* franchise paints a picture of a complex landscape in which online promotion functions alongside and is integrated with more traditional forms of promotional content, such as trailers and posters. In doing so, it demonstrates how online promotion supports, rather than competes with, more traditional marketing materials in a number of ways. First, as noted, the promotional infrastructure created by Lionsgate functioned as a site through which traditional promotional material was distributed to fan audiences. Second, the promotional infrastructure was supported through a range of cross-promotional campaigns – such as the involvement of Microsoft in the *Capitol Tour* and *The Hunger Games Explorer* or the involvement of CoverGirl with *Capitol Couture* – that facilitated the spread of the marketing for the movie to new audiences potentially unfamiliar with the franchise. Third, the campaign still relied extensively on traditional media for the distribution of promotional content. Although the first teaser trailer for *The Hunger Games: Catching Fire* was released online, it had its premiere as part of the MTV Movie Awards, in a major television event designed to generate interest in the movie's target audience of teens and young adults. Furthermore, Lionsgate used trailer releases to signal the launch of new promotional sites online, from the initial Capitol.pn site to *The Hunger Games Explorer*, indicating the reciprocal relationship between new and traditional media in the marketing of the movie. To see online marketing as in some ways opposed to, or taking away from, traditional forms of movie advertising is to misunderstand the ways in which Hollywood blockbusters are marketed. Rather, the online promotional infrastructure manages the dissemination and circulation of traditional marketing content such as trailers and posters to targeted audience groups, alongside their distribution through television and cinema. In this way it integrates and positions movies, and cinema-going, as part of the digital landscape of the internet.

However, such marketing campaigns play out on a global scale and the increased importance of international box office makes the role of local players particularly important in understanding the work of the promotional screen industries. The global distribution market for movies is highly concentrated and one of the central ways in which Hollywood secures its domination of the international film industry (Miller et al. 2001: 148–52). US distributors use economies of scale to control the international circulation of movies. The construction of the large campaigns typical of blockbuster marketing 'requires investments on a scale beyond the reach of smaller distributors everywhere' (ibid.: 151). As a consequence smaller low-budget and non-Hollywood movies are unable to compete with the marketing of the Hollywood blockbuster in terms of cost, scale and reach. Many Hollywood distributors manage the global circulation of their movies through their own international networks, while others operate joint ventures. Lionsgate, for example, has established a global infrastructure through distribution deals with partners across Europe, Australasia and Latin America (Lionsgate 2014). However, as we saw with the trailer industry in the last section, although these structures of international distribution function to facilitate the global domination of the Hollywood film industry, they also depend on the labour of promotional intermediaries within specific geographic territories.

In relation to distribution and marketing, the role of local actors can depend on the specific deals made on a film-by-film basis and whether a film is licensed to one or multiple markets (Kerrigan 2010: 155). Distributors have the right to release a movie only in the territories for which they are licensed and such licensing deals can, therefore, shape the promotional paratexts produced for a movie as well as the production cultures that create those texts. In the case of *The Hunger Games*, the first movie was created and distributed in the US and Canada by Lionsgate. However, according to the Internet Movie Database, sixty-one companies were responsible for distributing the movie in its theatrical and non-theatrical releases around the globe through Lionsgate's international distribution deals. In order to understand the global nature of Hollywood, therefore, we need to examine the role of local promotional intermediaries within the structures of distribution that shape the industry.

A brief examination of the UK marketing for *The Hunger Games* movies is revealing of the economic, structural and cultural factors that shape the processes through which Hollywood products are distributed and positioned globally.

Within the UK, the two *Hunger Games* movies that had been released by the summer of 2014 had both been distributed by Lionsgate's London-based subsidiary, Lionsgate UK. The case of Lionsgate UK's role in the promotion of the *Hunger Games* movies is instructive of the 'subtle negotiation of control' (Goldsmith et al. 2010: 29) that takes place between Hollywood and local partners in the creation of promotional paratexts. A significant proportion of the promotional work for *The Hunger Games* franchise was produced in Hollywood by creative agencies working to a brief designed by the marketing department at Lionsgate in the US, including the majority of the promotional infrastructure that shaped the marketing of the movie before tickets went on sale. Lionsgate's US marketing department also attempted to control the global release of promotional content. For the launch of the first teaser trailer for *The Hunger Games: Catching Fire* on 14 April 2013, the US office took control of the YouTube channels of its international distribution partners in order to upload the trailer simultaneously across the globe. The main trailer and the posters designed to promote the movie were also produced through Lionsgate's US office with no input from its local distributors.

However, Lionsgate's US office did not control all of the marketing for *The Hunger Games* in the UK, with the UK office taking responsibility, in particular, for promotion of the movies in the lead up to their theatrical release. Lionsgate UK worked with their media agency MEC to devise a specific media plan for the promotion of each movie based on their knowledge of the UK media landscape. In addition to advising on media buying, this involved UK-specific promotions such as an anti-piracy trailer produced with Find Any Film, part of the UK-based Industry Trust for IP Awareness. Local knowledge can also determine the phasing of a campaign with, for example, Lionsgate UK extending their Facebook spend to a week after release in order to capitalize on 'Orange Wednesday', a two-for-one ticket offer by the mobile phone company Orange. Lionsgate UK also produced a UK-specific television campaign in the lead up to the theatrical release of the first film. This included television spots that were created by the London-based creative agency Wonderland, a promotional tie-in with talent show *The X-Factor* (ITV, 2004–) and a 'hero spot' (a sixty-second television trailer) within the soap opera *Hollyoaks* (Channel 4, 1995–). Not only did this target the core teen and young adult demographics for the movie, but it also utilized forms of programming – reality television and the ongoing soap – that encourage live (or temporally proximate) viewing. As such, the global promotional infrastructure created and controlled by Lionsgate in the US for *The Hunger Games* movies sat alongside content produced by, and specifically for, the UK market.

However, the lack of geographical boundaries online can work against such attempts at localization. In interview, one former marketing assistant at Lionsgate UK gave the example of the Facebook page for *The Hunger Games*, noting that although there was a UK-specific site, many UK fans had liked the more official-looking US site that offered more content. As a consequence, these fans received marketing messages targeted at US audiences (such as competitions not accessible to UK fans). There are technological solutions to this, with Facebook now offering global companies the possibility of integrating their localized sites and then using information about users to push only the content relevant to their location. *The Hunger Games Explorer* site similarly uses the location of users to push only geographically and linguistically relevant content. Yet, elsewhere in the franchise's promotional infrastructure, the prioritization of the US market could be seen as contributing to the construction of the international viewer as second-class citizen in ways that undermine the argument that a global culture is emerging around certain transnational texts (Jung 2011). Not only does the promotional infrastructure favour English as a language, but it also includes content only accessible in the US (such as the US television spots posted on Capitol TV that are geo-blocked in the UK). In these ways US distributors structure the online interactions around movies in ways that can deprioritize global connections in favour of localized marketing messages (as in the case of Facebook) or prioritize the US audience (as in the case of the availability of audiovisual texts on Capitol TV).

Although a large franchise such as *The Hunger Games* has the budget to create a complex globalized promotional infrastructure, this is not open to all movies. Indeed, according to Katie Sexton non-blockbuster movie promotion, particularly for art-house movies, needs to be far more targeted because the marketing budgets are significantly reduced (2013). Both online and television advertising suffer as a consequence: television because the costs of buying advertising space are so high and online because, without the large promotional infrastructure and fan audience for a franchise like *The Hunger Games*, it is hard to ensure the effectiveness of the promotional content released online. As Sexton goes on to argue of online marketing:

> You often can't predict the full context of how your online ads will be experienced. When you buy a display ad in a newspaper you can buy it in the front half, on the right hand side and in a certain size, but when you buy display ads online there are so many more variables. Often your ads will appear in a rotation of other ads and you don't know what those are going to be, you don't know exactly what kind of editorial content is going to be next to them, you can't predict if your audience is using adblockers or if they're scrolling straight past, or if they're minimizing the page, or if they're clicking accidentally, or if they're even noticing them at all. You could be targeting an audience that have learned how to zone out all of the advertising noise online and thus wasting your money. But there are so many eyeballs in that space, to neglect it, isn't worth the risk.
>
> (2013)

In many ways, there is a rhetoric here that speaks of the complexities of the online marketing environment, particularly when compared to the long-standing practices of traditional newspaper advertising. Despite the decline of newspaper sales, newspaper advertising benefits from industry agreed conventions that have been established for understanding the value of different advertising formats – conventions that specify that larger adverts that are placed earlier in a newspaper or magazine will be more effective (and more costly). Sexton reveals the difficulty of translating these conventions into the different context of the internet. In particular she refers to the purchasing of a 'network' of advertising through companies that sell blocks of advertising space across a range of sites. Buying a network of advertising limits the control the marketer has over where the advertising is situated. Sexton also points to the uncertainties that arise around new media, however. While newspaper readers are just as likely to avoid an ad or put down a paper as an online reader is to minimize or skip advertising, her account of the internet speaks to a sense of the online space as fluid, difficult and unknowable. As Sexton later claimed of social media marketing in the same interview, 'it's so hit and miss. You could get it right one day and then the next day the hivemind has moved on and what you're talking about is no longer cool or relevant' (2013). While the creation of a promotional infrastructure for the online marketing of *The Hunger Games* was an attempt to manage this fluid environment, movies with smaller marketing budgets have less scope for taking risks with paid-for online advertising that might not return results.

This does not mean, though, that low-budget movies do not use online marketing. However, the use of the online space tends to be far more targeted. A former marketing assistant at Lionsgate described paying to link advertising for the studio's French-language movie *Jeune et Jolie* (2013) to searches on Google for the term 'French', as well as purchasing billboards on the Internet Movie Database website in order to target viewers specifically interested in film. Some independent film-makers are also using the internet to circumvent traditional routes to distribution and exhibition by promoting and releasing their movies online (Kerrigan 2010: 199–200, Vesey 2013). Yet for most lower-budget movies, the cinema trailer remains the main marketing cost. While distributing a trailer online can facilitate its exposure to a wide audience, it also depends on the viewer actively seeking out and selecting that trailer to view. By contrast, the cinema audience is both a captive one (unable to switch over during the trailers, even if they can talk through them) and an audience that has already demonstrated their interest in cinema-going (Sexton 2013). For movies that do not have the pre-sold features of a franchise like *The Hunger Games* or the budget for an extensive campaign, the cinema trailer is considered within the industry to be the most effective way of giving potential viewers a taste of the movie to come (Marich 2013: 10).

In this section we have demonstrated the ways in which Hollywood blockbusters are frequently positioned within a global promotional infrastructure that functions as a means of disseminating promotional content and managing the behaviour of viewers.[21] If, as Jonathan Wroot (2013) argues, paratextual content like DVD extras offer a way of interacting with a movie other than through its narrative, then the promotional infrastructure plays a similar role, allowing viewers to imagine themselves in a range of differentiated roles in relation to the world of the franchise. In doing so, the promotional infrastructure positions the movie as an event that is part of a larger and longer immersive experience that can be engaged with across multiple sites and in a variety of ways. Within this, the trailer is repositioned not simply as a text promoting a 'coming attraction' but as an engaging and anticipated form of content in its own right.

Conclusion

Over this chapter we have examined the function of promotional screen inter-mediaries in the film industry, focusing on the work of trailer houses and the marketing of the Hollywood blockbuster. We have demonstrated that despite the rising significance of online marketing, the trailer retains its status as a primary promotional text for the film industry. However, for the Hollywood blockbuster the trailer now figures as one component of a broader promotional infrastructure. These promotional infrastructures are created to construct ongoing, targeted and participative relationships with viewers. In doing so, cinema-going is positioned as part of a broader set of digital behaviours, from viewing promotional content online to playing games, producing UGC and interacting through social media. Rather than undermining the trailer, however, the promotional infrastructure can function to further reify traditional promo-tional content (such as trailers and posters) by positioning its release as a significant event in its own right.

Although the trailer is increasingly circulated online as a form of digital media, it is rhetorically positioned within the industry as akin to the cinematic experience. This symbolic hierarchy arguably shapes the trailer industry, which retains its centrality in the production of screen content to promote movies and has successfully exported this to other entertainment industries. Across our interviews with those working within Hollywood's promotional screen indus-tries, there was a strong sense that the trailer industry has significant value to its clients because of its ties to the Hollywood film business. This is a symbolic hierarchy that also has a global dimension as, despite the rise of international box office, the North American market tends to take precedence in the construction and circulation of promotional content.

Yet we must be wary of overstating the control of Hollywood in the global market. As we have demonstrated, the circulation of Hollywood movies is structured in part by local promotional intermediaries with their own specific production cultures. These are shaped by economic factors, such as reduced budgets, but also by cultural factors. In discussing the work of Create's London office, Suneil Beri (2012) described the experience of working with independent British movies as a point of differentiation from the trailer house's LA office. Here, Create London's *difference* from Hollywood becomes significant in gen-erating work from studio clients looking for promotional content 'that is a bit more independent' or that can 'bridge a transatlantic understanding' (ibid.). Along with the specificities of the production cultures of London's trailer industry (explored above), this reminds us that in an increasingly globalized media environment we need to attend to the negotiation between the local and the global not just in the texts, but also in the production cultures that shape the creation and circulation of promotional artefacts. This concern with the global scope of the promotional screen industries provides a point of focus for our last chapter. Moving beyond intermediaries based in Europe and North America, we consider, finally, the role of Chinese promotional screen expertise. This turns attention to the production of digital (animated) out-of-home and experiential materials used by corporate and organizational bodies to promote global media events such as the Olympic Games.

Notes

1 Consumer spending on VOD is on the increase, but there is a lack of public reporting about the income from VOD by the major players in the industry, making it difficult to ascertain the extent to which VOD might replace the income lost from the DVD market (Kaufman 2012).
2 A recent special edition of *Frames Cinema Journal* on 'Promotional Materials' (Issue 3, May 2013) took useful steps in this direction and included a series of interviews by Keith M. Johnston (2013) with trailer producers and editors.
3 Derek Johnson's (2012) account of Marvel Studios' independent film production between 2005 and 2009 and Kristin Thompson's (2008) examination of the production of the *Lord of the Rings* franchise offer other examples of franchise film-making by major independents.
4 Some studios and distributors (such as Disney) do retain in-house creative teams and have attempted to bring creative promotional work in-house to save costs (Marich 2013: 16–18). However, Suneil Beri (2012) claims that around 90 percent of promotional screen work is outsourced.
5 This is akin to the 'try it and see' philosophy that Allen (2009) argues has emerged in film production from the shift to tapeless editing.
6 See, for example, Stuart Heritage's regular trailer review feature for *The Guardian* (2014) and the fansite *Film Trailer Reviews* (2014).
7 James Deaville is currently undertaking a major study of the role of music and sound in film trailers in the project 'Re-framing film: music, trailers and meaning in the digital age' (funded by the Social Sciences and Humanities Research Council of Canada).
8 Marich claims that Hollywood's general rule of thumb is that creative costs should be about 5 percent of the cost of media buying (2013: 16).
9 Axis Animation is a Glasgow-based company made up of digital designers and animators that work across games, commercials, television and film.
10 This is in line with a broader recognition amongst the advertising industry in the US of the importance of the multicultural market (Palacios 2013).
11 Miller et al. also give examples of the ways in which Hollywood movies have been positioned in different international markets (2001: 153).
12 The major Hollywood studios all have distribution offices in London. London is also home to a number of other international distributors, such as Studiocanal and Eros (see the Film Distributors' Association (2014)).
13 The smaller scale of the UK trailer industry also leads to less specialization within creative agencies and editors are more likely to work across a wider range of genres.
14 Frank Frumento (2013) claimed that while in LA clients can afford twenty-five to thirty revisions, in the UK it is more typical for a trailer to go through only four or five revisions.

15 The three books that make up *The Hunger Games* trilogy were released by Scholastic between 2008 and 2010. The first movie, *The Hunger Games*, was released by Lionsgate in April 2012 and was followed by *The Hunger Games: Catching Fire* in November 2013. The final book is being adapted into two films, *The Hunger Games: Mockingjay Part 1* and *Part 2*, to be released in 2014 and 2015 respectively.

16 *The Hunger Games: Catching Fire* was the highest-grossing movie in the domestic market in 2013 (Box Office Mojo 2013b) and the third highest worldwide (Box Office Mojo 2013). *The Hunger Games* was the third-highest-grossing movie in the domestic box office market in 2012 (Box Office Mojo 2012) and the ninth highest worldwide (Box Office Mojo 2012a).

17 Caldwell (2008) makes a similar argument about the role of extras on the DVD, and it seems that with the decline of DVD sales, online promotion is providing an alternative outlet for these materials.

18 For example, a link to purchase tickets to the movie was accompanied by a reminder that all citizens are required by law to watch the Hunger Games.

19 This is reiterated across the promotional infrastructure for the franchise with, for example, the 'Capitol TV' YouTube channel (which shows trailers, clips and television spots) including a 'District Citizen Reel' in which user-generated videos tagged with CapitolTV can appear.

20 *The Hunger Games: Catching Fire* was released on different dates in each territory with, for example, the film opening in the UK on 21 November, but in the US and Canada on 22 November.

21 While this chapter has focused on *The Hunger Games* franchise, each of the top ten movies in 2013 in terms of box office gross had a promotional infrastructure that offered viewers a range of different ways of interacting with the movie, yet where the trailer occupied a prominent place. The range, extent and form of the promotional infrastructure did, however, vary from movie to movie.

Bibliography

Allen, M. (2009) 'Digital Cinema: Virtual Screens', in G. Creeber and R. Martin (eds) *Digital Cultures*, Maidenhead: Open University Press.

Baker-Whitelaw, G. (2013) '"Capitol Cuties" Mocks CoverGirl for Missing the Point of "The Hunger Games"', *The Daily Dot*, 4 December. Online. Available: http://www.dailydot.com/ (accessed 18 January 2014).

Beri, S. (2012) *Interview with authors*, 26 October.

Box Office Mojo (2012) '2012 Domestic Grosses'. Online. Available: http://boxofficemojo.com/yearly/chart/?yr=2012&p=.htm (accessed 20 November 2014).

——(2012a) '2012 Worldwide Grosses'. Online. Available: http://boxofficemojo.com/yearly/chart/?view2=worldwide&yr=2012&p=.htm (accessed 20 November 2014).

——(2013) '2013 Worldwide Grosses'. Online. Available: http://www.boxofficemojo.com/yearly/chart/?view2=worldwide&yr=2013&p=.htm (accessed 18 January 2014).

——(2013a) 'Box Office by Studio: Lionsgate'. Online. Available: http://boxofficemojo.com/studio/chart/?view2=allmovies&studio=lionsgate.htm (accessed 18 January 2014).

——(2013b) 'Yearly Box Office'. Online. Available: http://www.boxofficemojo.com/yearly/ (accessed 18 January 2014).

Brooker, W. (2009) 'Television Out of Time: Watching Cult Shows on Download', in R. Pearson (ed.) *Reading Lost: Perspectives on a Hit Television Show*, London: I. B. Tauris.

Brookey, R. A. (2010) *Hollywood Gamers: Digital Convergence in the Film and Video Game Industries*, Bloomington: Indiana University Press.

Caldwell, J. T. (2008) *Production Culture: Industrial Self-Reflexivity and Critical Practice in Film and Television*, Durham: Duke University Press.

——(2005) 'Welcome to the Viral Future of Cinema (Television)', *Cinema Journal*, 45 (1): 90–97.

Carlson, R. and Corliss, J. (2011) 'Imagined Commodities: Video Game Localization and Mythologies of Cultural Difference', *Games and Culture*, 6 (1): 61–82.

Drake, P. (2008) 'Distribution and Marketing in Contemporary Hollywood', in P. McDonald and J. Wasko (eds) *The Contemporary Hollywood Film Industry*, Oxford: Wiley-Blackwell.

Durrani, A. (2013) 'Mail Online and Guardian Lead Record Highs for Newspaper Sites in January', *Media Week*, 22 February. Online. Available: http://www.mediaweek.co.uk/article/1171927/mail-online-guardian-lead-record-highs-newspaper-sites-january (accessed 21 January 2014).

Film Distributors' Association (2014) *Links page*. Online. Available: http://www.launchingfilms.com/links/ (accessed 29 August 2014).

Film Trailer Reviews (2014) *Film Trailer Reviews*. Online. Available: http://filmtrailerreviews.com (accessed 29 August 2014).

Frumento, F. (2013) *Interview with authors*, 3 December.

Gerbrandt, L. (2010) 'Does Movie Marketing Matter?', *The Hollywood Reporter*, 6 October. Online. Available: http://www.hollywoodreporter.com/news/does-movie-marketing-matter-24514 (accessed 14 January 2014).

Goldsmith, B., Ward, S. and O'Regan, T. (2010) *Local Hollywood*, Queensland: Queensland University Press.

Grainge, P. (2008) *Brand Hollywood: Selling Entertainment in a Global Media Age*, London and New York: Routledge.

Gray, J. (2010) *Show Sold Separately: Promos, Spoilers and Other Media Paratexts*, New York: New York University Press.

Heritage, S. (2014) *Trailer Review* website. Online. Available: http://www.theguardian.com/film/series/trailer-review (accessed 29 August 2014).

Holliday, C. (2013) 'Footage Not Included: Pixar Animation Studios, Teaser Trailers and the Pleasurable Absence of Content', paper delivered at *Titles, Teasers and Trailers* conference, University of Edinburgh, 22–23 April.

Jenkins, H., Ford, S. and Green, J. (2013) *Spreadable Media: Creating Value and Meaning in a Networked Culture*, New York: New York University Press.

Johnson, D. (2013) *Media Franchising: Creative License and Collaboration in the Culture Industries*, New York: New York University Press.

——(2012) 'Cinematic Destiny: Marvel Studios and the Trade Stories of Industrial Convergence', *Cinema Journal*, 52 (1): 1–24.

Johnston, K. M. (2013) 'Interviews', *Frames Cinema Journal*, 3 May. Online. Available: http://framescinemajournal.com/?issue=issue3 (accessed 21 January 2014).

——(2009) *Coming Soon: Film Trailers and the Selling of Hollywood Technology*, Jefferson: McFarland.

Jung, S. (2011) 'K-pop, Indonesian Fandom, and Social Media', *Transformative Works and Cultures*, 8. Online. Available: http://journal.transformativeworks.org/index.php/twc/article/view/289 (accessed 21 January 2014).

Kaufman, A. (2012) 'Here's the 6 Reasons Why You Don't Know More About VOD Numbers', *Indiewire*, 4 April. Online. Available: http://www.indiewire.com/article/heres-the-6-reasons-why-you-dont-know-more-about-vod-numbers?page=1#articleHeaderPanel (accessed 12 August 2014).

Kehe, J. and Palmer, K. M. (2013) 'The Art of the Trailer', *Wired*, 18 June. Online. Available: http://www.wired.com/2013/06/art-of-movie-trailer/ (accessed 12 August 2014).

Kernan, L. (2004) *Coming Attractions: Reading American Movie Trailers*, Austin: University of Texas Press.

Kerrigan, F. (2010) *Film Marketing*, Oxford: Butterworth.

Lionsgate (2014) 'Lionsgate Company'. Online. Available: http://www.lionsgate.com/corporate/company/ (accessed 12 August 2014).

——(2013) 'Lionsgate Grosses Over a Billion Dollars at the Domestic Box Office and Another Billion Dollars Internationally For the Second Year in a Row'. Online. Available: http://www.lionsgate.com/corporate/press-releases/1561/ (accessed 18 January 2014).

McClintock, P. (2014) '$200 Million and Rising: Hollywood Struggles With Soaring Marketing Costs', *The Hollywood Reporter*, 31 July. Online. Available: http://www.hollywoodreporter.com/news/200-million-rising-hollywood-struggles-721818?mobile_redirect=false (accessed 12 August 2014).

McDonald, P. (2008) 'Britain: Hollywood, UK', in P. McDonald and J. Wasko (eds) *The Contemporary Hollywood Film Industry*, Oxford: Wiley-Blackwell.

Maltese, R. (2013) 'Catching Fire and the Most Unsettling Sandwich Advertising Campaign Ever', *Letters from Titan*, 30 November. Online. Available: http://lettersfromtitan.com/2013/11/30/catching-fire-and-the-most-unsettling-sandwich-advertising-campaign-ever/ (accessed 21 January 2014).

Marchand, A. and Hennig-Thurau, T. (2013) 'Value Creation in the Video Game Industry: Industry Economics, Consumer Benefits, and Research Opportunities', *Journal of Interactive Marketing*, 27 (3): 141–157. Online. Available: http://www.sciencedirect.com/science/article/pii/S1094996813000170 (accessed 21 January 2014).

Marich, R. (2013) *Marketing to Moviegoers: A Handbook of Strategies and Tactics*, 3rd edition, Carbondale and Edwardsville: Southern Illinois Press.

Miller, T., Govil, N., McMurria, J. and Maxwell, R. (2001) *Global Hollywood*, London: British Film Institute.

MPAA (2012) 'Theatrical Market Statistics 2012'. Online. Available: http://www.mpaa.org/wp-content/uploads/2014/03/2012-Theatrical-Market-Statistics-Report.pdf (accessed 20 November 2014).

O'Donnell, C. (2012) 'The North American Game Industry', in P. Zackariasson and T. L. Wilson (eds) *The Video Game Industry: Formation, Present State and Future*, London and New York: Routledge.

Ostrow, A. (2012) 'Ridley Scott's "Prometheus" Teased in TEDTalk from the Future', *Mashable*, 28 February. Online. Available: http://mashable.com/2012/02/28/prometheus-tedtalk-video/ (accessed 11 August 2014).

Palacios, S. (2013) 'Know the Multicultural Market and You'll Know the Key to Digital Success', *Ad Age*, 22 April. Online. Available: http://adage.com/article/the-big-tent/multicultural-consumers-hold-key-digital-success/241039/ (accessed 18 January 2014).

Pantozzi, J. (2013) 'Hunger Games Author Weighs In On Catching Fire Marketing', *The Mary Sue*, 18 November. Online. Available: http://www.themarysue.com/collins-hunger-games-marketing/ (accessed 20 November 2014).

Russo, J. L. (2009) 'User-Penetrated Content: Fan Video in the Age of Convergence', *Cinema Journal*, 48 (4): 125–30.

Schatz, T. (2008) 'The Studio System and Conglomerate Hollywood', in P. McDonald and J. Wasko (eds) *The Contemporary Hollywood Film Industry*, Oxford: Wiley-Blackwell.

Sexton, K. (2013) *Interview with authors*, 29 November.

Siwek, S. E. (2010) 'Video Games in the 21st Century: The 2010 Report', Entertainment Software Association. Online. Available: http://www.theesa.com/facts/pdfs/Video Games21stCentury_2010.pdf (accessed 18 January 2014).

Stern, D. (2012) *Interview with authors*, 13 November.

Thompson, K. (2008) *The Frodo Franchise: The Lord of the Rings and Modern Hollywood*, Berkeley: University of California Press.

Tornoe, J. (2013) 'This Is the Latino Community's Time – and It's About More Than Immigration', *The Guardian Online*, 21 June. Online. Available: http://www.theguar dian.com/commentisfree/2013/jun/21/latino-population-growth-united-states (accessed 18 January 2014).

Tryon, C. (2013) *On-demand Culture: Digital Delivery and the Future of Movies*, New Brunswick: Rutgers University Press.

——(2010) *Reinventing Cinema: Movies in the Age of Media Convergence*, New Brunswick: Rutgers University Press.

Vesey, A. (2013) 'Reading Between the Lines: Gender and Viral Marketing', *Cinema Journal*, 53 (1): 144–49.

Wroot, J. (2013) 'DVD Special Features and Stage Greetings: Whose Promotional Material Is It Anyway?', *Frames Cinema Journal*, 3. Online. Available: http://frames cinemajournal.com/?issue=issue3 (accessed 21 January 2014).

Zackariasson, P. and Wilson, T. L. (2012) 'Marketing of Video Games', in P. Zack-ariasson and T. L. Wilson (eds) *The Video Game Industry: Formation, Present State and Future*, London and New York: Routledge.

6 Events and Spaces
Digital Animation and Experiential Design

As a global media event, the 2008 Beijing Olympics provided China with a unique opportunity to promote itself as a nation. Following China's entry into the World Trade Organization in 2001, and a series of reforms aimed at opening the country to global cultural and economic markets, the Olympics became a means for China to project itself as modern and progressive. A sense of 'brand new China' (Wang 2008) was framed in no small part around the possibilities of digital technology. With the Chinese computer manufacturer Lenovo becoming a first-tier Olympic sponsor, and the Chinese Ministry of Information rushing to launch a new 3G mobile service in time for the Games, the Beijing Olympics offered 'the potential to send crucial messages to domestic and international audiences about China's ability to be both a technological pioneer and a producer of reliable technology' (Humphreys and Finlay 2008: 286). Companies like Lenovo and China Mobile were central to this message in corporate brand terms, promoting China's investment in computing and mobile services. However, the new media *look* of the Beijing Games, expressed most dramatically in the opening ceremony, was suggestive of a different area of Chinese technical and creative development at the turn of the twenty-first century – digital design.

Digital imaging was a distinguishing feature of the way that the Beijing Games were visualized as a global television spectacle. This included showpiece effects such as a digital scroll that unfurled in the centre of the Bird's Nest stadium during the opening ceremony on the biggest floor screen ever produced, an array of graphics that appeared on the ribbon screen atop the stadium in the largest circular projection ever attempted, and a dazzling firework display that was digitally 'faked' for broadcast television to ensure the ceremony's final moment of visual magnificence. Other digital forms created for the Beijing Olympics included 300 computer-generated Fuwa mascot animations and an extensive library of motion graphics accompanying individual Olympic disciplines. The company responsible for this work was a digital media firm based in the Haidian District of Beijing called Crystal CG. Providing digital design services across a range of media forms and texts, Crystal's history is aligned with a key period of Chinese creative industry development during the 1990s and 2000s. In this period, the Beijing Games provided a major platform for creative display and reputation building at both national and industry levels, providing a showcase for China's (and Crystal's) investment in digital media innovation. According to Li Wuwei, one of the principal architects of Chinese creative industry policy, Crystal's work for the opening ceremony was the very embodiment of 'China's creativity on the world stage' (Li 2011: 7).

So far, we have focused on Western companies that specialize in the production of promotional screen content for telecommunication firms, television broadcasters and film studios. This chapter uses Crystal to explore how the promotional screen industries can be analyzed beyond these regional and medium-specific contexts. Crystal has worked on a range of promotional projects for corporate, media and government clients around the world. In this final chapter, we use Crystal to open out perspectives on the promotional screen industries, moving beyond examples of mobile, television and film promotion to explore promotional screen forms designed for context-specific events and spaces. In doing so, the chapter demonstrates how any understanding of the promotional screen industries must extend beyond the confines, and companies, of Europe and North America. Indeed, if promotional screen design has yet to be fully explored as a sector of the creative industries, the role of East Asian companies in this field has barely been considered at all.

Crystal's breadth of work, from corporate promotional videos to large-scale projects for the Shanghai Expo and both the Beijing and London Olympics, brings into focus what William Boddy calls 'nondomestic reception sites' for promotional communication (2011: 76). This is a varied field of screen practice and has given rise to specialist industry subsectors. For example, Boddy examines the growth of the 'out-of-home' advertising market and the digital signage industry.[1] This includes the promotional use of video screens 'located in airport lounges, medical offices, sports venues, retail locations, and even site-specific services like the health club, grocery store, and elevator networks' (ibid.: 82). While billboard and point of sale advertising is nothing new, developments in digital technology in the mid- to late-2000s led to the growth and consolidation of the out-of-home advertising industry. In particular the market for digital signage was 'transformed by the rapidly falling costs of displays, the increasing use of networked programming, and the ability to offer interactive features' (ibid.: 83). Boddy outlines a range of companies in this sector, from those selling TV programming and advertising in locations such as taxis, petrol stations, pharmacies and car dealerships, to those responsible for the installation of large video screens in such places as London's Underground. While Boddy notes that the digital outdoor market is modest in terms of revenue, representing less than 2 percent of what is spent on network television advertising, it nevertheless represents a means of pursuing media audiences 'who are seen as increasingly fragmented, peripatetic and resistant to traditional mass media advertising' (ibid.). Within his account of mobile digital culture, nondomestic reception sites provide a key space where the 'new strategic imperatives of ubiquity, mobility and interactivity' are worked out.

Out-of-home media makes promotional use of spaces where people shop, eat, travel and gather. The context-specific nature of this media extends the discussion of the promotional screen industries beyond the production of branded entertainment, television promos and film trailers to other kinds of promotional design. If we take by way of example the 'context' of a long-haul flight – a potentially monotonous succession of captive spaces – the range of promotional screen encounters might include anything from interactive advertising shown in airport lounges, waiting rooms and washrooms, to useful media such as the safety videos shown on airline seat-back screens (Govil 2004). According to Will Case (2012), who animated the safety films for British Airways and was formerly the Executive Creative Director of Crystal's London office, these videos serve a calculated promotional function; safety films deliver information in a specific viewing context and are a point where consumers are 'touching a brand'. Promotional texts can take many forms and appear on various types of screen. As well as entertaining or ambient media (McCarthy 2001) produced for media and consumer brands, the work of the promotional screen industries can also include corporate media such as industry films and presentational videos that visualize projects and objects to potential investors. These promotional forms are used in business-to-business contexts and are produced for clients that are as likely to be architects or car manufacturers as networks and studios.

As specialists in computer-generated graphics and 3D animation, companies such as Crystal work on both out-of-home and corporate projects, producing computer-generated (CG) sequences as a key promotional tool. Analysing the 'computerization of audiovisual culture' at the beginning of the twenty-first century, Leon Gurevitch considers the specific promotional value of the computer-generated image, and suggests that CG special effects are now interchangeably deployed in adverts, Hollywood films and industrial promotional videos as 'digital attractions' (2010). Crystal is a purveyor of digital attractions; it has carried out digital imaging, post-production and multimedia work for automobile brands (Toyota, VW, Nissan), sports organizations (FIFA, Formula 1), television programmes (CCTV, BBC), films (specifically 3D special effects work), and for companies and government agencies staging live presentations and events. Positioning itself at 'the new frontiers of visual communication' (Crystal 2011b), Crystal's role as a promotional intermediary is based on its blend of creativity, technology and R&d in the digital field, partnering with other companies (ad agencies, film and TV studios, stadium companies, consumer brands) to create bespoke visual/promotional content for media within and beyond the home. Rather than develop brand campaigns, Crystal is largely project-driven and has a particular stake and reputation in 'spectaculars', the company's name for one-off ceremonies and events.

This chapter uses one of these spectaculars, the London 2012 Olympic and Paralympic Games, as a platform for analysing the production of promotional screen media that both surround live events and integrate into physical and media space. Based on its experience and delivery of work for the Beijing Games, Crystal was appointed 'Digital Imaging Services Supplier' of the London Olympics in 2007, and produced media ranging from fly-through CG animations and mascot films to stadium-based pixel animations for the opening and closing ceremonies. This provides a rich case study for exploring digital screen design, and the companies and creative work that support media events. First, extending the discussion of global and local exchanges in Chapter 5, the chapter examines how Crystal developed within and between the creative industry contexts of Beijing and London, and established itself as an agent of (Chinese) creative production within local and global image markets. Second, it considers Crystal's 'visualization', 'CG animation' and 'experiential' work for London 2012, and the promotional function this work assumed in helping to construct the address (and popular imagination) of the Games as the first 'digital Olympics'. Finally, the chapter considers the business of 'experience design', and the particular means by which events and spaces have become a site of promotional activity and screen expertise. Expanding the purview of promotional design, this chapter extends the questions that are central to any study of the promotional screen industries – what do we understand as promotion? And what do we understand as a screen?

'Created in China': digital design and the case of Crystal CG

In his study of creative industry development in China during the first decade of the twenty-first century, Michael Keane (2007) provides a detailed account of the cultural and structural challenges that would accompany a policy and brand shift in the 2000s, captured in the slogan 'From Made in China to Created in China'. This phrase took hold in 2006 after a series of policy forums held in Shanghai and Beijing on the Chinese cultural industries, and was associated with reforms designed to stimulate innovation rather than simply low-cost manufacturing as a source of productivity. Specifically, the slogan underscored the rehabilitation of 'creativity' as a signifier of cultural and economic progress, and of China's aspiration 'to be a serious contender for the spoils of the global cultural and service economies' (ibid.: 11). In policy terms, Keane points out that 'the provenance of the changes that would eventually sweep China was the UK Creative Industries Task Force' (ibid.: 80). This body represented New Labour's attempt in the late 1990s to give value to sectors such as advertising, architecture, arts and antiques, design, film, music, performing arts, publishing, software, new media, television and radio, and to connect these sectors to a rhetoric of enterprise and export development. During the 2000s, policy discourse emanating from the UK, which gained traction internationally, would influence a series of Chinese reforms aimed at developing the creative industries as a site of cultural and economic value. The development of Crystal CG can be set in this context. Before analysing the promotional work of Crystal as China's largest digital media company, it is necessary to establish the industrial context in which the company emerged and internationalized its operations. This connects our discussion to global developments in the promotional screen industries.

Established in 1995, Crystal was initially a specialist in architectural 3D visualization, its business wholly focused on the property sector. However, in 2001 Crystal was officially designated by the Beijing Olympic Bid Committee

(BOCOG) as its 3D Graphic Provider, tasked with producing promotion animation for the Beijing Olympic bid and helping government departments, artists and architects to develop 3D presentations of Olympic venues. This led to the company's diversification, Crystal providing digital imaging support to a range of other industry sectors and becoming a key supplier of visual effects and interactive digital media for live events, advertising and broadcast entertainment. In 2006, Crystal became the official 'Graphic Design Services Supplier' for the Beijing Games, undertaking 120 projects for BOCOG including films, event presentations, interactive media, exhibitions and Olympic mascots. The culmination of this relationship was the digital realization of the opening and closing ceremonies, a 290-strong creative team at Crystal working in close collaboration with Zhang Yimou to provide 3D simulations of the film director's vision of the ceremonies, including sixty minutes of unique digital content.

In business terms, Crystal's rapid growth in the 2000s was tied to the catalyzing force of the Beijing Olympics. More broadly, however, it was linked to the incorporation of the cultural and creative industries into municipal planning, especially marked in the mega-cities of Shanghai and Beijing (Hui 2006, Keane 2011). In Beijing, this involved the designation of ten infrastructural bases or clusters to support sectors such as publishing, news, design, advertising, software, and radio, television and film. Among these was the Zhongguancum Creative Industries Leading Base in the Haidian District of the city. Established in May 2005, Zhongguancum was established to provide a modern high-tech base for cultural industries and would become home to a wide range of digital media companies, internet-based industries, digital software enterprises, and cartoon and animation incubators. Crystal occupies several floors of the China Foreign Language Mansion within this district. Entering Crystal's offices, one is immediately struck by the sleek white-walled lounge, hi-tech screening space, corridors displaying graphic work, and the population of cool young creatives. Every inch the contemporary design space, Crystal is emblematic of the high-tech company spearheading China's digital design ambitions.

At the time of our fieldwork, Crystal employed 3,500 staff and had fourteen offices, including a number of Chinese hubs and international offices in London, Tokyo, Dubai, Hong Kong, Singapore and Los Angeles. It also ran an extensive educational programme in China, with seven digital education facilities training 16,000 students a year. In its own words, 'Crystal CG is a driving force for innovation and a rich source of expertise in 2D, 3D and animated digital imagery. We build collaborative partnerships to achieve extraordinary results – and have the global capability to deliver fast and cost-effectively' (Crystal 2011a). These technical and organizational attributes are geared to support five main industry sectors which the company describes as follows:

Property – architectural 3D visualizations to support design competitions, marketing campaigns and planning submissions.
Sport – to enhance sports marketing, promotion and presentation for sports organizations, sponsors and broadcasters.

Media and Events – visual effects and interactive digital media for events, advertising and broadcast entertainment.

Corporate – advanced digital imagery for corporate communication events, promotions and blended learning.

Public Sector – hyper-realistic virtual scenarios to help secure funding, raise awareness and gain approval.

(ibid.)

In pitching itself to clients, Crystal offers three main digital services that relate to the field of promotional communication – 'digital visualization' (describing the simulation of real environments using 3D graphics), 'film/animation' (referring to computer-generated characterization and animated effects), and 'experiential' (meaning the development of user experiences in physical and digital space). These services are underpinned by forms of technological and creative innovation that are suggestive of China's attempt to recalibrate its reputation as a low-cost manufacturing giant. The case of film/animation is indicative here. The outsourcing of cheap animation work to China is well told; the country remains a key destination for offshore production, with a significant amount of animation rendering for Western and Japanese studios carried out in Chinese animation 'factories'. However, Ted Tchang and Andrea Goldstein (2004) note that 3D animation was outsourced far less in the early 2000s. This was due in part to the complexity of 3D processes at companies such as Pixar but also to the lack of maturity in the global 3D industry. It is precisely in response to this lack of market maturity that Crystal staked a creative claim in 3D image development. In 2007, Crystal established the Beijing Crystal Film, TV and Media Technologies Co. as a branch of the larger company, positioning itself as 'one of the few CG companies in Asia which are able to do R&d, design and production of international-level 3D animations, film and TV special effects, documentaries and promos' (Crystal 2011c). In short, Crystal sought to associate itself with high-value CG production rather than low-cost animation rendering.

According to Li Wuwei, a senior Chinese policy advisor and Director of the Shanghai Creative Industries Association, the creative industries represent an alternative development model for the nation, China having 'vast potential in the high-value-added creative economy' (2011: 21). He observed that between 2006 and 2009, even in the midst of an economic downturn, China's creative enterprises had achieved average revenue growth of 60 percent and had become pillar industries in cities like Shanghai and Beijing. Notably, 'design services' experienced the biggest annual growth in 2009 (14 percent) with 'advertising and exhibition' (8 percent) and 'animation' (7 percent) also classified as high-growth creative industries (CIDA 2009). According to Li, China's economic development relies on raising productivity through industrial innovation and the commercialization of intellectual property.[2] Crystal is in many ways defining of the 'Made in China to Created in China' moniker on these terms – it is based in a key creative cluster in Beijing, sells proprietary technological and creative expertise in a high-tech field, and is increasingly positioned to compete in local and global markets.

As well as 3D animation, Crystal's proprietary imaging skills focus on 'digital visualization' and 'experiential'; it provides high-tech specialization in dynamic CG imagery and interactive virtual reality. This forms the basis of projects ranging from corporate promotional work at trade shows to major art exhibits at world Expos. In the latter case, one of Crystal's signature works after the Beijing Olympics was the interactive screen spectacle *Riverside Scene at Qingming Festival*, a huge animated mural of an ancient Chinese painting, paid for by Crystal and the Chinese government. This became the centrepiece of the China pavilion at the Shanghai Expo in 2010 and was later displayed at the Asia World-Expo in Hong Kong in 2010 and at exhibition domes in Macau, Taipei and Singapore. Crystal transformed the ancient painting, which depicts bustling urban and river life during the Song Dynasty, into a giant 3D animation. Measuring 130 metres long and 6 metres high, the digital version has moving characters and objects that are portrayed in a four-minute day-to-night cycle. Like the digital scroll at the Olympic opening ceremony, this exhibition piece served to promote Chinese cultural history and creativity on an international stage. In a series of ways Crystal's digital work dovetailed in the 2000s with efforts by the Chinese Communist Party to refresh its national image and build 'cultural soft power' (Li 2011: 23–4). The 'what' of screen promotion relates in this context not to the selling of entertainment media but to the promotion of a certain kind of national identity in which cutting-edge digital technology is applied to specific historical cultural forms.

As well as projecting the image of China internationally in the late 2000s, Crystal's digital expertise was at the same time sold to Western brands and corporate organizations. Significant to the company's global market positioning in this respect was the opening of the company's new office in London in 2007. This followed Crystal's having been awarded the contract of 'Digital Imaging Services Supplier' for the London 2012 Games. This was a symbolic move on a number of fronts, not least in that it placed Crystal in one of the world's design capitals. Breaking into the London media market was at the heart of Crystal's wider international growth strategy, and was seen to require careful steps. Terry Flew has argued that

> the internationalization strategies of large media companies need to be subjected to more empirical analysis to better understand the motivations that underpin international expansion, the relative success of these strategies, the relationships that emerge with nation-states of the host countries, and the effectiveness of the competition they face from local incumbents.
>
> (2011: 100)

While Flew is concerned with large multinational corporations, Crystal's entry into the London market points to the ground-level challenges of international expansion for media companies. It is worth briefly outlining Crystal's hub in London for it helps us think about two related issues – the logistics of delivering promotional work for an event on the scale of the Olympics and what 'Created in China' meant in the particular case of London 2012. In different ways, much like Create Advertising in Chapter 5, Crystal London provides a lens on the organizational dynamics that underlie the globalization of media production.

For Gilles Albaredes, former managing director of Crystal CG International, moving to London brought with it a set of 'guiding principles' for business. These involved recruiting local expertise, taking time to understand market dynamics, 'privileging strategic initiatives over aggressive commercial moves', and 'nurturing initiatives by adding value to the local communities' (cited in Sherwood 2010). Rather than deploy a Chinese management team, Crystal CG International effectively comported itself as a European business, employing twenty-five mostly British and European staff, and later renaming itself 'Crystal London'. Although half of its production work would be realized in China, Crystal CG International sought to move away from an offshore business model in order to sell digital visual expertise to Western organizations. Together with images and animations to assist in the planning and communication of London 2012, this included projects for clients ranging from Cisco, Intel and the BBC to London's Greenwich Council.

Despite the company's guiding principles, the spectre of Chinese outsourcing would nevertheless attach itself to Crystal. This was evident in early press coverage of Crystal's promotional work for London 2012, in particular its CG animation of the mascots Wenlock and Mandeville. In May 2010, the UK tabloid the *Daily Express* reported 'the fury' of British animation companies at Olympic work being produced by a Chinese-owned firm (Pilditch 2010). This tapped into a wider set of concerns about the health and global competitiveness of the British animation industry, the lobby group Animation UK campaigning against the lack of available tax breaks in Britain to combat outsourcing. The animation of the Olympic mascots focused these issues onto questions about the British creative economy, prompting Paul Deighton, Chief Executive of the London Organising Committee of the Olympic and Paralympic Games (LOCOG), to affirm that Crystal had a London office and employed British workers. The tabloid spat about Wenlock and Mandeville continued a seam of incredulity in the UK press at London's Olympic branding efforts, combining dismissive descriptions of the mascots ('strange blob-like creations') with LOCOG's pur-ported failure to back UK industries. While the Olympic mascots were con-ceived by the London creative agency Iris, their digital animation crystallized, in more ways than one, debates about UK creative labour. Whereas for Animation UK, Crystal's involvement went against 'the spirit of the 2012 Olympics and the year of the Cultural Olympiad' (Pilditch 2010), for LOCOG it represented the fact that 'the Olympic Games and Paralympic Games are global events, which attract global interest from businesses' (Deighton 2010).

In the production of promotional media, the Beijing and London Olympics demonstrate the cultural and work flows of the global creative industries. While the visual identity of the London Olympics was shaped by China's largest digital media company, the television branding of the Beijing Olympics was created for Chinese audiences by the London-based digital and communications company Red Bee Media (discussed in Chapters 2 and 4), the latter producing the opening title sequence for the Olympic programming of the Chinese state broadcaster CCTV.[3] In business terms, the Olympics were an opportunity for both Red Bee and Crystal to expand their regional client bases. For Crystal, in particular, this would involve significant co-exchange between the Beijing and London offices. It is necessary to understand the nuances of this relationship as they complicate theories of the 'international division of cultural labour' (Miller et al. 2005) that tend to associate China with outsourcing. While an increasing amount of 3D post-production work is bought in media capitals like London and Los Angeles and then carried out in China and India,[4] the tender for 3D effects and animation contracts is not always economically determined.

According to Will Case, the Executive Creative Director of Crystal London until 2013, Crystal won the tender for London 2012 for two principal reasons – because of the company's previous experience undertaking large-scale Olympic work and because it had the financial and production resources to undertake multiple projects at once. The opening and closing ceremonies alone involved forty subdivided projects totalling fourteen hours of animation content. These were produced alongside thirty minutes of mascot films, thirty-six minutes of performance visuals, 264 minutes of sports presentations, and the animation of twenty-six CG 'fly-throughs'. In creative terms these projects were led by Crystal London, combining small teams of art directors, animators, illustrators and technologists. To meet the logistical and infrastructural demands of this work, especially the volume of animation required for the four Olympic and Para-lympic opening/closing ceremonies, Crystal London supplemented its core staff with thirty-five freelance designers and bought the largest render file in the city. However, Crystal London also sent project work to Beijing in line with established company practice. Case commented, 'We've used their production facilities, their production workforce, and their engine room, as we like to call it, to help us deliver the work, because they can turn it round quicker and actually have got the pipeline to do it' (2012). As well as work for the ceremonies, CG mascot films were made in a matter of weeks using this pipeline, the creative story-boarding carried out in London and production work completed in Beijing. According to Albaredes, the mascot films involved fifty designers, at some points working seventy-two hours without sleep to meet LOCOG's deadline (2012). This, of course, raises pointed questions about the nature of digital design work and the demands of an industry sector that often requires long hours, and where new technologies and forms of design management have served to hasten, routi-nize and audit creative work (Julier and Moor 2009). In terms of delivering the scale of work required for the Olympics, LOCOG appointed Crystal for its track record at Beijing 2008 but also because of its status as a production powerhouse.

And yet, it would be a mistake to see Crystal CG simply as a production engine room. Not only has the company developed a wide portfolio of creative work for companies and organizations that operate in the Chinese market, but the growth of Crystal's London office – a small but significant satellite until it was scaled back after the Games – suggests ways in which creative processes have been shared between different parts of the company. For Case, Crystal Beijing is traditionally production-led in its approach; it functions according to work protocols where account directors and salesmen run projects, as opposed to creative directors and producers. Between 2007 and 2013, Crystal London occupied the role of 'a naughty brother' in this context. It was small, relatively autonomous and was positioned as a 'creative hub' in the company's global structure. Attuned to the language of Western brand marketing, the function of the London office was to get Western clients to 'buy into [Crystal's] creative services slightly differently' (Case 2012). However, the office would also assist on project work in China as Crystal Beijing, like the Chinese advertising industry more generally, embraced account business oriented towards brands (Wang 2008). In one sense, Crystal London's role was to educate and add value to the creative identity of the larger company as it sought to compete for brand business in local and global markets. While the severity of this competition saw Crystal CG reduce its workforce by 20 percent in 2013 – reducing its Beijing-based film, TV and media division and leaving just one intra-company liaison officer in London – Case described a host of creative opportunities that came about through working with Beijing during his tenure at the company. This relates not only to the scale of projects that came through the Beijing office but also to questions of creative outlook. Commenting in 2012, he said, 'we have got a lot to learn' from China's lack of scepticism when it comes to realizing promotional ideas and design projects, noting 'they just do it, I mean they'll work out a way of doing it, they haven't got that cynicism that we sometimes have, and I think they're much more prepared to try different things' (Case 2012). Moreover, Case would note 'there's a fascinating cool underground scene in China of design, fascinating, beautiful stuff, and I'd love to tap into a bit more of it if I could' (ibid.). The example of Crystal CG moves the discussion of Chinese cultural production beyond simple notions of outsourcing. It also demonstrates the degree to which 'Created in China' is a fluid concept at the level of the firm. In critical terms, Crystal illustrates the progressively more complex conditions of the global media environment and the 'liquid' way that global production networks and translocal creative processes play out on an everyday basis (Deuze 2007: 233–42).

According to Crystal's founder, Lu Zhenggang, 'what is most exciting and unique about this industry is being able to integrate the charm of technology with artistic creativity and then to carry out commercial operations' (cited in Li 2011: 36). Crystal's work for the London Olympics was symbolic on these terms, and provides a means of examining the particular way in which the company's specialist expertise in digital visualization, CG animation and experiential design were put to work. As can be seen from the five-point list of industry sectors that Crystal serves, mentioned earlier, sport is a locus of promotional design. This can range from the development of virtual advertising where digital billboards are inserted onto stadia and the surface of pitches, to multimedia technologies used to enhance sports viewing and analysis (Boddy 2004). The Olympic

Games provides a key platform for sports broadcasters to demonstrate their competitive edge in visual and graphic coverage and it is here that media design firms such as Crystal sell technological and creative know-how. However, the Olympics can also provide host nations with the opportunity to promote their own relation to new media technology. This was marked in the case of the Beijing and London Olympics. In brand terms, the London Games were especially quick to incorporate a sense of 'digital' experience into the look and language of their Olympic identity, and Crystal's work, as we shall see, was central to the construction of this promotional address.

Animating the Olympics

The London 2012 Games have been described as the first 'digital Olympics' (Royal Television Society 2013). Staged in a media period marked by increasingly fast internet speeds, the mainstream adoption of mobile and smartphones, the growth of mobile video, and the ability to stream live sporting events through various web, IPTV and connected TV services, this claim was especially made in relation to media coverage. Significantly, the BBC, as host broadcaster of the main Games (Channel 4 was host broadcaster of the Paralympics), sought to create the first 'fully digital' Olympics by broadcasting, live streaming, and making available for catch-up every single Olympic event (BBC 2012). This included over 2,500 hours of content made available on terrestrial television, through twenty-four additional live digital channels (via the BBC's red-button interactive service and website), as well as on tablets and mobile phones. This generated enormous digital traffic, the BBC reporting 106 million requests for online video content during the Games (Garside 2012). Together with this display of the BBC's multiplatform capability came opportunities for LOCOG to connect the Games with the wider policy discourse of 'digital Britain' introduced in Chapter 3. In the year that saw the nationwide switchover from analogue to digital television in the UK, the Olympics provided a catalyst for realizing the technological and cultural potentialities of 'being digital' (Carter 2009: 7). This section examines how the work of Crystal CG amplified this digital discourse in screen terms, creating a series of promotional texts that helped situate and define the Games as taking place within a transformed, and transforming, media environment.

The Olympic Games are especially useful for analysing the promotional screen industries because they magnetize a huge array of promotional screen media. This media is developed and produced by the range of promotional intermediaries outlined in Chapter 2, from advertising and media agencies and television promotion companies to digital media specialists. As the official 'Digital Imaging Services Supplier' of the 2012 Olympics, Crystal became a key promotional screen intermediary of the London Games, LOCOG harnessing the company's three main areas of expertise in 'digital visualization', 'film/animation' and 'experiential'. We will discuss these in turn. Not only do they illustrate different types of graphic, animation and digital design work, they also bring to light sub-genres of promotional screen media that are deployed at different points and places in the lifespan and staging of a large-scale media event.

Digital visualization: bid videos, business-to-business ads and presentational media

Digital visualization is central to Crystal's design expertise and is suggestive of a whole area of corporate and organizational promotion that is largely unexplored within screen studies. Through its development and application of 3D graphics, Crystal has worked with corporate clients in various sectors to produce business presentations that use digital and multimedia technology to pre-visualize products, buildings and services. From manufacturing companies to real estate developers, corporate promotional videos often use 3D technology to visually imagine objects, projects and constructions in development. By Crystal's own account, the benefits of 3D technology lie in its graphic ability to vividly simulate real environments, to explain and give life to complex ideas, to identify potential cost-savings before projects begin, and to distinguish business presentations from those of competitors (Crystal 2012a). Within the field of digital visualization, Crystal sub-divides its market into 'business presentations' and 'architectural visualization'. Both of these involve the creation of promotional content that uses computer-graphic technology to sell products and designs to clients, investors and other stakeholders.

While much of Crystal's work in digital visualization is for manufacturing and architectural companies, sport brings together the particular needs of business presentation and architectural visualization. For example, in bidding to hold a global sporting event such as the Olympic Games or the soccer World Cup, prospective host nations invariably use promotional videos to sell themselves to officiating bodies such as the IOC (International Olympic Committee) or FIFA (Fédération Internationale de Football Association). Bid videos are an interesting promotional sub-genre in their own right and often rely on digital visualization technologies to imagine sites, stadia and event scenarios. Crystal has produced a number of these, including the Beijing Olympic bid video and both Russia and Qatar's bid videos to host the World Cup in 2018 and 2022 respectively. In each case, these promotional texts are between one and three minutes long and combine dynamic 360-degree views of proposed stadia with computer-generated fly-throughs of cities and venues. Crystal was not involved in the bid video for London 2012 but did create the first unified 3D model of the Olympic Park, from which it developed a number of 3D visualizations of London 2012 venues.

This formed the basis of short-form content ranging from promotional images to support planning applications to mobile applications and 'wayfinding content' that helped to navigate and plan spectator journeys at the Olympic Park. 3D Visualizations also formed the basis of interstitial material used in broadcast and online coverage of the Games, Crystal collaborating with the BBC to

Figure 6.1 Digital visualization of the Olympic stadium (2012). Courtesy of Crystal CG.

produce animated sequences of CG flights between selected venues, the Olympic Park, and major London and UK landmarks.

Leon Gurevitch argues that CG flights are a characteristic 'digital attraction'; in audiovisual terms they are deployed in both industrial films and Hollywood blockbusters to create a sense of visual pleasure and astonishment. Noting the equivalence between industrial promotional videos (those of architects, aerospace agencies, car manufacturers) and Hollywood effects sequences, he notes

> an almost generic similarity in form and style of shot designed to create maximum effect. In such cases, wide, extremely long aerial shots are used to track and pan over the subjects: often feats of human engineering involving ant-like crowds of people to provide a sense of vast scale.
>
> (2010: 381)

Gurevitch suggests that panoramic CG sequences 'transfer most easily to the logic of promotion and self-promotion' and are often used prominently in publicity and advertising materials (ibid.). In broadcast terms, Crystal's 'venue to venue' 3D visualizations served a calculated promotional function for the BBC, underscoring the digital look and feel that the host broadcaster sought to give more generally to its coverage of the Games. This interstitial aesthetic extended more widely as the animations were also licensed by Crystal to eleven international broadcasters, including NBC and CCTV. Within European, American and East Asian television markets, Crystal's CG work was used as a digital attraction, visually transporting viewers between venues (and TV segments) via seamless and spectacular aerial flights.[5]

Digital visualization and related forms of graphic animation were also deployed in business-to-business ads and presentational media. In the former case, Crystal produced a ninety-second film for Cisco, the 'official network infrastructure partner of London 2012' and the company responsible for providing the switches, access points, cable TV outlets, telephones and ports that underpinned the communications infrastructure of the Games. Seeking to capitalize on its status as a second-tier Olympic partner, Cisco used Crystal to visualize the UK's router infrastructure in a 'business-to-business' advert that employed digital graphics to visualize the movement of data between desktops, laptops, smartphones, landlines, tablets and cameras. These graphic animations helped narrate a story of network technology whereby a family watch and share the athletic victory of their son and news organizations picture and report the triumph. In a different application, LOCOG used Crystal's visualization and animation expertise to create a series of sports presentation and brand visuals that were used on big screens at Olympic venues and 'live sites' (twenty-two spaces in urban centres around the country for people to gather and watch events). At live sites, this included kits of animated idents and images tailored to the local region. For sports presentations, Crystal produced digital content ranging from countdown clocks and performance visuals to a three-minute animated sequence (set to the Chemical Brothers' song 'Velodrome') that played before every cycle track race. This last example depicted a futuristic cycling duel reminiscent of the film *Tron* (1982), and assumed a very deliberate new media aesthetic. Like the other presentational short-forms produced by Crystal, these animated sequences were designed to engage spectators and build atmosphere within site-specific contexts, bringing 'a new level of entertainment to the Olympic spectator' (Crystal 2012b).

Presentational media were a form of entertainment but also served a calculated brand function, synchronizing with the style and compositional agility of

Figure 6.2 The digital aesthetic of presentation animation: *Velodrome* (2012). Courtesy of Crystal CG.

the London 2012 logo. In aesthetic terms, the graffiti-style logo of the London Games was defined by a sense of play within its form and movement within media space.[6] Rather than use a single fixed image, typical of past Olympic logos, the London 2012 logo was designed to be mobile in its graphic iterations and ability to transport across media platforms. According to Paul Deighton, the logo was 'dynamic, modern and flexible, reflecting a brand-savvy world where people, especially young people, no longer relate to static logos' (cited in Culf 2007). This sense of mobility – or 'logomotion' to use a contemporaneous term by *Design Week* (2010) – informed the brand language of the Games. As an intermediary, Crystal helped articulate this language in visual terms, working with LOCOG to create a repertoire of promotional texts that would surround and give identity to the Olympics as a cultural and media event. Crystal's 'visualization' of Olympic venues, data networks and sports disciplines inscribed the Games with a particular digital aesthetic. This was given a more explicit narrative and semiotic significance in Crystal's second main area of Olympic design work – CG character animation.

Film/animation: mascot films

Like the London 2012 logo and its ability to transmute on screen, the Olympic mascots were geared for a multimedia existence, connecting in this case with children. Based on a short story by the British children's author Michael Morpurgo, the mascots were conceived, as previously mentioned, by the London creative agency Iris. Having rejected a host of designs at the open pitch process – ranging from anthropomorphic pigeons to animated teapots – LOCOG selected a design that for some observers 'resembled characters dreamed up for a Pixar animation' (Gibson 2010) and for others 'appear to be conjured from Japanese comic books and computer games' (Glancey 2010). Distinguished by a huge Cyclopean eye functioning as a camera lens, Wenlock and Mandeville were designed 'to reflect and adapt to their surroundings, changing their appearance depending on the situation' (Crystal 2010).[7] The camera-eye was central to the brand premise, enabling children to interact with them and follow their journeys around the UK through Twitter, Facebook and an obligatory website. Generating revenue through toy-licensing deals, the mascots were also designed to embody the digital address of the Olympics. While their alien look would lead to some very un-childlike descriptions within international media coverage – *Vanity Fair* calling Wenlock a 'ghoulish cycloptic phallus', the *Toronto Sun* describing the mascots as 'walking penis monsters' and Twitter postings labelling them 'terror sperm' (Planet Sport 2010) – Wenlock and Mandeville were a deliberate departure from the history of cuddly Olympic mascots first embodied by the cartoon bear Misha at the 1980 Moscow Olympics and carried through to Beijing's Fuwa mascots. Phallic fears notwithstanding, they assumed the appearance of high-tech toys born from (and for) a digital world.

It was Crystal's job to animate the mascots, visualizing a series of animated shorts that could be viewed online, on British children's broadcast channels

Figure 6.3 Wenlock and Mandeville, London 2012 mascots. Courtesy of Crystal CG.

such as CBBC, as well as in movie theatres. These would function as promotional paratexts leading up to the Games, and consisted of *Out of a Rainbow* (released in May 2010), *Adventures on a Rainbow* (March 2011), *Rainbow Rescue* (December 2011) *and Rainbow to the Games* (May 2012). Ranging between four and sixteen minutes long, these animations developed a narrative of the mascots' journey to the London Olympics, depicting their interaction with an ordinary UK family and a selection of British Olympic and Paralympic team members. Within Jonathan Gray's typology of media paratexts, these shorts functioned as 'entryway paratexts' to the London Olympics (2010: 35), promotional forms that, as we saw in the last two chapters, work to create meanings, expectations and forms of engagement around a text. Like the Hollywood franchise products examined in Chapter 5, the modern Olympics have developed an apparatus of trailers, posters, previews and hype that shape the interpretive process surrounding the Games – an occasion textually constituted within and between the opening and closing ceremonies. While Gray focuses on the paratextual creativity surrounding films and television shows, one might equally point to the production of paratexts that surround transmedia events such as the Olympic Games. As with bid videos, mascot films are an underexamined promotional sub-genre. Rather than pitch projects, these films develop images, characters and storyworlds in the build-up to sporting spectacles.

Unlike Crystal's Fuwa mascot animations for the Beijing Games which borrowed from the slower, meditative traditions of Chinese cel animation and brush painting, Crystal's mascot films for London 2012 would use cutting-edge CG techniques to give everyday British life a distinct digital aesthetic. In narrative terms, *Out of a Rainbow* tells the story of George, a steelworker in the industrial city of Bolton, who, on his retirement day, takes as a memento two droplets of cooled steel from the last girder of the Olympic stadium. Cycling home to his wife and grandchildren, George crafts the droplets into two steel figures to give as toys to the children. Through some mystical alchemy, these are brought to life by a rainbow, upon which the adventures of Wenlock and Mandeville begin. The first mascot film turns on a comic sequence in the children's attic room. Reminiscent of Pixar films like *Toy Story* (1995) and *Monsters, Inc.* (2001) where the child's bedroom becomes a site for animation slapstick, the mascots amuse the children by taking the shape of British gymnasts, boxers, divers and Paralympic athletes, as well as taking on the celebratory lightning pose of Usain Bolt. In their animation style, but also in metaphoric terms, Wenlock and Mandeville are emblems of the 'liquid' media life – fast, fluid, and subject to change – that Mark Deuze (2007) associates with work and play in the digital age. In their transformation from steel droplets to agile electronic creatures, the mascots function as a symbol of the transition between the world of heavy manufacturing and the promise of a new digital economy. While UK factories are figured as central to building the physical infrastructure of the Games, the *meaning* of the Olympics is vested in the mobile, data-driven world of the mascots. *Out of a Rainbow* ends with the mascots high-fiving and waving goodbye to the children as they jump from the attic window and run along a rainbow to 'tell' people about the Olympics coming to London.

The second film, *Adventures on a Rainbow*, develops the sense of digital interaction. Resuming the story, the two mascots return to Bolton and send a picture/text message to the grandchildren's mobile phone. The animated short then follows the journey of the mascots as they swoop over motorways and through market towns (again drawing on Crystal's specialism in CG aerial panoramas) to visit British Olympic team members in training. In each case, the mascots take a photo of the athlete using their camera-eye; the photo is then remediated and projected as a signed Kodak print. In the final scene, the mascots zoom across London, taking the form of Coldstream Guards and Beefeaters as the rainbow flies over Buckingham Palace, the Tower of London, Big Ben and the London Eye. Criss-crossing London's night sky, the film ends with an aerial shot of two rainbows moving like tracers over the twinkling lights of the British Isles, with the words 'to be continued'. These journeys would be followed by the release of *Rainbow Rescue and Rainbow to the Games*, the latter, running at sixteen minutes, even having its own trailer. These final animated shorts would develop a more explicit adventure narrative, Wenlock and Mandeville texting various British Olympians on their smartphones to ask for help to rebuild a storm-ravaged school library and to be rescued themselves from a container ship heading to Brazil.

These animated shorts would serve a specific promotional function in the UK, selling the Games as a participatory national event and identifying a diverse and youth-friendly selection of British Olympians as its sporting face. The shorts also, importantly, develop a narrative of media engagement, antici-pating the Olympics through mobile screens and social networking sites aimed specifically at children. In their cyclopic look and customizable design, Wenlock and Mandeville ministered to the market for quirky character animations developed by social networking websites like Moshi Monsters;[8] they were fun and mutable figures that invited children to interact with an 'Olympic journey' through virtual encounters and consumable merchandise. In both the CG animation of the mascots and the foregrounding of cameras and text messaging, the mascot films were forms of promotional screen content that reinforced the address of the Olympics to a generation habituated to digital technology and the sharing of data. Accordingly, each short finished with the mascots' web address where viewers could extend their involvement by uploading comments, videos and photos of their encounters with Wenlock and Mandeville, and find other opportunities to play games and make and display customized mascots.

In their creative design, the mascot films can be set within a recent tradition of Olympic promotional animation in the UK. By way of comparison, the BBC commissioned a 2D trailer called 'Monkey' four years before to promote and frame its coverage of the Beijing Olympics. Created by the pop star Damon Albarn and the graphic artist Jamie Hewlett, this work drew multiple influences from Chinese illustration, Japanese Manga, Western television and post-punk animation. If, as Karen Lury (2008) suggests, 'Monkey' offered itself as a 'cross-platform, cross-culture concept', Wenlock and Mandeville were similarly conceived, given the ability to move between media and incorporating national and international stylistic references. In a representational sense, the mascot films were steeped in familiar and exportable referents of 'Britishness' but were animated more in the tradition of anime than Aardman. This was partly the result of the multi-level collaboration taking place between British and Chinese creative personnel in producing the shorts, but it was also consistent with attempts to align the Games with popular cultural styles associated with a young, digital media generation.[9] The fact that Wenlock and Mandeville reminded critics of Pixar animations *and* Japanese comic book characters is not incidental; the mascot films would bear the hallmarks of both as CG reference points. While, for some, the mascots were 'appalling computurised smurfs for the iPhone generation' (Bayley 2010), the shorts would animate the London 2012 brand in ways that were designed to speak precisely *to* this generation. Selling itself as 'expert at delivering creative digital media solutions that captivate and inspire target audiences' (Crystal 2011a), Crystal produced entryway paratexts that used a visual style attuned to the cultural and multimedia literacy of the 'young people' that LOCOG placed at the centre of its Olympic promotional pitch (Tomlinson 2008). Blending contemporary CG animation styles, Crystal inscribed the mascot films with a new media aesthetic that resonated with the digital aspirations of London 2012.

Experiential: pixel animations and live event media

The realization of the Olympics' digital theme was perhaps most fully expressed at the opening and closing ceremonies. This provides the context for Crystal's third main area of Olympic promotional screen work – 'experiential'. Directed by Danny Boyle, the 2012 Olympic opening ceremony provided a paean to 'the isles of wonder', an elaborate and sometimes idiosyncratic staging of Britain's industrial, social and cultural contribution to the world. Over many acts, the opening ceremony would develop a sub-narrative about modern life and new technology, sequences moving from the depiction of the heavy technology of the industrial revolution to the network technology of the mobile and social media age. The latter included a miniature soap opera on contemporary digital life that culminated in the revealing onstage of the inventor of the World Wide Web, Tim Berners-Lee. Presented as a living symbol of Britain's contribution to the digital present, his appearance was accompanied by a graphic rendering of his quote 'this is for everyone', which appeared as a giant stadium message.

Ever since the 1970s, made-for-television Olympic ceremonies have been a major source of audience figures, the Los Angeles Games in 1984 providing a watershed in the production of the Olympics as television extravaganza (Tomlinson 1996). To achieve the requisite degree of visual spectacle for a global audience of 900 million people, the opening and closing ceremonies of the London Games combined live performance with a unique form of pixel animation developed by Crystal. This made use of 70,500 paddles that were attached to the seats of the stadium to create a gigantic 360-degree screen. These paddles were used to project a host of sweeping and rhythmic pixel animations around the Olympic stadium, from graphic words such as those of Berners-Lee to lyrics, colours and animations of clocks, cogs, seagulls, silhouettes, sonic reverberations, people and pinball machines. Crystal was responsible for the creative design of this 'experiential' effect. While pixel animation had been tried at the Doha World Athletics Championships in 2010, with the use of one pixel to create colour

Figure 6.4 Pixel animations at the Paralympic closing ceremony, 9 September 2012. Courtesy of Crystal CG.

washes in the main stadium, Danny Boyle sought to use 'audience pixels' on a different creative scale. According to Will Case, who led the project for Crystal, Boyle wanted 'to somehow bring the audience into the stadium, and find a way of immersing it'; the animations were designed to 'expand the narrative from the field of play out into the audience and make them feel part of the show' (Crystal 2012c).

In her discussion of the affordances of digital media, Janet H. Murray suggests that 'an immersive environment is one that captivates and holds our attention because it feels expansive, detailed and complete' (2012: 101–102). She continues: 'Immersion is the experience produced by the pleasurable exploration of a limitless, consistent, familiar yet surprising environment' (ibid.). At the opening and closing ceremonies, a sense of immersion was created by choreographing the pixel animations with the live performance on the main stage.[10] In visual terms, the ceremonies were defined by the ability of the pixel animations to transform the physical space of the stadium into a living screen, animations gliding, pulsating and constellating within and between the very aisles of the auditorium. Compared to the Bird's Nest in Beijing, the London Olympic stadium was unremarkable in terms of its architectural design. However, it was enlivened at the ceremonies and made to feel 'expansive' and 'surprising' by the way it collapsed boundaries between spectators (who could each touch a paddle) and the main stage. This, again, gave the ceremonies a distinctive digital look, and they became a site of promotional spectacle for the Games as a whole. In turning the stadium into a screen, the pixel animations created spectacle for those watching on television as much as it did for those in the stadium.

As a form of paratextual content, the pixel animations existed on the physical and interpretive perimeter of the ceremonies. This meant that certain pixel animations representing months of creative labour could be missed. Will Case describes a sequence used in the opening ceremony where the image of Jesse Owens ran around the stadium, the creative outcome of a complex animation process that used motion capture and archival data to build a detailed 3D replica of the athlete. Despite it being, for Case, 'one of the most beautiful things we created for the opening ceremony' (2012), the content was never seen or recorded as it was displayed on the paddles at the very moment that Muhammad Ali physically appeared and was given a standing ovation. Despite these contingencies, the pixel animations gave the ceremonies a dynamic visual surround, heightening a sense of involvement and interactivity in the stadium. A signature example was the digital rendering of Freddie Mercury in the closing ceremony. This involved a sequence of musical call and response between a digitized image of Mercury and the stadium audience. Using giant screens in the centre stage, Crystal used rotoscoped footage of Mercury and a process called real-time rendering to create the effect of Mercury vocally conducting the crowd. This was an experiential application of a digitextual phenomenon, popularized in the 2000s, of bringing pop stars back to life. Previously seen in adverts and television programmes that used digital compositing and effects technology to make icons such as Elvis Presley sing beyond the grave (Grainge 2010), the closing

ceremony used digital 3D effects and audience pixels to create a sonorous relationship between the stadium crowd and Queen's lead singer. In its production
of bespoke visual content such as this – experienced within the stadium and
represented on television around the world – Crystal helped digitally animate
the London Olympics in moments of maximum media exposure. Attracting
significant amounts of press coverage, the ceremonies, and the pixel animations
in particular, helped position the UK and London as a site of digital creativity.

From the pre-visualization of venues and the animation of mascots to the
production of digital content used within broadcast television, online media and
stadium shows, Crystal helped realize the promotional identity of London 2012
across a range of platforms and screen sites. While the Olympics are, of course,
a promotional bonanza for corporate sponsors, promotional screen content
goes beyond the output of heavy-spending commercial brands like Coca-Cola,
McDonald's and Proctor & Gamble. It also involves a host of promotional
media – bid films, business-to-business adverts, outdoor presentational videos,
mascot shorts and live event media – which specialists like Crystal produce for
corporations, governments and organizational bodies such as LOCOG. In its
role as 'Digital Imaging Services Supplier', Crystal helped frame the promotional and presentational look of the Olympics, producing screen content that,
in different ways, shaped the aesthetic, semiotic and experiential meaning of
the Games.

The Olympics also served a promotional function for Crystal itself, however.
In an interview with us directly after the Games, Will Case said,

> The fact of the matter is that people now know who Crystal are and the
> investment it took us. We've ended up working on the biggest show on Earth,
> [we have] huge exposure, huge presence out there now globally, you can't
> buy that stuff.
>
> (2012)

This provides insight into the level of self-promotion required in a highly competitive design market, but it also highlights the importance of the ceremonies
(and the pixel animations) for Crystal in consolidating its global position. Gilles
Albaredes, who managed Crystal London until the end of the Games, described
experiential work as 'the real driver of growth' for the company moving forward, owing to the potentially high financial returns (2012). Case also saw
experiential as a key to future development, remarking: 'I think our focus will
be much more in the brand experiences and finding companies and agencies to
work with who are looking for something different' (2012). In the last section,
we consider the rise of 'experiential' as an emerging facet of the promotional
screen industries. Having examined promotional screen design in relation to
Crystal and the Olympics – the Beijing and London Games being two of the
biggest global media events in this book's period of study – we conclude by
turning attention to wider movements and horizons within the digital design

sector, opening out perspectives on experiential as a strand of promotional design work that seeks, in Case's terms, to 'break down the screen' (ibid.).

Context is king: experience design

Within critical and industry discourse, 'experiential' or 'experience design' connotes a specific way of thinking about interactivity. For Tricia Austin and Richard Doust, experiential suggests how 'interactive graphics which are effectively combined with sound and embedded in objects and architecture can not only communicate ideas but provoke very strong bodily and emotional responses as well' (2007: 52). Although, as they point out, the term is contested as a design category of its own – owing a debt to other disciplines such as environmental signage, animation and even film and theatre design – 'experiential' has been taken up within the promotional screen sector to denote a particular set of creative and marketing practices.

As we saw in Chapter 2, Crystal CG is one of a number of companies with roots in visual effects, like R/GA and MPC, which sell expertise in experiential design. For such companies, experiential denotes the creation of 'user experiences' (UX) in physical and digital space. This ranges from interactive installations in retail environments to live events that connect to digital campaigns. In two examples, the 'experiential' division of the ad agency Mother turned to MPC in November 2012 to create a tropical 3D aquarium for the computer brand ACER, resulting in an installation that was situated in twenty-five major European shopping centres. Comprising a large physical tank made up of twelve screens, this installation encouraged shoppers to engage with a CG dolphin which appeared to swim and play. Meanwhile, R/GA developed a live event for Nike's online 'Signature Moves' campaign in 2012, creating an application that captured the movement of participants on a live green-screen basketball court that generated data used to produce digital images of on-court play. Although creating different kinds of audience interaction, these examples used screen technologies to 'activate' campaigns within and between real and virtual environments. The former was designed to draw in passing crowds – the dolphin installation framing a display of ACER's latest product range and its slogan 'explore, beyond limits' – and the latter was designed as a sports educational event, with children invited to learn from NBA players in the 'Nike Film Room' at basketball festivals. Both examples brought to life brand campaigns in the physical world and are illustrative of 'experiential marketing', what Liz Moor describes as 'the attempt to approach consumers in an expanded range of everyday spaces' (2003: 40).

While event-based marketing is hardly new, Moor describes 'a "powering-up" of the spatial and experiential dimensions of marketing' in the 2000s, companies using an increasing range of 'live strategies' to communicate and socialize the experience of brands (ibid.: 43). As Moor suggests, and as we saw in Chapter 3 with T-Mobile, live music events have become a site for affective marketing initiatives.[11] However, like sport, music events such as festivals, concerts and stadium shows provide a context for promotional screen media beyond the campaign ambitions of consumer brands. They can also incorporate a variety of screen experiences that promotionally surround events and shows themselves. The Glastonbury Festival in 2009, for example, saw an interactive public video installation called 'Picnic on the Screen', a work commissioned for the BBC's Village Screen that used blue-screen mats to encourage creative play between the festival audience and a large-format public video screen (Gould and Sermon 2009). On a miniaturized scale, interactive LED wristbands were given out at Coldplay concerts in 2012 that created wearable screen displays, digitally controlled so as to flash, text and change colour at specific moments.[12] In these examples, experiential design was used to facilitate audience involvement in particular spatial and temporal performances.

'Experiential' initiatives such as those mentioned above expand the scope and focus of the promotional screen industries. In 2006 the UK-based National Endowment for Science, Technology and the Arts (NESTA) proposed a model of the creative industries organized around four clusters defined by commonalities in business models, markets and products. As outlined in Chapter 2 (see note 5), these clusters included 'creative content providers' (including film, broadcasting and interactive media), 'creative service providers' (including advertising and design), 'creative experience providers' (encompassing live music, performing arts, spectator sports, visitor attractions, museums and exhibitions) and 'creative originals producers' (including crafts and designer-makers). Promotional screen intermediaries like Crystal, R/GA and MPC operate within and between all of the first three groupings – they produce digital *content* that is directly distributed to audiences, they supply visual *services* to other businesses and organizations, and they develop location-specific *experiences* that become part of public and commercial events. As we have shown, Crystal's work for the London Olympics encompassed each of these areas, demonstrating just how interlocking NESTA's groupings can be, even within the organization of a single company.

At the same time, experiential design reinforces the sense of promotional screen work as a creative discipline. Notably, it underscores a rule of experiential design summarized by Will Case in the maxim 'context is king'. As Crystal's Director of Experiential during the Olympics, it is worth quoting Case at length:

> The point is it is all about the context; it's where you put it that makes it relevant. You can make the most beautiful piece of content and stick it somewhere and it's irrelevant. So my job is to be mindful of where it's going. Television is easy, it's a TV, it sits in your house and that's what you do, you sit and watch it. If I put a screen in Trafalgar Square I have to be mindful of the fact that it's in Trafalgar Square, who's looking at it, how are people looking at it. It's a completely different mindset of how to do that. You can create incredible experiences that are rubbish, because if the context is not right and it's not relevant it's a complete waste of time,

so the thing that we ask ourselves every time is: is it relevant? Is it contextually right? If it is then we're going in the right direction.

(2012)

It is instructive to return to the pixel animations to show how this contextual principle applies. In this case being 'contextually right' meant being sympathetic to the architecture of the Olympic stadium. This involved creating a giant screen that accounted for the holes and gantries where people would walk and also designing content that would be legible when animated on panels that curved. It also meant being sympathetic to the context of the ceremonies. Case notes that 'the creativity must lead the technology; if you let the technology lead you're doomed' (ibid.). As a visual experience embedded into the place and space of the Olympic ceremonies, the pixel animations had to create effects that were consistent with and completing of the live show. In a contextual sense, they had to expand rather than disrupt the performance environment of the ceremonies. Like other experiential forms, the pixels can be seen as part of the attempt by digital agencies to design for spatial contexts, moving beyond traditional concepts of what a screen is, where it can be used, and how audiences interact with it.

In her broad-ranging discussion of interaction design, Janet Murray notes that 'as computational environments move beyond the two-dimensional screen, designers are experimenting with placing virtual objects in real space' (2012: 176). This ranges from the development of augmented reality applications that 'superimpose images and texts on places in the actual world using GPS and special viewing devices' to the use of 'wireless, location-based and sensor technologies that actively sense our presence, calculate our location, and communicate with one another with and without our conscious intervention' (ibid.: 178). The promotional screen industries intersect with the questions of design that emerge from this convergence of physical and digital space. From interactive billboards to holographic product launches, the media and marketing industries have sought to capitalize on the new opportunities opened up by the dispersal of screens and the comingling of real and virtual environments.

As we discussed in Part I, actors in the media and marketing industries have responded to the proliferation of platforms and the fragmentation of audiences by pursuing 'the new strategic imperatives of ubiquity, mobility and interactivity' (Boddy 2011: 76). In this context, 'out-of-home' and 'experiential' media have been taken up as strategies for addressing, engaging and monitoring consumers on the move. According to William Boddy, the dispersal of screens beyond the home in the 2000s 'provoked a proliferation of distinct textual forms, business models and viewing practices' that collectively challenged the traditional status and domestic setting of broadcast television as an advertising medium (ibid.: 77). In related ways, Liz Moor connects the diversification of media audiences to the scope of 'new marketing', suggesting that 'experiential marketing is one of a number of ways in which marketers are currently exploring what might count as marketing media and, through this, what kinds of spaces they might be able to build around their brands' (2003: 46). These observations provide a background to the way in which certain kinds of promotional intermediary have sought to navigate, and design for, changes in the media environment. While agencies like Saatchi & Saatchi, Red Bee Media and Create Advertising have focused on the promotional screen economy of mobile communication, television and film, Crystal are specialists in the textual forms and viewing practices – the digital image content and user journeys – that have become integrated into the physical world, notably at live events.

Conclusion

This chapter has focused on the companies and creative work involved in making promotional screen content and experiential media for events and spaces. This brings into focus design agencies that specialize in the production of 'digital attractions'. Through the pregnant case of the London Olympics, we have shown how digital animated content has been used to surround and enhance the viewing experience of media 'spectaculars'. Not only does Crystal's work point to promotional screen content made for organizational purposes and semi-public spaces (such as bid videos), it also demonstrates the range of digital paratexts that help constitute global sporting events. In the case of London 2012, promotional screen content was made for screens large and small, mobile and static, and was designed to circulate and become a site of interactivity within physical as well as virtual sites.

Crystal's digital work was part of a rich variety of official and unofficial paratexts that framed the Games. While many of these were celebratory in nature, like Channel 4's 'Meet the Superhumans' trailer that introduced this book, others were less triumphal. Parallel to the release of the four Olympic mascot films, for example, a mock documentary was run on BBC Two called *Twenty Twelve* (2011–12). This focused on the trials and tribulations of the 'Olympic Delivery Committee', a fictional executive body tasked with organizing the London Olympics. Satirizing the language and pratfalls of managerial culture, the series lampooned with special bite the 'Head of Brand' for the Olympics. Seeking to produce feature blogs ('flogs') and 'sonic branding' for the Olympics, promotional efforts were linked in the series to inane management orthodoxies. While it is easy to dismiss the promos, publicity and hype made to sell media events – and *Twenty Twelve* is very funny when skewering public relations brandspeak – we would argue that the promotion of London 2012 and the role of specialist companies like Crystal CG suggests a more complex and ranging picture of promotional design than is often acknowledged in academic and popular representations of such work. Not only does Crystal reveal developments in the global creative industries – notably the rise of Chinese digital media expertise – it illustrates the variety of promotional screen work undertaken for large-scale media events, and the way that digital forms connect with techno-narratives within host countries (Humphreys and Finlay 2008). Crystal's corporate and creative history demonstrates how, between the cultural and policy contexts of China and Britain, media promotion can involve animating the digital dream life of nations, as much as imagining new communication technologies or enlivening the latest films and television shows.

Notes

1 Developments in digital signage have expanded the scope of promotional communication for brands. In 2011 Global Industry Analysts (GIA) projected that the global digital signage industry would reach $13.8 billion by 2017, a growth tied to the decline of television as the advertising medium of choice (Giza 2011).

2 In Crystal's case this was symbolically realized by forty short films that the company made for the Chinese International Property Rights Office, using 3D animated characters to, in its own words, 'educate the importance of [*sic*] and how to protect international property rights' (Crystal 2011d).

3 This would include a signature motion graphic sequence devised by Red Bee that combined athletes with the five Chinese elements and the iconic CCTV building and logo. Broadcast to over 380 million households and a potential audience of one billion viewers, the CCTV commission symbolized for Red Bee's Director of Creative, Andy Bryant, 'the coming of age for Red Bee Media as a truly global creative player' (Garside 2008: 8). Despite its work for CCTV, the 'complexities of working in China' would lead Red Bee to close its Beijing office after the Olympics. This owed in part to the bureaucratic difficulties of being a wholly-owned foreign enterprise in China but also to cultural and work differences, notably the expectation among Chinese clients of seeing finished work at early conceptual stages (Bryant 2011).

4 The post-production facility Prime Focus, for example, which is owned by an Indian conglomerate, often sells effects work at slightly less than market rates in London and then produces this work in cheaper industry settings such as Mumbai and Chandigarh.

5 Considering the way that 'digital technologies have transformed the two-dimensional screen into increasingly realized three-dimensional spaces', Janet H. Murray argues that one of the emerging design challenges in three-dimensional environments is establishing clear conventions for point of view (2012: 73). Crystal's 3D visualizations of products, constructions, maps and landscapes are engaged with these design challenges. In terms of sports coverage, Crystal also developed an on-air 3D effect called 'venue-vu', first used by the BBC at Wimbledon in 2011, that involved the integration of virtual flights between courts with live video feeds.

6 Created by the brand consultants Wolff Olins, the London Olympic logo used four jagged and chunky shapes to create the number 2012, bearing the Olympic rings and the word 'London'. Despite descriptions of the 'vitality' and 'edginess' of the design from LOCOG, the logo met with a barrage of criticism in the British press, and was likened to a deconstructed swastika and even associated with triggering epileptic seizures (Glendinning 2007). Pouring scorn on corporate logos is a minor journalistic sport in the UK so these reactions were predictable. However, the vociferousness of the criticism was in itself revealing, moving beyond aesthetic and design judgements to questions of how people could (or not) relate to logos.

7 Wenlock was named after the UK town that helped inspire Pierre de Coubertin to launch the modern Olympics, and Mandeville was named after the UK town where the Paralympics was founded.

8 Launched in 2008 and targeted at seven- to twelve-year-olds, Moshi Monsters invites children to adopt a 'moshling' character and then interact, share and comment through a moderated social networking site, via an online television channel (Moshi TV), and through merchandise. By 2011, Moshi Monsters had 38 million registered pre-teen users and estimated merchandise sales of £62 million (Kiss 2011).

9 While the production work was carried out by Crystal's offices in London and Beijing, the shorts were written, produced, directed, narrated and scored by British artists, the music performed by the National Youth Orchestra, and the films narrated by Stephen Fry who had previously voiced the English version of pan-regional children's TV programmes such as the CG animated series *Pocoyo* (Clan TVE, 2005–2010).

10 It is not coincidence that the effect of these pixel animations was achieved by mapping software called 'Immersive'.

11 This extends to the film and television industries, which use conventions and expos such as Comic-Con to launch the promotional campaigns for movies and TV series and to premiere trailers.

12 These were given the trade name 'Xylobands' and followed other digital wristbands used for experiential marketing purposes such as the Nike 'FuelBand' developed by R/GA.

Bibliography

Albaredes, G. (2012) *Interview with authors*, 16 June.

Austin, T. and Doust, R. (2007) *New Media Design*, London: Laurence King.

Bayley, S. (2010) 'The 2012 Olympic Mascots', *The Observer*, 23 May: 35.

BBC (2012) 'BBC Sport Breaks Online Records with First Truly Digital Olympics'. Online. Available: http://www.bbc.co.uk/mediacentre/latestnews/2012/olympic-online-figures (accessed 20 November 2014).

Boddy, W. (2011) '"Is it TV Yet?" The Dislocated Screens of Television in a Mobile Digital Culture', in J. Bennett and N. Strange (eds) *Television as Digital Media*, Durham: Duke University Press.

——(2004) *New Media and Popular Imagination*, Oxford: Oxford University Press.

Bryant, A. (2011) *Interview with authors*, 23 July.

Carter, S. (2009) *Digital Britain*, London: HM Government, Department of Business Innovation & Skills and Department for Culture, Media & Sport.

Case, W. (2012) *Interview with authors*, 18 September.

CIDA (2009) 'China's High-Growth Creative Enterprise Report', Creative Industries Assessment Centre Report. Online. Available: http://www.techweb.com.cn/commerce/2009-11-27/482707.shtml (accessed 8 March 2011).

Crystal (2012a) 'Business presentation'. Online. Available: http://www.crystalcg.com/en/business_presentation.html (accessed 10 March 2011).

——(2012b) 'Sport Presentation Sampler – London 2012'. Online. Available: http://crystalcg.co.uk/#/work/46486131 (accessed 10 March 2013).

——(2012c) 'Olympic Opening Ceremony – London 2012'. Online. Available: http://crystalcg.co.uk/#/work/46687821 (accessed 15 March 2013).

——(2011a) 'Sectors'. Online. Available: http://www.crystalcg.co.uk/sectors (accessed 14 June 2011).

——(2011b) 'Organisation'. Online. Available: http://www.crystalcg.co.uk/about/organisation (accessed 14 June 2011).

——(2011c) 'Digital Entertainment'. Online. Available: http://www.crystalcg.com/en/digital_entertainment.html (accessed 12 June 2011).

——(2011d) 'Digital Imaging Design'. Online. Available: http://www.crystalcg.com/en/Audio_video.html (accessed 14 March 2011).

——(2010) 'London 2012 Mascots Launched to the World'. Online. Available: http://www.crystalcg.com/en/news.aspx?nid=150 (accessed 18 September 2011).

Culf, A. (2007) 'Edgy Symbol of Digital Age or Artistic Flop – London Unveils Olympic Logo', *Guardian*, 5 June: 3.

Deighton, P. (2010) 'Launch of 2012 Mascots Was Showcase for Britain', *Daily Express*, 26 May: 37.

Design Week (2010) 'Animation: Logomotion', 6 May: 14.

Deuze, M. (2007) *Media Work*, Cambridge: Polity.

Flew, T. (2011) 'Media as Creative Industries: Conglomeration and Globalization as Accumulation Strategies in an Age of Digital Media', in D. Winseck and D. Yong Jin (eds) *The Political Economies of Media*, London: Bloomsbury Academic.

Garside, J. (2012) 'Huge Spikes in Data Use Reveal Hits of the Games', *Guardian*, 15 August: 10.

——(2008) 'British Firm Strikes Gold in Beijing', *Sunday Telegraph* (City Section), 8 June: 2.

Gibson, O. (2010) 'One Eyed Aliens With Taxi Lights on their Heads – It Must Be the Olympic Mascots', *Guardian*, 20 May: 3.

Giza, M. (2011) 'Digital Signage Market to Hit $14B by 2017', *Commercial Integrator*, 1 September. Online. Available: http://www.commercialintegrator.com/article/digital_signage_market_to_hit_14b_by_2017 (accessed 9 September 2013).

Glancey, J. (2010) 'Part CCTV Camera, All Cash Cow', *Guardian*, 20 May: 3.

Glendinning, L. (2007) 'Please Look Away. It's the 2012 Logo', *Guardian*, 6 June: 1.

Gould, C. and Sermon, P. (2009) 'Picnic on the Screen'. Online. Available: http://creative technology.salford.ac.uk/paulsermon/picnic/ (accessed 7 March 2013).

Govil, N. (2004) 'Something Spatial in the Air: In-flight Entertainment and the Topographies of Modern Air Travel', in N. Couldry and A. McCarthy (eds) *Mediaspace: Place, Scale and Culture in a Media Age*, London and New York: Routledge.

Grainge, P. (2010) 'Elvis Sings for the BBC: Broadcast Branding and Digital Media Design', *Media, Culture & Society*, 32 (1): 45–61.

Gray, J. (2010) *Show Sold Separately: Promos, Spoilers and Other Media Paratexts*, New York: New York University Press.

Gurevitch, L. (2010) 'The Cinema of Transactions: The Exchangeable Currency of the Digital Attraction', *Television & New Media*, 11 (5): 367–85.

Hesmondhalgh, D. and Baker, S. (2011) *Creative Labour: Media Work in Three Cultural Industries*, London and New York: Routledge.

Hui, D. (2006) 'From Cultural to Creative Industries: Strategies for Chaoyang District, Beijing', *International Journal of Cultural Studies*, 9 (3): 317–31.

Humphreys, L. and Finlay, C. J. (2008) 'New Technologies, New Narratives', in M. E. Price and D. Dayan (eds) *Owning the Olympics: Narratives of the New China*, Ann Arbor: University of Michigan Press.

Julier, G. and Moor, L. (eds) (2009) *Design and Creativity: Policy, Management and Practice*, Oxford: Berg.

Keane, M. (2011) *China's New Creative Clusters*, London and New York: Routledge.

——(2007) *Created in China: The Great New Leap Forward*, London and New York: Routledge.

Kiss, J. (2011) 'Monster Obsession Sparks New TV Service for Children', *Guardian*, 2 April: 7.

Li, W. (2011) *How Creativity Is Changing China*, London: Bloomsbury Academic.

Lury, K. (2008) 'Monkey Magic'. Online. Available: http://www.flowtv.org/2008/08/monkey-magickaren-lury-university-of-glasgow/ (accessed 4 July 2012).

McCarthy, A. (2001) *Ambient Television: Visual Culture and Public Space*, Durham: Duke University Press.

Miller, T., Govil, N., McMurria, J., Maxwell, R. and Wang, T. (2005) *Global Hollywood 2*, Berkeley: University of California Press.

Moor, E. (2003) 'Branded Spaces: The Scope of "New Marketing"', *Journal of Consumer Culture*, 3 (1): 39–60.

Murray, J. H. (2012) *Inventing the Medium: Principles of Interaction Design as a Cultural Practice*, Cambridge, Mass: MIT Press.

Pilditch, D. (2010) 'British Firms' Fury as 2012 Olympics Promo Film is Made in China', *Daily Express*, 24 May: 5.

Planet Sport (2010) 'Canada', *The Observer*, 23 May: 18.

R/GA (2012) 'What We Do in 11 Minutes'. Online. Available: http://www.rga.com/about/featured/what-we-do/ (accessed 20 November 2014).

Royal Television Society (2013) 'The First Digital Olympics'. Online. Available: http://www.rts.org.uk/2012-first-digital-olympics (accessed 14 March 2013).

Sherwood, B. (2010) 'London Olympics Pave Way Towards Crystal CG's European Credentials', *Financial Times*, 2 August: 16.

Tchang, T. and Goldstein, A. (2004) 'Production and Political Economy in the Animation Industry: Why Insourcing and Outsourcing Occur'. Paper presented at the *DRUID* conference, Elsinore, Denmark, June.

Tomlinson, A. (2008) 'Olympic Values, Beijing's Olympic Games, and the Universal Market', in M. E. Price and D. Dayan (eds) *Owning the Olympics: Narratives of the New China*, Ann Arbor: University of Michigan Press.

——(1996) 'Olympic Spectacle: Opening Ceremonies and Some Paradoxes of Globalization', *Media, Culture & Society*, 18 (4): 583–602.

Wang, J. (2008) *Brand New China: Advertising, Media and Commercial Culture*, Cambridge, MA: Harvard University Press.

Conclusion

Only Promotion

In *W1A* (BBC, 2014), the follow-up to the BBC's London Olympics satire *Twenty-Twelve*, the Corporation turned the spotlight on itself, the programme following the pitfalls of former Head of the Olympic Deliverance Commission, Ian Fletcher (Hugh Bonneville), as he took up his new role as BBC Head of Values. The four-part comedy offered plenty of opportunities to mock the bureaucratic workings of 'Auntie', including the Corporation's appointment of external brand agency, Perfect Curve. In a moment of characteristic satirical piquancy, the series depicted the Perfect Curve team turning their hand to re-designing the BBC logo, concluding that it simply had too many letters. Their solution? That it should be replaced by a design bearing a striking resemblance to the Star of David. In lampooning Perfect Curve, *W1A* exemplified the broader derision of promotional intermediaries, the agency's brand consultant Siobhan Sharpe (Jessica Hynes) being described by one reviewer as 'verbally incontinent PR propelled entirely by the hot gas of media buzzwords' (Raeside 2014). *W1A*, as with *Twenty-Twelve* before it, speaks to a perception of the creeping centrality of promotional practice to the operations of contemporary organizations like the BBC and LOCOG; its satire of brandspeak reveals a nagging cultural anxiety about promotional screen intermediaries and the role they play. It is the complex reality of this intermediary work, beyond the caricatures, that has formed the subject of this book. Using a critical industrial framework, we have attempted to move away from comedic derision that positions promotional screen practice in negative or overtly mocking terms. In these conclusions we want to ask what it means to take the promotional screen industries seriously.

In his classic 1992 study *Only Entertainment*, Richard Dyer argued against the commonplace, pejorative dismissal of the idea of entertainment, claiming that it masked a tendency to assume that the meaning(s) of entertainment were already known or easily understood. His eclectic collection of essays on subjects ranging from disco to musicals to pornography aimed to analyse 'given instances of entertainment *as* entertainment, neither assuming one already understands what this is nor pushing the analysis too quickly on to other things' (2002: 1). Our purpose has been different from Dyer's, but it has had similar ambitions, namely to take promotion seriously – to recognize the complexities and creativity involved in the production of promotional forms and to consider the industrial and cultural functions they serve. Much as Dyer's collection of essays presented a challenge to what counts as an object of academic study, so this book has sought to demonstrate the value of analysing screen promotion, both textually and industrially. Building on recent work within film, television, cultural and advertising studies, we have argued that screen promotion can be understood not just as a textual category, but also as a screen discipline with its own opportunities and challenges. Rather than lament promotion, or view it as a symptom of increasing commercialization, we have sought to understand promotion on its own terms. This involves neither denying the promotional intent of screen forms like ads, promos, trailers and digital shorts, nor letting promotional intent determine the cultural meanings (and pleasures) that such forms provide.

Dyer stressed that entertainment always needs to be understood within its cultural and historical specificity. While screen promotion has a history as long as the audiovisual media industries themselves, this book has focused on the first decades of the twenty-first century. As evidenced in the discourse of promotion *as content* explored in Chapter 1, this is a period in which the definitions and functions of promotional screen forms were explicitly up for debate. Our intention is not to imply that promotion deserves particular attention at this time *because* of its increased tendency to function as 'content'. Rather, we suggest that the discourses surrounding promotion as content point to the central place that screen promotion has occupied, and continues to occupy, within a moment of (digital) media transition.

Indeed, across the book we have explored the ways in which the promotional screen industries have functioned as navigators of the changes produced by digital culture. In Part I we examined formal and industrial developments in screen promotion as part of a broader set of transformations in the media landscape. We argued that developments in screen promotion in the 2000s and early 2010s can be understood in relation to 'the new strategic imperatives of ubiquity, mobility and interactivity' (Boddy 2011: 76) that have challenged the relationships between audiences, producers and distributors of moving image content. Within this industrial context, the boundaries between the fields of advertising, film and television, and digital design have become more fluid as companies across these sectors compete and collaborate in the production of promotional content for a variety of clients. As we have seen, these clients range from consumer brands such as T-Mobile and Chipotle, to media companies such as the BBC and Lionsgate, to organizations including the London and Beijing Olympic Organizing Committees.

Although promotional screen intermediaries often proffer expertise in relation to particular industries, across these different industries promotional screen content and the companies responsible for creating it are navigating clients through the infrastructural, ideological and imaginative transitions produced by digital culture. Chapter 3 examined the rhetorical shift in advertising approach encapsulated within the concept of the 'participation economy', a term that responds to the growing function of mobile and social network communication in everyday life. Establishing tendencies in the digital promotional environment, this chapter demonstrated how the dynamics of spreadable marketing and consumer co-production are shaping promotional screen practice through the creation and dispersal of content that aims to facilitate social connections and audience activity rather than to aggregate attention through centralized channels. Through campaigns such as T-Mobile's 'Life's for Sharing' and corporate theorizations such as 'Lovemarks', advertising agencies like Saatchi & Saatchi engaged consumers in the late 2000s and early 2010s by creating promotional texts that fulfilled the social use of mobile technology, part of a broader cultural moment when mobile phones were being repositioned as platforms for screen content.

If telecommunication companies such as T-Mobile have pursued promotional strategies that represent mobile social media as a means of circulating and sharing audiovisual material, the television and film industries (examined in Chapters 4 and 5 respectively) have sought to embrace, but also manage, contemporary developments in digital media. Once again, promotional intermediaries play a central role here. The 'new strategic imperatives of ubiquity, mobility and interactivity' present a potential threat to the established business models and industrial practices of the television and film industries. Promotional screen intermediaries, such as Red Bee Media, position themselves explicitly as 'thought leaders' able to navigate their clients through the maze of new opportunities (and dangers) wrought by digitalization. From the routine digital promotional forms developed around prime-time family audience programmes like *Planet Earth Live* to the experimental second screen Walkers' Kill Count app, Chapter 4 revealed how promotional screen content attempts to manage the potentially unruly behaviour of the television viewer. Accordingly, promotional screen intermediaries play an active role in ongoing trade debates about the changing relationship between the television industry and its audience. The relation between the film industry and its audience has also been affected by digitalization. With the blockbuster movie becoming part of an entertainment event that is increasingly played out online, Chapter 5 demonstrated the ways in which Hollywood studios and their agencies create promotional infrastructures that attempt to construct sustained, targeted and participative relationships with their audiences.

Chapter 6 moved beyond the more extensively examined areas of advertising, television and film into the production of audiovisual content for live events and spaces. The case example of Crystal CG's work for the Olympic and Paralympic Games demonstrated how promotional screen content extends to out-of-home and experiential media, in this case used by corporate and organizational bodies. Here, promotional screen intermediaries such as Crystal were called upon to create digital attractions, contextually specific promotional forms that would surround the Olympic Games in 2012 (and 2008) as a global media spectacle. Across the different fields and disciplines discussed in Part II, promotional screen intermediaries were revealed to play a key role in navigating and negotiating the transitions wrought by digitalization. Agencies like Saatchi & Saatchi, Red Bee Media, Create Advertising and Crystal CG have shaped, and are continuing to shape, the promotional screen forms that have become so much a part of audiovisual culture in the contemporary 'attention economy'.

Indeed, promotional screen texts have assumed an expanded role within the media landscape of the early twenty-first century. This has been explored most explicitly within film and television studies in work on media paratexts. As Jonathan Gray argues, 'Film and television shows ... are only a small part of the massive, extended presence of filmic and televisual texts across our lived environments' (2010: 2). With a wider range of sites for accessing audiovisual media, we are far more likely to have seen the trailer for a movie or television programme than to have seen the 'primary' text itself. However, as we have shown, promotional screen forms don't just promote movies and television programmes, but also events, organizations, products and services, becoming an important strategy for marketers across a range of sectors. As such, the para-textual function of promotional texts that Gray examines in relation to film and television can be understood to extend far more widely in digital media culture.

At the same time, the function of promotional screen content is not *just* paratextual; promotional screen materials do not solely operate as frames and filters for the meanings of other works. Over the course of the book, we have encountered promotional texts that can stand as self-contained artefacts of screen culture, from the crowdsourced flashmob ads examined in Chapter 3, to the teaser trailers comprised of original footage explored in Chapter 5, to the mascot films created for the London Olympic Games discussed in Chapter 6. Analysing Pixar teaser trailers as vignettes in the wider life of studio franchises – specifically, those teasers made up of original animated footage and that function as shorts – Christopher Holliday suggests that we might 'argue whether it is the *teaser* that is being "franchised", and in an adjustment of hierarchy, more demand is being placed on the feature-films to fill in the narrative lacunae between the teaser and any subsequent shorts' (2013). In this, as in other examples, promotional short-forms can be dislocated from the texts and brands they are promoting. In looking to create promotional screen forms that audiences are motivated to engage with and share (rather than avoid), promotional texts can assume meanings and values that extend beyond their role as a paratext or form of marketing for another product, event or service. They can be, at once, marketing and short film, promotion and content.

This is not to deny the important marketing function of promotional screen content, whether as applied to movies and television programmes or consumer products and live sporting and entertainment spectacles. However, critical understanding of this marketing function deserves further interrogation. Gray argues that the use of terms such as 'hype, promotion, promos, and synergy', stemming as they do from the realm of profits, business and accounting, 'may prove a barrier for us to conceive of them as creating meaning, and as being situated in the realms of enjoyment, interpretive work and play, and the social function of media narratives' (2010: 5–6). Across this book, we have endeavoured to keep the industrial context and market imperatives of promotional screen forms in balance with the enjoyment, interpretive work and play they potentially offer. In maintaining this balance, we have sought to understand the role of promotional audiovisual media in a particular historical moment. Specifically, it has been our argument that promotional screen content in the 2000s and early 2010s has functioned to construct a digital 'popular imagination' and to manage digital behaviour in response to shifting conditions in the marketing and media environment.

Across Part II, we have examined forms of promotional screen content that, in various ways, position our engagement with the world *as* digital, and that offer models for 'being digital'. The T-Mobile 'Life's for Sharing' campaign examined in Chapter 3 literalized themes of sociality and media sharing as central to 'being digital' through the use of flashmobs. In Chapter 4 the promotional screen content for *Planet Earth Live* and *The Walking Dead* positioned television viewing as a digital activity shaped by 'connected' television viewing, from going online in-between episodes, to tweeting or playing along while watching. The promotional infrastructure for *The Hunger Games* franchise discussed in Chapter 5 constructed cinema-going as part of a larger digital social experience to be enacted online, addressing a central question for the Hollywood movie industry: how to make the digitally literate downloader go to the cinema. Chapter 6 demonstrated how promotional screen content became linked to national narratives of digital media engagement, computer-generated animation being used within a range of promotional media to help project the London Games as the first 'digital Olympics'.

Analysing how popular cultural texts act as forms of 'training' for 'new ways of seeing, acting and thinking' in a digital world, Will Brooker remains ambivalent about whether the narratives of digital mastery offered by the movies, video games and advertisements he examines can offer the space for the development of a critical mentality towards digitalization (2010: 554). Promotional screen content can offer digital resources for creativity, communication and expression (Tryon 2009). At the same time, however, marketing and promotion are tied up with discourses of control and manipulation, imbricated with increased surveillance and attempts to manage consumer behaviour (Andrejevic 2007). Promotional screen content is often constructed and/or circulated in ways that enhance the ability of the media producer to monitor (and sell on) data about consumer behaviour (Lee and Andrejevic 2014: 54). In Chapter 3, for example, 'Josh's Band' was shown to leverage content in exchange for data that T-Mobile could exploit and commercialize. Beyond this, in providing cues about digital media life, promotional screen content can attempt to manage or discipline viewer behaviour. The promotion of models of 'digital viewing', discussed in Chapter 4, privileged watching television as broadcast. Similarly, although the marketing of *The Hunger Games* situated the movies of the franchise as part of a broader interactive digital infrastructure, it did so with the intention of driving cinema-going. Meanwhile, the mascot films in Chapter 6 constructed a narrative of media engagement around the London Olympics that facilitated and framed children's social media interaction around the event. Recognizing that promotional screen forms attempt to train or manage viewer behaviour does not mean that such forms cannot also be understood as playful, pleasurable or potentially beneficial. As with all texts, we cannot assume that viewers simply accept the intended meanings of promotional content. Over and above this, in offering models of digital behaviour, promotional screen texts have the potential to be useful resources for viewers adjusting to the affordances of digital living.

In Part II we looked at rich instances of media promotion. As well as examining the industrial and cultural function of promotional texts, however, our study has served to reflect more broadly on the status of promotional screen content as a *creative* artefact. The issue of creativity recurred in our industrial fieldwork, both at trade gatherings and in many of the interviews we undertook with marketing professionals. As part of its critical project, *Promotional Screen Industries* has drawn attention to the forms of creativity and expertise that sit behind promotional screen content at the 'meso' industrial level. Across the various examples of promotional screen work that we consider are content forms that involve significant creative and technical skill. In their digital design work for the London Olympics, for instance, Crystal CG innovated with the possibilities of new technological developments to transform the stadium itself into a screen on which complex audiovisual content could be displayed. Beyond the technological difficulties of rendering and processing Crystal's 'pixel animations' for the London Games were the creative challenges of producing two and a half hours of content – content that could not only be accurately reproduced on a massive curved screen, but that also integrated with the live performances of the opening and closing ceremonies taking place in the centre of the stadium. Promotional and paratextual work such as this pushes our understanding and conceptualization of expressive (experiential) content in ways that also broaden the scope of what screen-based media can be.

Yet even on the more traditional screens of the television set and movie theatre, promotional media offer particular opportunities for artistry and creativity. According to Mandy Combes, who moved to Red Bee from a previous career as a children's television producer at the BBC, promotion is one of the few places within the contemporary television industry to 'push the boundaries of creativity', in comparison with programme production which is constrained by accountability and tighter budgets (2012). Combes pointed out that the durative shortness of much promotional screen content means that it needs to grab audience attention quickly and to stand out against the higher-budget advertising within which it often sits. At the same time, short-form promotional content often has higher production values than long-form programmes (i.e. higher budgets per minute of screen time). As such, she argued that promotional content can offer a bigger creative challenge than traditional programme-making.

Although Combes was talking specifically about television promotion, Frank Frumento also emphasized the creative skill involved in cutting movie trailers, arguing that beyond the movie editor, the trailer editor is the person who probably has the best knowledge of the film, having spent days and hours unpacking it into a series of elements that can be repackaged in multiple ways (2013). Although Frumento argued that a good trailer should be 'entertaining in and of itself ... and could stand alone as a two minute short film', he also emphasized the specificity of trailers as a cultural form that needs to combine 'storytelling and allure' (ibid.). In similar ways, the Executive Creative Director of Red Bee Media, Charlie Mawer, outlined the specific skills needed to create television idents, commenting:

> Trying to do something you can watch 3,600 times without getting irritated by it is a particular challenge and it necessitates a particular type of story-telling and a particular type of engagement that is less about grabbing you by the jumper and shaking you and is much more about giving you something you can sit back and be immersed in, that you can take stuff from. It's a different level of engagement.
>
> (cited in Grainge 2011: 94)

In both instances, these practitioners are describing a different kind of creativity than that of conventional television programme-making or film-making, one that requires a sophisticated appreciation of the nature of short-form media and the specific demands of screen-based marketing.

Taking the work of the promotional screen industries seriously, then, means thinking more broadly and fluidly about creativity and the skill-sets involved in the production of promotional screen materials. The agencies and departments explored in this book produce work that demands particular skills in design, animation, editing, motion graphics and strategic thinking, with staff often expected to be multidisciplinary and agile in their working practices. This labour is typically characterized by a culture of competition and collaboration based around con-tract and project work that is subject to client approval. The need for approval could be seen to undermine the creative autonomy of workers within the pro-motional screen industries. M. J. Clarke describes the ways in which the approval culture of freelance transmedia comic book artists encourages standardized and 'safe' products designed to fulfil the expectations of the client (2013: 46). However, these labour arrangements also ask us to be attuned to the specific skill-sets involved in working within the parameters of creative briefs and client approval. In short, promotional labour invites greater scrutiny of the nature of the relationship between agency and client and the extent to which the competitive environment of contract work might offer spaces for innovation as much as it encourages tendencies for playing safe. The complexities of this work culture are beyond the scope of this book but they do point to the potential value that an examination of the promotional screen industries might pose to our understanding of the organization and management of creative labour.

In critical terms, placing the promotional screen industries centre stage helps remind us that the media industries are composed of far more than just the film studios and television broadcasters that often dominate media industry studies.

It points to the value of pushing at the traditional boundaries of what counts as 'media' industries. Charles Acland has recently advocated an approach to media industry research that pursues the 'dirt and depth of cultural economies' (2014: 9), insisting on the need to 'expand the boundaries of media industries studies to encompass some of the foundational resource requirements and implications of the production and distribution of media works' (ibid.: 8). Although the promotional screen industries are of a different order to the industries of plastics, microchips, processing units and electrical power that Acland argues underlie the media industries, this book has demonstrated that promotional intermediaries play a fundamental part in the production and distribution of media works. Responding to calls for research into the 'dirt' (Acland 2014) and 'mess' (Caldwell 2013) of the media industries, this book contributes to a growing body of work that foregrounds seemingly peripheral sectors of the media industries (Santo 2010).

In focusing critical attention on the promotional screen industries, our study has attempted to 'build and share critical understandings of how media industries shape public knowledge and aesthetic experience' (Hesmondhalgh 2014: 24). In calling for critical media industries studies David Hesmondhalgh warns against the creeping menace of instrumentalism in academic research, particularly in a context in which 'universities are increasingly encouraged to service the requirements of governments and businesses' (ibid.: 23). In some senses this book, stemming in part from a piece of (government-funded) research council 'knowledge exchange' with Red Bee Media, can be situated precisely within this instrumental move; it has emerged in a broader context within which academic research is required to have a use and 'impact' value to industry and society. Every time we have presented the results of our fieldwork with Red Bee at academic conferences we have been asked about how we intend to retain critical distance and avoid the perils and pitfalls of 'going native'. Yet such questions perhaps pose too strong a division between a company such as Red Bee (and many of the other promotional screen intermediaries that we interviewed) and our own academic position. The questions that we have as academics attempting to understand a period of transition for the media industries are ones that are also being asked by promotional screen intermediaries whose job it is to sell expertise and thought leadership in the wake of media change. Each visit to Red Bee or interview with a promotional screen intermediary was an intellectually stimulating experience – a chance to gain insight into the ways in which different people, professions and organizations are trying, like us, to make sense of the instability of the present moment.

For many of our interviewees the experience of being interviewed was described as akin to 'therapy', a rare chance to reflect on their own working practices and assumptions. For others it was a chance to put forward and promote a particular position or corporate line on contemporary media developments. Either way, all of our interviewees were engaged, to different degrees, in a process of critical theorizing. For promotional intermediaries this critical theorization can present a commercial advantage in gaining or maintaining clients, and can sometimes solidify into proprietary models such as Red Bee's 'on-brand TV' proposition (Chapter 1). On the whole, however, in their day-to-day work, promotional intermediaries seek to mobilize their theorizations and lack the privileged opportunities that we have, as academics, for sustained reflection on our shared questions.

And this is, perhaps, the point of divergence between academics and the promotional screen intermediaries who, in our case, generously allowed us into their working lives. If Red Bee is explicitly concerned with theorizing media change in order to capitalize on new opportunities for content, engagement and commercialization, our work is informed by a cultural studies training that sees transitions in media history as a precise context for examining the production of social and cultural relationships. Moving beyond Red Bee's interests in how to navigate clients and viewers through a new media landscape, we have been concerned with broader developments in industrial and cultural practice in the 2000s and early 2010s. In one sense, we have been attuned to the particularities of the promotional sector as an increasingly hybrid site of media production and screen work. Overlaying this analysis, however, is an examination of the vernaculars of digital living and digital behaviour that have been inscribed, or enacted, through promotional screen content. With the increased ubiquity, mobility and interactivity of screen media, it has been our contention that pro-motional screen forms (and the industries that produce them) play a powerful role in shaping the contexts within which everyday life is played out during the first decades of the twenty-first century.

The roots of this book lie in our shared and long-standing enjoyment of promotional screen content. While, of course, promotional screen content can be crass, poorly executed or even boring, at their best promotional screen texts can offer beautiful, funny, sometimes deeply moving experiences that reward just as much (if not more) repeat viewing as movies and television shows. Screen output such as trailers, promos, idents, ads, companion apps, online videos, experiential media and digital shorts warrant examination not only for their potential for artistry and creativity, but also for the significant role they play in the industrial, social and cultural formation of twenty-first-century media life. This book represents a first step towards moving beyond the pejorative dismissal of such forms as 'only promotion' and taking promotional screen content and the industries that produce it seriously.

Bibliography

Acland, C. (2014) 'Dirt Research for Media Industries', *Media Industries Journal*, 1 (1): 6–10.

Andrejevic, M. (2007) *iSpy: Surveillance and Power in the Interactive Era*, Lawrence: The University Press of Kansas.

Boddy, W. (2011) '"Is it TV Yet?" The Dislocated Screens of Television in a Mobile Digital Culture', in J. Bennett and N. Strange (eds) *Television as Digital Media*, Durham: Duke University Press.

Brooker, W. (2010) '"Now You're Thinking With Portals": Media Training for a Digital World', *International Journal of Cultural Studies*, 13 (6): 553–73.

Caldwell, J. T. (2013) 'Para-Industry: Researching Hollywood's Backwaters', *Cinema Journal*, 52 (3): 157–65.

Clarke, M. J. (2013) *Transmedia Television: New Trends in Network Serial Production*, New York and London: Bloomsbury.

Combes, M. (2012) *Interview with authors*, 29 May.

Dyer, R. (2002) *Only Entertainment*, 2nd edition, London and New York: Routledge.

Frumento, F. (2013) *Interview with authors*, 3 December.

Grainge, P. (2011) 'TV Promotion and Broadcast Design: An Interview with Charlie Mawer, Red Bee Media', in P. Grainge (ed.) *Ephemeral Media: Transitory Screen Culture from Television to YouTube*, London: British Film Institute.

Gray, J. (2010) *Show Sold Separately: Promos, Spoilers and Other Media Paratexts*, New York: New York University Press.

Hesmondhalgh, D. (2014) 'The Menace of Instrumentalism in Media Industries Research and Education', *Media Industries Journal*, 1 (1): 21–26.

Holliday, C. (2013) 'Footage Not Included: Pixar Animation Studios, Teaser Trailers and the Pleasurable Absence of Content', paper delivered at *Titles, Teasers and Trailers* conference, University of Edinburgh, 22–23 April.

Lee, H. J. and Andrejevic, M. (2014) 'Second-Screen Theory: From the Democratic Surround to the Digital Enclosure', in J. Holt and K. Sanson (eds) *Connected Viewing: Selling, Streaming, and Sharing Media in the Digital Era*, London and New York: Routledge.

Raeside, J. (2014) 'Have you been watching … W1A?', *Guardian*, 2 April. Online. Available: http://www.theguardian.com/tv-and-radio/tvandradioblog/2014/apr/02/have-you-been-watching-w1a (accessed 21 August 2014).

Santo, A. (2010) 'Batman Versus The Green Hornet: The Merchandisable TV Text and the Paradox of Licensing in the Classical Network Era', *Cinema Journal*, 49 (2): 63–85.

Tryon, C. (2009) *Reinventing Cinema: Movies in the Age of Media Convergence*, New Brunswick: Rutgers University Press.

Index